FOR REFERENCE

Do Not Take From This Room

MAN, MYTH, AND MAGIC

MAN, MYTH,
AND MAGIC

Legendary Creatures and Monsters

Cavendish
Square

New York

Published in 2014 by Cavendish Square Publishing, LLC
303 Park Avenue South, Suite 1247, New York, NY 10010

Library of Congress Cataloging-in-Publication Data

Armstrong, E. A.
Legendary creatures and monsters / by E. A. Armstrong.
p. cm. — (Man, myth, and magic)
Includes index.
ISBN 978-1-62712-578-9 (hardcover) ISBN 978-1-62712-579-6 (paperback) ISBN 978-1-62712-580-2 (ebook)
1. Animals, Mythical. 2. Legends. 3. Mythical animals. I. Title.
GR825.A76 2014
398.24—d23

Editorial Director: Dean Miller
Editor: Fran Hatton
Art Director: Jeffrey Talbot
Designers: Jennifer Ryder-Talbot, Amy Greenan, and Joseph Macri
Photo Researcher: Laurie Platt Winfrey, Carousel Research, Inc
Production Manager: Jennifer Ryder-Talbot
Production Editor: Andrew Coddington

Photo Credits: Cover photos by John Linnell/The Bridgeman Art Library/Getty Images, Eugene Grasset/The Bridgeman Art Library/Getty Images, Hendrik Goltzius (1558–1617)/Hendrick Goltzius Cadmus Statens Museum for Kunst 1183/ Deposit of the Statens Kunstsamlinger/*; AlejandroLinaresGarcia/DevMaskTocMAPDF/*, 1; Kano Tan'yu/Kano Tan'yu - Phoenixes by Paulownia Trees - Google Art Project/*, 2–3; Gustave Moreau/Gustave Moreau - Galatée (Museo Thyssen-Bornemisza)/*, 5t; Hendrik Goltzius/Hendrick Goltzius Cadmus Statens Museum for Kunst 1183/*, 5c; Andreas F. Borchert/Clonfert Cathedral Mermaid 2009 09 17/*, 5b; PD-ART/Manuscript Odinn/*, 9; Friedrich Johann Justin Bertuch/Bertuch-Basilisk/*, 5c; John Bauer/The Bridgeman Art Library/Getty Images, 7t; Photo-Beard/Shutterstock.com, 9; Vladimir Egorovic Makovsky/Getty Images, 12b; John Linnell/Getty Images, 13; Mathiasrex Maciej Szczepa?czyk/Medal (12 ducats) commemorating voctories of Polish King Vladislaus IV over Russia, Turkey and Sweden 1637/*, 15; Gustave Moreau/Gustave Moreau - Galatée (Museo Thyssen-Bornemisza)/* 17; Hendrik Goltzius/Hendrick Goltzius Cadmus Statens Museum for Kunst 1183/*, 18; Bibi Saint-Pol/Sea thiasos Nereides Triton Glyptothek Munich 239 right/*, 19; Piero di Lorenzo/Piero di Cosimo - Liberazione di Andromeda - Google Art Project/*, 20–21; Arthur Rackham/Siegfried and the Twilight of the Gods p 056/*, 22; Mike Peel/Chinese New Year dragon, Manchester/*, 24; Leonard Bramer/Leonard Bramer - Mors Thriumphans/*, 28; Fountain Posters/Battle with Mara/*, 29; Jean Edouard Dargent/Getty Images, 30–31; Mikhail Alexandrovich Vrubel/Mikhail Vrubel - Flying Demon - Google Art Project/*, 31; AlejandroLinaresGarcia/DevMaskTocMAPDF/*, 32; Suad Al-Attar/Getty Images, 33; John Atkinson Grimshaw/Getty Images, 36; Joseph Noel Paton/Sir Joseph Noel Paton - The Quarrel of Oberon and Titania - Google Art Project 2/*, 37; Richard Dadd/Richard Dadd - The Fairy Feller's Master-Stroke - Google Art Project/*, 39; August Malmström/August Malstrom - Dancing Fairies/*, 40–41; Charles Prosper Sainton/Getty Images, 42; E Gertrude Thomson/Emily's Fairies WA MVAS/Allingham W The Fairies/*, 44–45; ease/Placement for initiation in Apangai, Papua New Guinea 1984/Own work/*, 47t; Eugene Grasset/Getty Images, 47b; Odilon Redon/Getty Images, 48; Baron Mikhail Petrovich Klodt von Jurgensburg/Getty Images, 49; Stanislav Pobytov/Getty Images, 50; Utagawa Kuniyoshi/Apparition of the monstrous cat./*, 52–53; De Agostini/Getty Images, 54; Utagawa Kuniyoshi/The poet Dainagon sees an apparition/*, 55; Richard Doyle/Jack and the Giants image17/*, 56; Sridhar1000/The Demon Kumbhakarna Is Defeated by Rama and Lakshmana/*, 57; Francisco Jose de Goya y Lucientes/Getty Images, 58; De Agostini/Getty Images, 59; Heinrich Schlitt/Goblins/*, 60; Michal Ma?as/Clay-golem/*, 63; Buchhändler/Rabbi Löw Saloun/*, 65; sailko/Arte italo-etrusca, antefissa con testa di gorgone, VI sec. ac/*, 66; jorchr/Malmö griffin/*, 67; Ollios/Hitit Grifini/*, 68; Franz Xaver Simm/Homunculus Simm Faust/*, 70; sailko/Artista mantovano, ercole e l'idra di lerna, argento, 1530s/*, 71; DEA/G. DAGLI ORTI/Getty Images, 72t; Frans II Francken the Younger/Getty Images/*, 72b; Mansell/Time & Life Pictures/Getty Images, 73; Richard Cummins/Getty Images, 74; Bettmann/Corbis/AP Images, 75l; General Photographic Agency/Getty Images, 75r; Marie Birkl/AP Images, 76; De Clercq Collection/Dancing maenads Louvre Ma3626/Jastrow/*, 77; Blacas Collection/Dancing maenad Python BM VaseF253/Jastrow/*, 78; Wolfgang Sauber/St. Jakob Kastelaz - Phantastische Lebewesen rechts 3 Meerjungfrau/*, 79; Andreas F. Borchert/Clonfert Cathedral Mermaid 2009 09 17/*, 81; Gustave Moreau/Gustave Moreau - Galat/*, 82; Werner Forman/Universal Images Group/Getty Images, 84; J. R. Skelton/Stories of beowulf grendel/*, 85; Friedrich Johann Justin Bertuch/Phoenix-Fabelwesen/*, 86; Bernard Gagnon/Longshan Temple - Fenghuang/*, 87; Kano Tan'yu/Kano Tan'yu - Phoenixes by Paulownia Trees - Google Art Project/*, 88–89; Bibi Saint-Pol/Dionysos satyrs Cdm Paris 575/Own work/*, 91; 1822: ceded to Louis XVIII by Vienne, France/Faunus Vienna Ma528/Marie-Lan Nguyen/*, 92; Vassil/Gargouille Cathedrale dE Moulins/Own work/*, 93; John William Waterhouse/John William Waterhouse - Ulysses and the Sirens - Google Art Project/*, 96–97; Luis García (Zaqarbal)/Sirena de Canosa s. IV adC (M.A.N. Madrid) 01/*, 98; Wolfgang Sauber/St.Jakob Kastelaz - Phantastische Lebewesen links 6 Sirene/Own work/*, 99; Viktor M. Vasnetsov/*, 100; Sundar1/Budhanilkantha0861/Own work/*, 101; National Park Service Digital Image Archives/Mammoth Cave National Park INDIANMI/*, 103; McKay Savage/Peru - Cusco Sacred Valley & Incan Ruins 040 - Pukapukara (7092597645)/*, 104; HighInBC Attribute to Ryan Bushby/Kwakwaka'wakw big house/Own work/*, 105; John bauer/Ett gammalt bergtroll/*, 107; John Bauer/The Bridgeman Art Library/Getty Images, 108t; Gage Skidmore/The Hobbit - Troll statues/*, 108b; Sidney Hall/Monoceros, Canis Minor, Atelier Typographique 3g10076u/Library of Congress/*, 110–111; Martin Schonauer/Unicorn hunt - Martin Schongauer (circle)/Own work/*, 112; Man vyi/Buckingham Palace December 2012 22/Own work.*, 113; Hulton Archive/Getty Images, 115; Bin im Garten/Vampire skeleton of Sozopol in Sofia PD 2012 06/Own work/*, 116; FluoritLaufer/Arsenalantivampires/Own work/*, 118; Shawn Allen/Vampire Children/*, 119; DEA/G.DAGLI ORTI/Getty Images, 120; El Comandante/Monolito de Coatlicue (con colores)/Own work/*, 121; Werner Forman/Universal Images Group/Getty Images, 123; Werner Forman/Universal Images Group/Getty Images, 124; WeirdTales36n2pg038 The Werewolf Howls/*, 127; Lucas Cranach the Elder/Werwolf/*, 128; Paramount Pictures/Museum of the City Of New York/Getty Images, 131; Wonderlane/Maschera Yeti/*, 133; Moises Rosas/LatinContent/Getty Images, 134; HECTOR RETAMAL/AFP/Getty Images.   * Wikimedia Commons.

Cavendish Square would like to acknowledge the outstanding work, research, writing, and professionalism of Man, Myth, and Magic's original Editor-in-Chief Richard Cavendish, Executive Editor Brian Innes, Editorial Advisory Board Members and Consultants C.A. Burland, Glyn Daniel, E.R Dodds, Mircea Eliade, William Sargent, John Symonds, RJ. Zwi Werblowsky, and R.C. Zaechner, as well as the numerous authors, consultants, and contributors that shaped the original Man, Myth, and Magic that served as the basis and model for these new books.

Printed in the United States of America

Contents

A Reader's Guide to *Man, Myth, and Magic: Legendary Creatures and Monsters*

Wherever cultures have grown up, there are common universal themes running through their religions, storytelling, and mythologies. Throughout history, humans have imagined fantastic beasts as the source of both legends and nightmares. There exists a fascinating combination of supernatural beings specific to an individual society and creatures that are universal in their presence in the folklore of civilizations around the world.

Dragons, fairies, dwarfs, centaurs, gorgons, and harpies all impinge on us in their different ways, showing us a glimpse of the terror, frailty, and enchantment that lurks inside us all: 'charm'd magic casements, opening on the foam of perilous seas.' Every society from the dawn of time has revered and feared creatures and monsters that were not part of the known natural order, and a number of the beasts of legends can be found across multiple civilizations.

Man, Myth, and Magic: Legendary Creatures and Monsters is a work derived from a set of volumes with two decades of bestselling and award-winning history. It is a comprehensive guide to the supernatural beings that appear in our oldest myths, are represented in the legacy of our collective art, and indeed in our dreams and consciousness. These creatures fascinate us when we are young, and the desire to read about, and perhaps spot, a mythological beast never completely fades as we age. From modern interest in vampires, Bigfoot, and the Loch Ness Monster, interest in legendary creatures has grown in recent years.*

Objectives of *Man, Myth, and Magic*

The guiding principle of the *Man, Myth, and Magic* series takes the stance of unbiased exploration. It shows the myriad ways in which different cultures have questioned and explained the mysterious nature of the world about them, and will lead teachers and students toward a broader understanding of their own and other people's beliefs and customs.

The Text

Within *Man, Myth, and Magic: Legendary Creatures and Monsters*, expert international contributors have created articles, which are arranged alphabetically, and the depth of coverage varies from major pieces of up to 10,000 words to concise, glossary-type entries in short paragraphs. From the Abominable Snowman to zombies, key creatures, monsters, and beasts from every continent are profiled, with articles focusing on how different cultures viewed these supernatural entities as either benevolent or evil. Several of the entries cover monsters and creatures that have universal versions, including dragons, ghosts, vampires, and werewolves.

The book is written in an engaging style, is heavily illustrated, and subjects of major interest are provided with individual bibliographies of further reading on the subject at the end of each article. What made it possible to create this work was the fact that the last century has seen a powerful revival of interest in these magical and mythological subjects at both the academic and the popular levels. The revival of scholarly interest has created the modern study of comparative religion and shapes and further expands modern anthropology with its investigation of so-called indigenous or first peoples and their beliefs and rituals (which have been found far more complex that originally believed). At the same time there has been a flourishing revival of popular interest in ancient civilizations, cross-cultural understanding, and alternative paths to truth. This interest

> *Whereas in the ancient Middle East and in medieval Europe the dragon remains an essentially sombre and forbidding monster, lurking in the mythical depths, as it were, in the Orient and particularly in China and Japan he has a certain splendour and panache.*

The Troll and the Boy, John Bauer (1882–1918)

has shown no sign of diminishing during this century; on the contrary, the trend has grown stronger and has explored new pathways. Scholarly investigation of the subjects included in the series as a whole has continued and has thrown much new light on some of our topics. The present edition of *Man, Myth and Magic* takes account of both these developments. Articles have been updated to cover fresh discoveries and new theories since they first appeared.

With all this, *Man, Myth, and Magic* is not intended to convert you to or from any belief or set of beliefs and attitudes. The purpose of the articles is not to persuade or

justify, but to describe what people have believed and trace the consequences of those beliefs in action. The editorial attitude is one of sympathetic neutrality. It is for the reader to decide where truth and value may lie. We hope that there is as much interest, pleasure, and satisfaction in reading these pages as all those involved took in creating them.

Illustrations

Since much of what we know about myth, folklore, and religion has been passed down over the centuries by word of mouth, and recorded only comparatively recently, visual images are often the most powerful and vivid links we have with the past. The wealth of illustrations in *Man, Myth, and Magic: Legendary Creatures and Monsters* is invaluable, not only because of the diversity of sources, but also because of the superb quality of color reproduction. Unicorns, mermaids, goblins, and so many other beasts are all recorded here in infinite variety, including tomb and wall paintings, and artifacts in metal, pottery, and wood. Examples of artwork from all over the world are represented.

Back Matter

Near the end of the book is a glossary that defines words that are most likely new to students, edifying their comprehension of the material. The A–Z index provides immediate access to any specific item sought by the reader. This reference tool distinguishes the nature of the entry in terms of a main entry, supplementary subject entries, and illustrations.

Skill Development for Students

The books of the *Man, Myth, and Magic* series can be consulted as the basic text for a subject or as a source of enrichment for students. It can act as a reference for a simple reading or writing assignment, and as the inspiration for a major research or term paper. The additional readings suggested at the end of many entries is an invaluable resource for students looking to further their studies on a specific topic. *Man, Myth, and Magic* offers an opportunity for students that is extremely enlightening; twenty volumes that are both multi-disciplinary and inter-disciplinary; a wealth of fine illustrations; a research source well-suited to a variety of age levels that will provoke interest and encourage speculation in both teachers and students.

Scope

As well as being a major asset to social studies teaching, the book provides students from a wide range of disciplines with a stimulating, accessible, and beautifully illustrated reference work.

The *Man, Myth, and Magic* series lends itself easily to a multi-disciplinary approach to study. In *Man, Myth, and Magic: Legendary Creatures and Monsters*, literature students will be interested in the legends, fairy tales and folk plays, the written works of prose and poetry that incorporate these fantastical beings. The symbolism and representation of these beasts shown in the marvelous illustrations will expand the minds of students of art, whether as practitioners or scholars.

Students of music can learn how the grandeur of such beasts lends itself to inspire compositions. History buffs can see how, springing from our hopes and fears, certain of these creatures became emblematic of various armies and nations. As well as its relevance to study areas already mentioned, the book will provide strong background reference in anthropology, philosophy, and comparative religion.

Conceptual Themes

As students delve into this volume, they will gradually become sensitive to the major concepts emerging from the text. Students can begin to understand the prevalence of mythological creatures, with their exaggerated features and oftentimes human characteristics, across the globe. They can grasp the development of patterns and motifs that accompany this amazing menagerie. The themes that recur throughout these stories of the supernatural are, in fact, reflections of mankind's history, what society expects and the individual experiences. The creatures and their actions are details of our eternal story and adventure.

The concept of magic appears in folklore tales all over the world, in the good fortune brought by fairies and leprechauns, in the cries of the banshees heard at the deathbed. What similarities and differences exist in the imaginary beasts among all cultures? There is a primal threat of the unknown dangerous prowlers of the night, the similarities in the sightings of yeti in the Himalayas, skunk apes in Appalachia, and Sasquatch in the Pacific Northwest. Mythological creatures have been alongside every heroic endeavor of legends. Understanding how civilizations from the earliest days of creation have always incorporated unbelievable, but somehow necessary, animals into their stories can make for a keener understanding of our history and of our selves. These areas of man's belief in magic and the expressions of the human condition through legends and myths are challenging ways for more advanced students to use both this individual volume and the other title selections in this set.

Abominable Snowman

The abominable snowman of the Himalayas is supposed to be a creature half-human and half-animal, hairy and about the size of a child of twelve or fourteen, which walks erect on two legs, swinging its arms. Its hair is described as reddish or light brown, and not very thick. European travelers called the snowman 'abominable' because of the horror with which the Sherpas, a Himalayan people, regard the creatures, which they call yeti.

Expeditions have searched without success for the yeti. Mountaineers have found what were thought to be its footprints in the snow, but research has revealed that these tracks were made by other animals. Anthropologists have shown that the Sherpas' stories are questionable, and the view that the snowman is a legend is now widely accepted. Legends of hairy mountainmen have also been reported from the Gobi desert, Mongolia, and the Rockies near Canada's Pacific coast.

According to Sherpa folklore, a monkey king was converted to Buddhism and lived as a hermit in the mountains; an ogress fell in love with him and he abandoned his solitary life to marry her. The children she bore him were covered in hair and had tails, and they were the first yeti.

Alien Visitors

In many mythologies the great gods live in the sky or on top of a high mountain, from which they look down and see the doings of human beings on the earth. Sometimes they come down to Earth, often in disguise, and intervene in events on the human plane. Early in the Old Testament story the 'sons of God' look down from heaven and see that the daughters of men are fair, so they descend to Earth and beget children with them. The Greek gods have numerous amatory encounters with human beings in mythology, and in Norse mythology the god Odin is a frequent wanderer upon the earth. In Jewish, Christian, and Moslem tradition, God sends angels to the earth as messengers to men. The belief that spirits from a different plane can invade human beings' bodies and minds is known all over the world.

This ancient theme has taken on a new lease of life in the theory that travelers from outer space visited the earth in spaceships in the past and intervened in earthly matters. They are credited with using their superior knowledge and technique to teach the earthlings and create the basis of human civilization. The awed earthlings regarded the visitants as gods and weaved mythologies about them. These alien visitors are still coming, it is claimed, and there are reports of them being seen by human beings, communicating with members of our species, and sometimes abducting or 'space-napping' people.

Visitor from Venus

All sorts of strange things have been seen, or imagined, in the sky for centuries past—armies marching in the clouds, airy chariots, pillars of flame, wheels, bow-shaped objects, globes, and flying crosses. In 1646 in England many 'honest, sober, and civil persons and men of good credit' were reported to have seen men struggling in the air and tugging at each other, one of them holding a drawn sword. In 1878 a farmer in Texas used a significant word in describing something bright orange he had seen in the sky, moving very fast. He said it was 'the size of a large saucer and evidently at great height.'

The expression 'flying saucer' did not come into general use until a man named Kenneth Arnold saw nine mysterious objects flying at blistering speed near Mt. Rainier in Washington State in 1947 and described them as looking like 'saucers when skipped over water.' Five years later, in 1952, a Californian named George Adamski claimed he had met an alien from a flying saucer from Venus. The alien was about 5 feet 6 inches tall, blond, tanned, and long-haired, wore a brown uniform without pockets or fasteners, and struck Adamski as beautiful and profoundly wise. He said he had felt 'like a child in the presence of one with great wisdom and much love.' Communicating with Adamski telepathically, the alien told him that his people on Venus were greatly alarmed by the development of nuclear weapons on Earth.

There are many conspiracy theories surrounding alien visitations to Earth.

This was a theme that was to recur frequently in accounts of encounters with aliens, who were often credited with the same kind of vaguely uplifting and mushily benevolent sentiments about peace and love as many of the 'spirits' purporting to communicate through mediums and channelers. An opportunity to get high-minded sentiments of this kind across to the public appears to be one of the motives, conscious or unconscious, of many mediums, channelers, and alien visitor contactees.

Adamski's experience was reported to the world, in 1953, in a book called *Flying Saucers Have Landed*, which sold like hot cakes and brought him much short-term notoriety. He afterward claimed many more meetings with alien humanoids, but few students of Unidentified Flying Objects have ever taken him seriously. The publicity he gained, however, set off a wave of revelations from other people who claimed to have encountered mysterious beings from space.

Hypnosis Has Landed

There was a sensational and significant development when a couple named Betty and Barney Hill were driving through the White Mountains in New Hampshire, in 1961, and saw a large object shaped like a pancake with windows descend from the sky. They forgot what happened next, but they found themselves further down the road than they could account for and they seemed to have lost two hours of time. They both began to experience disturbing dreams. In 1963, they consulted a psychiatrist in Boston and under hypnosis they 'remembered' what had happened to them. They said they were taken on board the spacecraft, undressed, and medically examined by the crew—aliens who

were about 5 feet tall, hairless, with blue-grey skin, pear-shaped heads, domed foreheads, and slanting, catlike eyes. The aliens came from a star named Zeta Reticuli. They were fascinated by Barney Hill's false teeth and, apparently, they took a sperm sample from him and subjected Betty to a pregnancy test.

The psychiatrist had no doubt that the Hills were fantasizing, but their story was written up in a successful book and later made into a film. The Hill case set an unfortunate precedent for the use of regression hypnosis to elicit supposedly suppressed memories of 'encounters of the fourth kind,' which have too often been accepted as gospel despite their unverifiability

> Then suddenly, with a strange buzzing noise, three extraordinary creatures flew through the kitchen and into the lounge. They were only about 36 inches tall . . .

and the lack of corroborating evidence. It also sparked off theories about the extraterrestrials conducting human breeding programmes, which seem to have ministered to a need deep in human psychology.

'We Shall Return'

Not all the reported cases have needed hypnosis to bring them back to memory, by any means. In 1957, Antonio Villas Boas, a 23-year-old Brazilian, was ploughing a field at night—to escape the ferocious heat of the day—when something descended to the ground close to him, and small creatures emerged. They were about 5 feet tall and wore 'space suits' with helmets and breathing apparatus. They seized him and took him to their spacecraft, where his clothes were stripped off and a strange-

looking naked woman, red-haired, fair-skinned, and high-cheekboned, made forcible love to him. Afterward she pointed to her belly and then to the sky, evidently meaning that she would bear his baby in her own world far away among the stars. His clothes were given back to him and he was shown round the strange beings' craft before they finally let him go.

The sexual motif in this account, reminiscent of much of the world's heritage of mythology, is one that has recurred frequently. Serious students of UFOs were unhappy with the publicity given to the story when it came to public attention in 1964. They did not believe it and feared it would bring the whole subject into disrepute. A doctor who examined Villas Boas in Rio de Janeiro in 1958, however, was favourably impressed by him and said he showed symptoms consistent with exposure to radiation.

Many more stories of alien visitors emerged from South America. In Chile, in 1977, a patrol of six young soldiers and a corporal in the early hours of the morning saw lights in the sky. An object landed not far away from them and the corporal, telling the others to stay put, walked toward it in the darkness. They waited anxiously for fifteen minutes until the corporal returned. He was in a strange, trancelike state, mumbling to himself, 'You do not know who we are or where we come from, but I tell you we shall return.' Then he passed out.

At dawn, the soldiers were surprised to see several days' growth of beard on the corporal's face and to discover that his digital watch showed a date five days ahead. They took him to the town of Putre, where the authorities hushed up the whole affair. All the corporal would say when he was at last allowed to talk to the media was that he could not remember what had happened.

The detail about the date on the watch recalls old traditions about fairylands and spiritual realms where time runs differently from on earth.

The Astronaut God

In the late 1960s and for a time in the 1970s, a Swiss author, Erich von Däniken, made himself a fortune and attracted excited attention in the media with a series of books in which he maintained that far in the remote past, some 10,000 years ago, the earth had been visited by advanced beings from outer space who created the human race in their own image by altering the genes of monkeys. These early astronauts were worshipped as gods by their creation, and the world's mythologies and sacred books are disguised accounts of their period on earth. He cited various ancient artefacts as proof of his theories, including the Olmec heads of ancient Mexico, the Easter Island statues, the mysterious Nazca lines of Peru and the Great Pyramid of Egypt.

Von Däniken's first book, *Chariots of the Gods?*, came out in German in 1967 and proved to be a best seller in 26 different languages, including Bengali, Chinese, and Hebrew, as well as English, but his 'evidence' proved lamentably unconvincing. The craze presently died away, but it had demonstrated the urgent need with which many people, at a time of declining confidence in the established religions, wanted to believe in powerful superhuman forces at work in the universe.

Alien Corn

Many observers have pointed out the link between reported contacts with alien intruders and science fiction. Long before the 1950s and the subsequent crop of stories of abductions and rapes, writers like Jules Verne, H. G. Wells, and Edgar Rice Burroughs, and an army of pulp fiction authors, had told vivid stories of alien beings

coming to earth. In 1951, the year before George Adamski supposedly met his amiable Venusian, the film *The Day the Earth Stood Still* had well-intentioned aliens coming to earth and landing in Washington D.C. to warn the world of the danger. In 1953, the film *Invaders From Mars* probably helped to stimulate the rash of reports of unfriendly aliens landing and kidnapping humans.

One of the unsatisfactory things about the reports is that the aliens' appearance varies so enormously. They are sometimes tall and sometimes short, sometimes fat and sometimes thin, sometimes furry and sometimes hairless. They may have long arms or short arms, large heads or small heads or no heads at all, slanting eyes or goggle eyes. Some of them are diminutive figures, recalling the fairies and goblins of traditional European folklore.

In 1976, two women in County Durham, England, described aliens they claimed to have seen as little creatures only 18 inches tall, with long white hair and huge eyes. In 1978, there was an abduction involving three adults and two children in Oxfordshire, England. Under hypnotic regression, one of the children described the aliens as small, goblinlike creatures with big ears, but the others said they were human in appearance, tall and fair with blue eyes, wearing silver suits and black shoes, but with unnaturally large ears.

It is hard to believe that aliens from so many different civilizations are busy dropping in on the earth and difficult not to conclude that they do not come from outer space at all, but from the inner spaces of the human mind. Again, however, they do reflect the age-old human need for otherworldly figures and, although some of them are all sweetness and light, others are evil. One persistent motif is that of the Men in Black, sinister bureaucrats who arrive on the scene after an abduction

is over and warn the victims to keep quiet. They may be aliens themselves or zombielike humans in league with the aliens.

Extraterrestrials seem to have penetrated even behind the Iron Curtain. In 1989, Tass reported a claim that three 10 foot humanoids with tiny heads and three eyes apiece, wearing silver suits and accompanied by a robot, had landed at Voronezh in a spaceship like a shining ball. Several children claimed to have seen them, but were unable to back up their story.

'Take Me To Your Larder'

This headline topped media reports in Britain of a case in 1979 that had its comical aspects. A 45-year-old woman in the West Midlands saw her husband off to work as usual at seven one morning and thought she saw a light in the garden. She looked to see if the carport light was on, but it was not, so she thought no more of it. She put down food for the family Alsatian dog and called him. When the dog came in from the garden, he flopped down, glassy-eyed as if he had been drugged. Then suddenly, with a strange buzzing noise, three extraordinary creatures flew through the kitchen and into the lounge. They were only about 36 inches tall and had white, waxy faces and black eyes, with thin slits of mouths and no eyebrows. They had wings and wore silvery clothes.

The woman found herself floating involuntarily into the lounge, where she had to shield her eyes from glowing light. The three peculiar intruders were attentively examining the ornaments on the Christmas tree. They probed into her mind telepathically, telling her not to be afraid as they would not harm her, and that they came from the sky. She told them that the decorations were up to celebrate the birthday of Jesus and they telegraphed back that they knew all about Jesus.

She gave them mince pies, but they did not eat them. They said they often came 'down here' to talk to people, but people did not seem to be interested. When she lit a cigarette, they seemed terrified and dashed off, each of them taking a mince pie. Outside she saw them go into an egg-shaped object, which took off. She found that the electric clock in the house had stopped and that all her cassette tapes were magnetized and unplayable. Her eyes were sore and she felt sick for a week.

Alien Communions

The American novelist Whitley Strieber believed that he had been visited by alien beings on numerous occasions. They were of different physical types. Some were short and stocky with broad faces, deep-set eyes, pug noses, and wide mouths. Others were about 5 feet tall, slender and delicate, with slanted, prominent, and mesmerizing black eyes, and only a vestigial nose and mouth. There were smaller ones with round black eyes like buttons. The beings subjected him to thorough, painful, and unpleasant physical examination. They also injected something into his brain.

The book describing his experiences, *Communion*, came out in 1987, was hyped in the media, and duly proved to be a successful seller. Unfortunately it was entirely based on 'memories' elicited under hypnosis. Jenny Randles, the British investigator, has commented on 'the almost wild and semihysterical zeal' with which believers in alien abduction greet figures like Strieber and Kathie Davis (an American abductee who claimed to have been made pregnant by an alien and had her unborn foetus taken from her body by aliens to be brought up elsewhere). Casting doubt on claims of this kind offends the need to believe, but the belief itself may be extremely dangerous. In 1986, a case was reported in England in which two small girls were murdered by their grandmother, who allegedly believed it the only way to save them from aliens who were trying to beam them up into space.

FURTHER READING: J. Spencer and H. Evans ed., Phenomenon: From Flying Saucers to UFOs. *(Macdonald, 1988); Richard Hall.* Uninvited Guests. *(Aurora Press, 1988); J. Randles.* Abduction. *(Hale, 1988); E. Fiore.* Abductions. *(Sidgwick & Jackson, 1989).*

Banshee

In Irish folklore, the banshee is a female spirit whose keening or wailing voice is believed to be the harbinger of imminent death. On occasion, the banshee may herald the death of someone away from home or even overseas. The wailing is most often heard at night, sometimes on several successive nights. The banshee is usually an auditory rather than a visual phenomenon, although, if visible, she may take the form of a woman with long pale hair. Individual banshees are associated with particular family

Boaters are terrorized by banshees in the Vladimir Makovsky work *Terrible Vengeance* (1874).

names. The banshee is found also in Norse, Scottish, and Welsh mythology as well as in North American folklore.

Basilisk

The basilisk was the king of serpents, a creature with the body and feet of a winged cockerel and the tail of a snake, which was believed to be so lethal that it could kill by simply looking at its victim. Its hiss and smell were also believed to be fatal. These beliefs were

Basilisk out of Bertuch's *Fabelwesen*

widespread across medieval Europe and had a long lineage. The basilisk was described in his *Natural History*, written about AD 79, by Pliny the Elder, who noted that an attempt by a horseman to kill the beast with a spear would result in the toxin traveling up the spear to destroy both rider and horse. He recorded that the only animal able to overcome the basilisk was the weasel. Some 1,300 years later, the power of the basilisk was still active in the popular imagination when the poet Geoffrey Chaucer referred in *The Canterbury Tales* to the creature's ability to kill by sight. In early Christian symbolism, the basilisk was thought to represent the Devil, and the English translation of the Latin Vulgate Bible made at Douai in the late sixteenth century makes several references to the power of the basilisk.

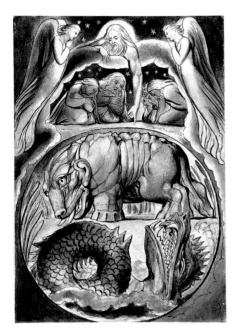

William Blake's *Behemoth and Leviathan*, from his work *The Book of Job* (1825).

Behemoth

From Old Testament times Behemoth was the king of the beasts. The prophet Job described him as 'a tyrant over his fellow creatures' that no one 'under wide heaven' could ever attack and emerge from the encounter unscathed. As insurance against famine, should the ravenous Behemoth and his offspring devour the earth's resources, the monster was created with no sexual desire and forced to live in barren territory. In reality, Behemoth was probably a hippopotamus, or possibly an elephant, despite the fact that modern Biblical translations call him 'crocodile'. His name derives from the plural of the Hebrew *behemah*, meaning 'beast'.

Bigfoot

Known to Native Americans as Sasquatch—'hairy man'—this giant hominid creature, similar to the Himalayan yeti, has been recorded in various parts of the United States for close to two centuries, and given the popular name of Bigfoot.

As early as 1851, a local newspaper in Greene County, Arkansas, reported that two hunters had seen a herd of cattle being chased by 'an animal bearing the unmistakable likeness of humanity.' This 'wild man' was of gigantic stature and, after watching the hunters, turned and ran away, leaping 12 to 14 feet at a time, and leaving footprints 13 inches long.

Indian legends picture the creature as a giant 8 or 9 feet tall, with a wide, flat nose and very long arms. It is said to be particularly concentrated in the region of Morris Mountain, some 60 miles inland from Vancouver.

Well over a thousand sightings of Bigfoot have been reported over the past 150 years. Most have been in the northwest USA and Canada, but in recent years a similar creature, known locally as the 'skunk ape,' has been reported from as far south as Florida.

One of the more convincing sightings dates from 1967, when Roger Patterson and Bob Gimlin were riding through the remote forest of the Bluff Creek area of northern California. They came upon a huge humanoid creature, some 7 feet tall and covered all over with dark hair, squatting beside a creek. Patterson had his movie camera with him and, as the creature rose and hurried away, he leapt from his horse and followed it, filming as he ran. He shot 30 feet of colour film before the being disappeared into the trees; but he was also able to take casts of footprints, twice the size of a man's.

Critics have dismissed the film as that of an actor dressed in a gorilla suit, but footprints reported from other sightings have matched the casts, and many descriptions, by apparently objective observers, correspond with the appearance of the creature in the film.

Bigfoot is said to be shy but inquisitive, coming close to people camping in the forest, and pawing through their belongings at night.

Sceptics dismiss sightings as poorly observed bears, but since the earliest reports the descriptions of Bigfoot have remained consistent.

Several people claim to have had the opportunity to observe the creature from hiding, and all agree that it is some 6 to 8 feet in height and heavily built; humanlike, although covered with dark hair, and walking upright. Perhaps the most remarkable report was that of Albert Ostman, who alleged in 1924 that he had been kidnapped by a Bigfoot near Toba Inlet in British Columbia, and held captive by a family of four for several days. He finally escaped by offering the father of the family a large amount of snuff, and fleeing as the creature gasped for breath.

Several searches have been mounted for Bigfoot, but its mountain home is difficult terrain, broken by impassable ravines. Some caves were found near Morris Mountain that showed signs of past habitation, though whether by long-dead Indians or hairy hominids no one can say. Bigfoot seems destined to remain a representative of the universal mythic wild man, from the yeti and 'Neanderthal' survivors of central Asia to the Tarzans of modern fiction.

Centaur

Centaurs were monsters in the classical sense, in that these legendary creatures combined two species in one skin. They had human heads, arms and torsos, merging into the bodies of horses. Centaurs were often savage and unbridled, according to report. Yet they had much mysterious wisdom and virtues far surpassing those of ordinary men.

The ancient Greeks regarded the centaurs as fanciful celebrants who danced in the train of Dionysus, the wine god, but also believed that their own forefathers had both befriended and fought against centaurs in the days of old. The latter conviction probably had some basis in fact, for the name centaurs signifies 'those who round up bulls' and the idea of the centaur may well have sprung from the cattle-breeders of Thessaly in northern Greece, who spent much of their time on horseback and whose manners were rough and barbarous. Alternatively, it has been suggested that the original centaurs were Cimmerian and Scythian raiders, rough-riding nomads from the north, who often invaded Thrace in the northeast.

In mythology, the origin of the centaur was more poetic. It was said that a most reprehensible mortal man named Ixion had founded the race. This Ixion committed the outrageous offence of daring to attempt to seduce Hera, wife to Zeus and queen of heaven itself. To see how far Ixion's impudence would go, Zeus formed a cloud image of Hera and substituted it for the goddess. A monster, Centaurus, was born of this strange union, and when grown to maturity, united with the mares of Mt. Pelion and so produced the centaurs.

Another, more austere legend has it that Chiron was the first centaur. Chiron had begun life as a Titan, a primeval son of Cronus and the ocean nymph Philyra. He dared make war against the young gods of Olympus, but they defeated him. Apollo, the god of light and reason, punished Chiron by making him half horse.

He had been educated by the gods and in turn undertook the instruction of hero after hero: Actaeon, Jason, Castor and Polydeuces, and Achilles, each served an apprenticeship with Chiron in the wilderness.

But Chiron's own fate was an unhappy one. He fell wounded by a poisoned arrow in a tragic accident. The arrow came from the quiver of a good friend, the best of men, impetuous Hercules. There was no

antidote to its poison. To escape the wound's unending agony, Chiron renounced immortality in favour of his fellow-Titan, Prometheus. Zeus then generously set the kindly centaur's image in the heavens as the constellation Sagittarius, the Archer.

Feast of the Lapiths

Artists have always delighted in the challenge centaurs offer them. Arnold Böcklin, the nineteenth-century German artist, once painted a huge centaur who stoops into a blacksmith's shop to have his shoes repaired. Rubens sketched a boyish Achilles astride Chiron's broad back; the ageless tutor turns halfway round in mid-gallop to explain some abstruse point. One of Michelangelo's first sculptures was a bas-relief *Battle of the Centaurs*. His source was the Roman poet Ovid, who vividly describes a feast held by the Lapith tribe, a legendary people of Thessaly, to celebrate the nuptials of their chieftain Peirithous.

The centaurs were invited to attend that feast as friends but they got drunk and tried to drag the Lapith women forcibly off into the bushes. A brawl ensued, with slaughter on both sides, and the centaurs were driven away as darkness fell. According to another version, the centaur Eurytion was invited to the feast but became excited with the wine, attempted to abduct the bride, and was restrained by Theseus. Eurytion then returned to the attack with a band of centaurs, who were armed with slabs of stone and trunks of pine trees. A long battle followed, from which the Lapiths eventually emerged victorious. The centaurs were driven to the frontiers of Epirus and sought shelter on Mt. Pindus. It was this quarrel that sadly put an end to the ancient friendship between man-kind and the centaurs.

Today in Greece, the peasants will tell you of *kallikantzaroi*, 'good centaurs', who appear to be descended

from the old legendary creatures. But the 'good' that has been prefixed to their names in modern times is a precaution taken out of fear, as when a superstitious northerner refers to elves or fairies as 'the good people'. The kallikantzaroi come up out of the ground on winter nights. They are hoofed, shaggy, swift, stupid, and mischievous. In short, they are 'monsters' in the modern, and not the ancient, sense.

ALEXANDER ELIOT

Cerberus

Cerberus, the three-headed, serpent-tailed 'dog of Hades', resided at the entrance to the Greek underworld. Here, on the far side of the River Styx, this offspring of Typhon, the monstrous being associated with the winds, and Echinda, the creature who was half woman half serpent, guarded the entrance to the underworld, in order to prevent the souls, or 'shades', of the dead from leaving. As they were rowed in by Charon, the ferryman, Cerberus would greet the newly deceased—sometimes with courtesy, sometimes with ferocious snarling. To help ensure a friendly welcome, the dead were provided with honey-cakes with which to placate the creature and keep him occupied as they passed. These 'sops to Cerberus' have since become a metaphor for any small sweetener offered temporarily to avert a threat. Where the saliva of the hell-dog Cerberus dripped, it is alleged to have stimulated the growth of the deadly poisonous monkshood plant (*Aconitum napellus*), also known as wolfsbane, at the gates of Hades.

Even the Gods lived in fear of Cerberus. In an attempt to lull the creature into submission, Orpheus successfully sent the creature to sleep with the sound of his lyre, while the Sibyl produced the same soporific effect by

Cerberus depicted on a coin (1637) commemorating victories of Polish King Vladislaus IV over Russia, Turkey, and Sweden

throwing into each of the dog's mouths some pieces of cake seasoned with poppies and honey. The Greek hero Hercules confronted the hellhound in his twelfth and most challenging labour. Despite being bitten by its tail, Hercules managed to seize the animal's head and carry it back, as ordered by Apollo, to King Eurystheus.

The legend of Cerberus is thought to originate in the Egyptian custom of using dogs to guard graves; in Egyptian mythology the jackal-headed god Anubis performed a similar role. However, the number of his heads was not fixed at three until Roman times. When first described by the Greek poet Hesiod in the 8th century BC, he was said to have no fewer than fifty.

Changeling

The birth of a deformed, moronic, or exceptionally ugly child is an old tragedy. One way to make the parents feel better is to decide that the child is not their own at all but a substitute, left by the fairies in place of the child they have stolen. How much pain has been suffered by children believed to be changelings no one can measure, but a hundred years ago in Ireland a changeling child was burned to death on a hot shovel. In 1894, near Clonmel in Ireland, a young woman was burned to death as a changeling by her husband and family. There are many stories of a child being thrown out on a dungheap to die of exposure, and a favourite way of dealing with a changeling was to whip it until the fairies came to take it back.

A changeling can also be made to reveal its true form by making it laugh or making it cross water. It is some-times a fairy child but more often an old, even senile fairy, disguised as an infant. A typical English changeling story tells how a woman's baby never grew, was always hungry, failed to learn to walk, and lay in its cradle year after year. The woman's older son, a soldier, coming home after a long absence, saw the child's strange and hairy face, and took an empty eggshell, which he filled with malt and hops, and heated on the fire. There was a laugh from the cradle. 'I am old, old, ever so old,' said the changeling, 'but I never saw a soldier brewing beer in an eggshell before.' Now he knew for sure that it was a changeling, the soldier went for it with a whip, and it vanished through the door.

A baby was likely to be snatched away by the fairies before he had been christened, that is before he had been made a Christian and before he had been officially named, and so became a person in his own right. Ways to protect him were to draw a circle of fire round him, hang a pair of open scissors over him, or put his father's trousers across the cradle.

Chupacabra

Stories of a mysterious blood-sucking animal that preyed on and killed livestock at night began to circulate in 1995 in Puerto Rico, an island in the Caribbean. Sheep were the first reported victims, whose bodies were allegedly drained of blood by the attacker, and some five months later a large number of agricultural animals, including poultry, were found dead, bearing the same incision marks as the sheep. The unknown predator was given the name Chupacabra from the Spanish *chupar* meaning 'to suck' and *cabra* for 'goat', although the creature appeared to be indiscriminate in its liking for a wide range of prey. Initially, the killings were thought to be part of an occult ritual.

Reports of similar attacks occurred in Mexico as well as the southern United States the following year.

Sightings of the beast became widespread as the fear of the vampirelike creature increased. There was speculation that the Chupacabra was a supernatural or alien being who also attacked people. Descriptions of it by eyewitnesses included talons, a reptilian skin and glowing red eyes, although it was also said to resemble a strange wild dog with large teeth.

The scientific and veterinary community expressed scepticism about the mythology of the Chupacabra. One theory regarding its origin is that the Chupacabra is as much a victim as an aggressor, being a wild dog or coyote infested with a particularly virulent form of mange, which causes the animal's coat to drop out and the skin to thicken giving it a leathery appearance. An infected animal is also vulnerable to secondary infection, which could account for the reported unpleasant smell of the Chupacabra. Lacking the strength to hunt the small mammals that usually form their diet, sick coyotes resort to preying on agricultural and domestic animals, following their preferred pattern of nocturnal hunting.

Chimaera

The Chimaera was a monster compounded of parts from three creatures: lion, goat, and serpent. It appears in Homer's *Iliad* (books 6 and 16) as located in Lycia, in Asia Minor, where it is killed by the hero Bellerophon. Bellerophon's legend contains many more adventures than his battle with the Chimaera, but these additional features belong to other, unrelated, parts of the legend and need not concern us here.

Bellerophon was already disliked by his ruler, Proetus, the king of Ephyre in Argolis, a place usually identified with Corinth. He was also disliked by Proetus's wife Antea, who tried to

seduce him and failed. In revenge, she accused him of making advances to her. Proetus did not try to kill him directly, but sent him to Iobates of Lycia, his father-in-law. Bellerophon was at first well received by Iobates, but when the king read the calumnious letter that he brought, containing secret instructions that Bellerophon should be killed, he plotted his death by ordering him to slay the Chimaera.

The Chimaera was of divine, not human origin, being 'a lion at the front, a serpent at the rear, and in the middle a chimaera.' This word, which seems to leave part of its body unexplained, meant 'goat'. 'The Chimaera breathed flashing fire. But Bellerophon killed it, relying on marvels from the gods.'

He then fought his way through other perils until he married the king's daughter. The Chimaera is called *amaimaketos*, an epithet which is otherwise used of fire and probably means 'raging', though some ancient writers used it to mean 'invincible'. In Hesiod's *Theogony*, probably written in the 8th century BC, the Chimaera is mentioned as born by Echidna to Typhon with other monsters: Orthus, Geryon's hound, Cerberus, and the Hydra. Typhon's origin was certainly in Lycia, so that scholars who say that the Chimaera's location there is only secondary are probably wrong.

Hesiod says that the Chimaera had three heads, one belonging to each component animal, that it was killed by Pegasus and Bellerophon, and that by Orthus it was the mother of the Sphinx and the Nemean lion. A fragment of Hesiod's *Catalogue of Women*, which mentions the legend of Bellerophon, seems to be our earliest explicit reference to Pegasus as the name of his horse. Pindar alludes very briefly to Bellerophon's killing of the Chimaera.

Apollodorus, at the end of his history of Greek mythology, written in the 2nd century BC, once more

gives the story of Bellerophon. Of the Chimaera, he says that it was more than a match for many men, and that through its middle head, that of a goat, it belched fire. It was a single creature with the power of three beasts. Bellerophon, soaring high on his winged horse, Pegasus, shot down the Chimaera. Pegasus was thus a necessary means for its killing.

The name of this mythical monster, which once described a beast compounded of a lion, a goat, and a serpent, has come to be used for any hybrid plant or animal or, in a metaphorical sense, for any imaginary fear.

This has an affinity with a Hittite winged lion from Carchemish on the Euphrates, which has a snake for its tail and a second and human head rising from its back. The fiery breath of the Chimaera may be a mythical rendering of the flaming gas that rises from the ground here and there in the southwest of Anatolia.

Alternatively, it has been said that the Chimaera was a personification of the storm cloud. Today, it describes any fantastic or horrible imaginary creature, and is also the term applied by biologists to plants and animals having hybrid characteristics.

Cyclops

Cyclops, or 'circle-eye', is the name given to the one-eyed giants of Greek myth. Divine craftsmen, they were the forgers of Zeus's thunderbolt. Best known is Polyphemus, who, in Homer's *Odyssey*, imprisons Odysseus and his men, but is outwitted by the hero. The cyclops is generally depicted in classical literature as a figure of burlesque and fun.

Opposite page:
Galathea by Gustave Moreau (1826–1898) depicts a scene from Ovid's narrative poem *Metamorphoses*.

Demons

Evil spirits: derived from the Greek *daimon* (hence 'daemon'), a spirit which might be good or bad. The Christians condemned all pagan spirits as evil beings under the sway of the Devil, which gave the word 'demon' its invariably evil modern connotation.

Dracula

The most famous vampire of fiction, central character of Bram Stoker's novel *Dracula*, published in 1897, and of a celebrated film version, made in 1931 and starring Bela Lugosi. A walking corpse that sucks the blood of the living, Dracula has appeared in many other horror films.

Dragon

Where there are myths, there are usually dragons. But although it would be easy to recognize a dragon, and descriptions and artistic representations of dragons abound, it is not so easy to define the beast. Like other fabulous monsters, such as the Chimaera and griffin, the dragon is a mixture of several creatures. One of the earliest dragons to leave a permanent mark in the world (he is depicted in white glaze against a blue background on a gate in ancient Babylon) appears to have the head and horns of a ram, the forelegs of a lion, a scaly, reptilian body and tail, and the hind legs of an eagle. Each race has naturally drawn on the part of the animal world with which it is familiar in putting this composite beast together. The dragon of the ancient Egyptians is a close relation of the crocodile, while elephant dragons appear in Indian myths, and stag dragons in Chinese.

The dragon is even more dangerously equipped than any of his mythical rivals. The forked tongue and tail, the glaring eyes and ominously flared nostrils, the scorching breath, the sharp teeth and talons, and the armour-plating of the body add up to a formidable array of weapons. But strangely enough, the dragon is by no means always hostile to man. In the East, particularly, he is often a symbol or a portent of prosperity, and there are many tales of individual acts of kindness performed by dragons for the benefit of men.

Cadmus Slays the Dragon, Hendrik Goltzius (1558–1617)

So-called *Altar of Domitius Ahenobarbus* or *Statue Base of Marcus Antonius*, relief frieze of a monumental statue group base

Though most people now would associate the dragon with fire, his primeval element is water, whether the sea, rivers, lakes, water-spouts, or rain clouds, and this watery connection is what chiefly distinguishes the dragon from other mythical hybrids. Even desert-dwelling people insist on it, and their dragons spend a lot of time lurking at the bottom of wells. Indeed, the bottom of a well is often identified with the dragon's eye, and this is a link with another distinguishing characteristic of the dragon: its baleful and searching gaze. There is little doubt that the word 'dragon' is derived ultimately from an ancient Greek word meaning 'to see'. In the Old Testament the dragon is mentioned several times in the same breath as the owl, another creature with large, bleak eyes.

Descended from Serpents

Like other creatures, both mythical and real, the dragon has evolved. The giant saurians—the whale-sized fish-lizards, the 50 foot tyrannosaurs, and the tanklike dinosaurs—disappeared from the face of the earth millions of years before man appeared, but it is possible that their fossils and remains inspired the earliest stories about dragons. Amongst extant creatures, however, the dragon's earliest identifiable progenitor is the serpent, and some authorities believe that they can trace the lineage of dragons all over the world back to one common ancestor, Zu, the monster of watery chaos in Sumerian mythology.

The Sumerians settled in Mesopotamia in the 5th millennium BC, and their struggle to tame the rivers in that country inspired several myths. Their most important god was Enlil, who himself started life as a river god, but was promoted to the dry land and the upper world. The serpent or dragon Zu stole the tablets, worn by Enlil on his breast, on which were set out the laws governing the universe. On Enlil's orders, Zu was slain by the sun god Ninurta, who thus set the precedent for sun gods who battle with dragons in the myths of other ancient peoples.

The Sumerians were superseded, around 1800 BC, by the Babylonians, a Semitic people who took over many of their myths and religious beliefs. The legend of Zu left traces in the great Babylonian epic of creation, Enuma Elish, in which the sea goddess Tiamat leads the forces of primeval watery chaos against the gods. In her army she has sharp-fanged serpents and ferocious dragons, with crowns of flames, made so much like gods that all who look at them die of fright. She is defeated nevertheless by Marduk, champion of the gods, and son of Ea (Enki in Sumerian), the god of wisdom. After the battle, Marduk cuts Tiamat's body in two, leaving one half to form the sea and lifting up the other half to form the sky. Marduk was originally the local god of the unimportant town of Babilu, but his power grew with that of his people, the Babylonians, and he became eventually the god of creation. Every New Year, which the Babylonians celebrated in the spring, his victory over the dragons of chaos was reenacted through the recital by priests of the creation epic.

It seems likely that Babylonian or Sumerian influence were at work from an early period in Egypt. The dragon

Andromeda Freed by Perseus, Piero di Cosimo (1462–1521)

myth in particular is thought to have reached there toward the end of the 3rd millennium BC, and to have inspired the legend of the gigantic serpent Apophis (or Apep, or Apop), the enemy of the sun god. Later in Egyptian mythol-ogy, the captive Apophis was identi-fied with the ocean that girt the earth and held it together, but at the same time threatened to break its fetters and destroy the world. The Egyptians gradually adapted the dragon myth from one of creation to one of the daily combat between light and dark-ness. The sunset was interpreted as the swallowing of the sun by Apophis, or alternatively the sun was imagined to do battle with the dragon every night

as it traveled through the underworld. The dragon rose from a dark river to attack the sun's boat, but by morning had been cut to pieces, or, in other versions of the myth, had been forced to disgorge the sun.

There was a similar story of battle between the sun and storm clouds, also represented as a conflict between the god and a dragon or water monster. In a related Asiatic myth, which also derives from the Sumerian

and Babylonian stories of battles between the dragons and a god, the dragons survived but were held on the seabed by fetters or by the hands of the gods; their struggles to free themselves caused earthquakes and violent storms.

Servant of the Devil

At a later period in Egypt, the dragon was identified with the god Seth, the violent 'Lord of the South', god of earthquakes, hurricanes, thunder, and destruction, who shook the very sea itself. The belief arose, too, that after death the souls of the wicked would be cast before a fire-breathing dragon or devoured by the 'Swallower of the West', a dragonlike hybrid which was made up from the crocodile, the lion, and the hippopotamus.

In the oldest writings in the Old Testament, Yahweh is represented as a storm god, at whose coming 'the earth trembled, and the heavens dropped, yea, the clouds dropped water, the mountains quaked before the Lord' (Judges 5.4–5). His power over sea, sky, cloud, and serpent is celebrated in passages reminiscent of the Babylonian and Egyptian dragon-myths. 'Thou didst break the heads of the dragons on the waters,' says the Psalmist (Psalm 74.13), and, according to Isaiah (27.1), 'The Lord . . . shall slay the dragon that is in the sea.' In fact, the battle between Yahweh and the dragons is a familiar theme in the visions of the later Hebrew prophets, for whom, however, the dragon has a purely symbolic meaning as the enemy—Assyrian, Babylonian, or Egyptian—of Israel. The prophet Ezekiel speaks of the Lord God's hostility toward Pharaoh, 'the great dragon that lies in the midst of his streams', into whose jaws he will put hooks and whom he will have thrown into the wilderness (Ezekiel 29). During the Babylonian exile, another prophet calls upon the Lord with the cry, 'Was it not thou that didst cut Rahab in pieces, that didst pierce the dragon?' (Isaiah 51.9).

Elsewhere in the Old Testament, and in Jewish writings of the 1st century AD, the dragon is a symbol of mourning and desolation. In early Christian texts the dragon represents the Devil or the Devil's servant, an identification suggested by the leathery webbed feet and forked tail common to both beings, and one which is in line with the general conception of the dragon as the enemy or adversary, especially of God or the gods. In the Book of Revelation (chapter 12), the dragon is described in some detail. He is big and red, and has seven heads and ten horns, and in the war in heaven Michael and his angels fight against the dragon and his angels 'and the great dragon was thrown down, that ancient serpent who is called the Devil and Satan, the deceiver of the whole world; he was thrown down to the earth, and his angels were thrown down with him.'

The process in which different peoples develop and adapt a vague concept in a way which suits their own needs and experience can be traced in the treatment of the dragon myth by the ancient Iranians and Indians. In Iran, where a dualistic view of the universe prevailed, there were many forms of the myth of conflict between the god of light and the dragon. In one of these myths, the great god

Siegfried Kills Fafner, Arthur Rackham (1867–1939)

of creation Ahura Mazdah struggles with the three-jawed, three-headed, six-eyed dragon Azhi Dahaka, 'an imp of the spirit of deceit'. In a later version of the same story, prevalent in the 4th century AD, it is the fire god Atar, originally a lesser deity in a polytheistic system, but now the son of Ahura Mazdah, who fights the dragon Azhi. The dragon also evolves with the passage of time, and becomes a human monster with two serpents springing from his shoulders, a guise in which he has passed into the folklore of the Armenians and other people of the Middle East.

In the ancient Hindu hymns known collectively as the Rig Veda (c. 1200 BC), the dragon is represented as the demon of drought, and is slain by the god Indra, who thereby releases the waters from the storm clouds. In a parallel development to the Iranian version, another version of the myth describes how Trita, god of healing and life, and bringer of fire from heaven, slays the three-headed, six-eyed serpent Visvarupa. In both these myths there are details which recall the Sumerian Ninurta's battle with the dragons. In Vedic mythology, however, the dragon is occasionally depicted as a friend of man, and in later Hindu sacred texts Indra's defeat of the dragon meets with only qualified approval.

The dragon is described as a three-headed creature in the earliest mention of him in ancient Greek literature (in the *Iliad*), where Agamemnon's sword-belt is decorated with a blue enamel dragon and there are three dragons on his cuirass, which was made in Cyprus. The reference to Cyprus may be connected with the fact that the Greeks probably imported the dragon from Palestine, as is reflected in the myth of Perseus and Andromeda, the daughter of the Ethiopian King of Joppa (Jaffa). Andromeda was chained to a cliff on the coast of Philistia (Palestine) when Perseus saw

her, fell instantly in love with her, and rescued her from the female sea-dragon. Robert Graves has suggested that Andromeda's story was inspired by a Palestinian or Syrian icon of the Babylonian god Marduk. The Greek myth did introduce a new element into the tradition about dragons, however, and that is the idea that the dragon must be propitiated by human sacrifice, preferably of a royal virgin.

Another peculiarly Greek notion is that of the sowing of dragon's teeth, from which spring the founders of the city. The dragon has survived in modern Greek folklore as the *drakos*, a word usually translated as 'ogre'. These creatures maintain the time-honoured dragon role of the adversary, and in some stories they have more specific dragon traits: they sleep with their eyes open, and see with them shut, a characteristic suggested by fish, which is also attributed to the Dragon King in some Chinese legends. They are also, in some stories, assigned the role of guarding precious treasure.

Guardian of Treasure

The earliest mention of dragons in connection with treasure appears to be by a Greek author, Artemidorus (2nd century AD) an expert on the interpretation of dreams. Dreams about dragons, he says, indicate wealth and riches, 'because dragons make their fixed abode over treasures.' There may well be some remoter, more obscure link between dragons and treasure that has so far not been explained, because in a culture quite unrelated to any of those we have discussed so far, that of the Maori in New Zealand, the dragon's first cousin, the lizard, is also revered as the guardian of funerary caves, and this is said to be because the lizard represents Whiro, the god of sickness and death. The sacred crocodiles of ancient Egypt may also have had a similar function.

The Terror of Smaug

Bilbo the hobbit ventures into the underground lair of Smaug, the dragon:

As he went forward it grew and grew, till there was no doubt about it. It was a red light steadily getting redder and redder. Also it was now undoubtedly hot in the tunnel. Wisps of vapour floated up and past him and he began to sweat. A sound, too, began to throb in his ears, a sort of bubbling like the noise of a large pot galloping on the fire, mixed with a rumble as of a gigantic tom-cat purring. This grew to the unmistakable gurgling noise of some vast animal snoring in its sleep down there in the red glow in front of him.

It was at this point that Bilbo stopped. Going on from there was the bravest thing he ever did. The tremendous things that happened afterward were as nothing compared to it. He fought the real battle in the tunnel alone, before he ever saw the vast danger that lay in wait. At any rate after a short halt go on he did; and you can picture him coming to the end of the tunnel, an opening of much the same size and shape as the door above. Through it peeps the hobbit's little head. Before him lies the great bottom-most cellar or dungeon-hole of the ancient dwarves right at the Mountain's root. It is almost dark so that its vastness can only be dimly guessed, but rising from the near side of the rocky floor there is a great glow. The glow of Smaug!

There he lay, a vast red-golden dragon, fast asleep; a thrumming came from his jaws and nostrils, and wisps of smoke, but his fires were low in slumber. Beneath him, under all his limbs and his huge coiled tail, and about him on all sides stretching away across the unseen floors, lay countless piles of precious things, gold wrought and unwrought, gems and jewels, and silver red-stained in the ruddy light.

Smaug lay, with wings folded like an immeasurable bat, turned partly on one side, so that the hobbit could see his underparts and his long pale belly crusted with gems and fragments of gold from his long lying on his costly bed. Behind him where the walls were nearest could dimly be seen coats of mail, helms and axes, swords and spears hanging; and there in rows stood great jars and vessels filled with a wealth that could not be guessed.

J. R. R. Tolkien, *The Hobbit*

Chinese New Year celebrations dragon

The association between dragons, caves, and treasure became very popular in the early Christian period and in the Middle Ages. In a Roman legend of the fifth century, St. Sylvester conquers a dragon which lies at the bottom of a cave on the Tarpeian rock outside Rome, to which maidens had been sacrificed. The legend incorporates much of the typical symbolism of dragon lore. There are 365 steps leading down to the cave, an allusion to the sun (linked, as we have seen, with dragons in Sumerian and Egyptian mythology) and its annual journey round the earth, according to the cosmology of the time. In this Roman legend the cave is also a symbol of death, as in the Maori lizard cult.

In Teutonic mythology the dragon Fafnir slain by Siegfried lurks in a cave, watching over a treasure hoard which is the source of life and power. Siegfried is made invulnerable by bathing in the dragon's blood, and through drinking it acquires the language of the birds—symbolic of domination over nature. In the myths of many races, heroes obtain boundless courage by eating a dragon's heart or drinking its blood, or acquire its penetrating gaze by killing it.

In early Christian thought the dragon has the allegorical role, already seen in the book of Revelation, of representing the Devil or the Antichrist, or more generally, evil passions, paganism, or the oppressive powers of this world. Whatever the connection between the historical and the legendary St. George, the origin of the story of St. George and the dragon seems to lie in this general idea, but as worked up in the Middle Ages, particularly under the influence of the Crusades, the story obviously owes much to the Greek myth of Perseus and Andromeda. The hold of the dragon on the medieval mind is also exemplified in heraldry, where the dragon is featured often, both for charges and supporters. The use of the dragon as an emblem in modern times is, of course, suggested by this heraldic tradition.

The Dragon of the East

Whereas in the ancient Middle East and in medieval Europe the dragon remains an essentially sombre and forbidding monster, lurking in the mythical depths, as it were, in the Orient and particularly in China and Japan, he has a certain splendour and panache. Indeed, there can be few mythological figures which have so stimulated the oriental imagination. The mere description of the dragon given by the ancient Chinese writer Wang Fu shows an exuberance not to be found in the West: it has a triple-jointed body, the head of a camel, the horns of a stag, the eyes of a demon, the ears of a cow, the neck of a snake, the belly of a clam, the scales of a carp, the claws of an eagle, and the soles of a tiger. The Chinese dragon is, however, just as intimately concerned with water, caves, and treasure as his cousins in the West. And cousins all these dragons are, sharing common ancestors, though the Chinese dragon has picked up some of the traits of the Burmese lotus-serpent on his journey from Mesopotamia and India, has assimilated a Buddhist adaptation of ancient Asiatic snake cults, and has acquired some distinctively Chinese features on his native soil.

The most striking of these is that the dragon in China is not, as in the West, a representative or symbol of the powers of evil. On the contrary, according to the old Chinese Book of Rites, the dragon as the chief of all scaly animals is one of the four benevolent spiritual animals, the unicorn, phoenix, and tortoise being the others. How this transformation came about can only be guessed. It reflects the general principle stated by Jung that 'every psychological extreme secretly contains its own opposite', which is expressed in Chinese thought through the classical doctrine of Yang and Yin, the good and bad influences. That this principle underlies the dragon's transformation into a beneficent being is confirmed by Wang Fu's statement that the dragon's scales number 117, of which eighty-one are imbued with Yang and thirty-six with Yin, because the dragon is partly a preserver and partly a destroyer. Yang is also the male element and, as its representative, the dragon also became at an early

period a symbol of the Emperor, and appeared on the Chinese flag (which may have suggested its use in heraldry later in the West). During the Manchu dynasty (1644–1912) the dragon was held in especial esteem, and everything used by the Emperor was described in terms of it: there was the dragon throne, dragon bed, and dragon boat.

This kindly view of the dragon entailed significant changes in the dragon lore which the Chinese adopted from other Asiatic peoples. Whereas the Sumerian Zu stole the tablets of destiny from the god Enlil, Chinese dragons frequently appear as the givers of laws. They are also instructors in magic and givers of swords, while the art of painting was

In the myths of many races, heroes obtain boundless courage by eating a dragon's heart or drinking its blood, or acquire its penetrating gaze by killing it.

introduced to China by a dragon.

Although Chinese dragons appeared at favourable moments to presage periods of prosperity, and had been known to emit foam which had supernatural powers of fertilization, they could also, when offended or disturbed, cause a drought by gathering up all the water of a district in baskets, or they could eclipse the sun. To propitiate them, the Chinese flew dragon kites, especially at the mumming parade in the New Year.

In Japanese legends the dragon is a more ambivalent creature than in Chinese. There are dragons who demand the sacrifice of a young virgin every year, and in one myth the storm god Susa-no-wo rescues the princess Inada by making the dragon drink saki and then chopping it to pieces. In Japan, too, the dragon is associated

with water. The Dragon King lives in a mysterious marine realm, with a retinue of serpents, fishes, and other sea monsters, and tribes of dragons have power over rain and storms. There are many stories of wise Buddhist priests who can take these creatures and make them give rain in time of drought, or of holy men on pilgrimages who command the dragons to calm the stormy sea.

The Beast Within Us

The dragon is known in many other parts of the world: in Hanoi, which was once known as the Dragon City; in Iceland, where the god Loki has associations with a female dragon; in the British Isles, where there are dragon caves and dragon-haunted lochs; and in Hawaii, where all the dragons are descended from the mother goddess Mo-o-inanea, the 'self-reliant dragon'.

According to some modern psychologists, the dragon is still with us, representing, says Jung, the 'negative mother-imago, and thus expressing resistance to incest, or the fear of it.' The dragon's guardianship of treasure represents, according to the same author, the mother's apparent possession of the son's libido: in psychological terms, the treasure which is hard to attain lies hidden in the unconscious. While this theory can be neither proved nor disproved, the consistency with which a number of well-defined traits have adhered to such a monster in many countries throughout fifty or sixty centuries, at the very least, poses an interesting problem. One thing is clear: broadly speaking, people get the dragons they deserve, and the same might be said to be true of psychologists and anthropologists, each of whom will give his own solution of the problem.

DAVID PHILLIPS

Dryad

In Greek mythology, a dryad was a nymph of the forests and woods. Although the etymology of the name suggests that dryads were originally associated with oak trees in particular, dryads came to be seen as general woodland spirits. Hamadryads were identified with individual trees—their lives were integral to and dependent on those of the trees—so the destruction of a tree meant the destruction of its attendant spirit. Dryads occur in C. S. Lewis's *The Chronicles of Narnia*, and the sculptor Eric Gill carved the figure of a nymph showing the leaves of her woodland setting almost indistinguishable from her flowing hair.

Dwarfs

In folk legends and fairytales, dwarfs were always described as creatures of small stature, ranging from the size of a man's thumb to the height of a two-year-old child. In appearance and feeling, they roughly resembled human beings, but magical powers endowed them with special skills and wisdom far beyond those of any mortal men. Inhabiting the dark and secret places of the earth, dwarfs could appear or disappear with bewildering rapidity.

Although dwarfs were a regular feature of northern folklore, references to such diminutive beings can be found in Greek literature. Crowds of tiny men climbed ladders to reach the top of Hercules's wine cup, when that hero visited their country; and in Greek paintings they were depicted as hewing ears of corn with miniature axes. Such writers as Pliny and Aristotle claimed that tribes of these minute people dwelt in caves on the banks of the River Nile.

Very occasionally, dwarfs were described as incredibly beautiful. Fair Idun, of Norse mythology, was utterly unlike her dark, ugly brothers and father, dwarfs who were skilled smiths. Old Ivaldir sometimes allowed his lovely daughter to walk abroad in the sunlight, which she much preferred to their gloomy underground kingdom of Svartalfheim. Because she was so beautiful the sun's rays did not turn her to stone, a fate which befell other members of the race of dwarfs. Bragi, the handsome god of poetry and eloquence, fell in love with Idun, and married her; and she was given the special task of keeping the golden apples, which gave the gods eternal youth and vigour.

The more usual Scandinavian and Teutonic dwarfs were hump-backed,

> *. . . dwarfs were always described as creatures of small stature, ranging from the size of a man's thumb to the height of a two-year-old child.*

dark little men with large, wise heads and long beards. Sometimes their feet resembled those of a goat, or a goose. All lived to a great age, and considered unwholesome food to be the cause of the brief span of human life. Their kingdoms and tribes were ruled over by kings and chieftains, who possessed large armies. Dwarf territories were situated deep inside mountains, mines, or under water. In the main, the creatures feared and detested sunlight, and one named Alviss, who was compelled to remain all day above ground, was turned to stone by exposure to the sun's bright rays. Garbed in black, brown, or grey, they found no difficulty in merging into rock clefts and cave mouths, or gaining unseen access to their dark, subterranean abodes.

All that Glitters

Dwarfs were particularly the jealous custodians of gold, precious metals, and jewels, and this guardianship also included the glitter of the sun's and moon's rays. Their vast underground halls were reputed to contain the most priceless of treasures. Anyone who stole from these hoards suffered great misfortune, and if a robber did manage to transport some of the gold to his home, he would abruptly discover that the fortune had turned into a pile of dead leaves.

To the mortal men they favoured, dwarfs were the givers of wise counsel, for they were considered to be the repositories of great knowledge. This secret wisdom evidently invested them with the power to foresee the future, make themselves invisible, and assume other forms. They were also adept at magic songs and runes, and brewed the heady mead of poetry, which was guarded by the gods. Anyone aiding them was treated with the utmost kindness and courtesy, and generously rewarded from the storehouses of treasure. Legend tells of human midwives given gold in grateful return for their special services.

The dwarfs were chiefly renowned for their ability to produce magnificent metalwork. The foremost craftsmen among their numbers were generally the kings. It was these ugly and often ill-tempered little men who could create wondrous works of art and magic. They forged the armour for the gods, and the strong chain called Gleipnir with which the gods bound the terrible Fenris Wolf. Magic swords and golden rings, so highly prized in many legends, were fashioned by the deft fingers of dwarfs. Fair Idun's two brothers made Gungnir, Odin's magical spear. They also produced for the goddess Sif, the beautiful wife of Thor, exquisite, long golden tresses, to replace her own hair after the mischievous god Loki had shorn it off.

Another dwarf, Sindri, forced to compete against Ivaldir's two sons by the boasting of his brother Brökk, wrought many wonderful things, including Thor's mighty battle hammer, Mjblnir, which no matter how far it was hurled always returned to its thrower's hands. For the god Freyr, the dwarf made Gollinborsti. This great boar could either be ridden or draw a chariot, and it traveled as easily through water or air as upon land. The lights from Gollinborsti's special golden bristles ensured that Freyr never rode in darkness, not even in the deepest night. For Odin, Sindri fashioned Draupnir, a golden arm ring. Every ninth night, eight rings, all of similar weight, were formed and fell from this magical piece of jewellery, so that by the end of only one year the owner of the dwarf's handiwork would have amassed a great treasure.

Lords of the Mine

Anyone who forced the dwarfs to give or make one of their exquisite articles was doomed, and their gain brought only misery. An enchanted sword, Tyrfing, which two dwarfs were compelled to forge, had a curse laid upon it. It could never be drawn from out of its sheath without bringing death.

Those dwarfs who lived in the mines were regarded very warily by men, and considered more vicious and unpredictable than those inhabiting mountains. Miners often heard them moving about far below in the darkness, and now and then glimpsed the little men. Within the mines, all kinds of catastrophes, from broken tools to roof falls and sudden fires, were attributed to the fury of these dwarfs. This was their method of punishing over-inquisitive humans, who appeared to treat the tiny 'lords' of the mine without proper respect. However, if mollified with presents of

food, dwarfs were known to help with the work in hand, and give advance warning of danger by tapping in the mine shafts. The tales of the 'knockers' from Cornwall and Staffordshire belong among those of the rest of Europe relating to mine dwarfs.

Generally, it was human beings who had cause to grumble about the dwarfs' behaviour. These mischievous and sometimes malicious beings teased farm animals, abducted children and beautiful maidens, and stole bread and corn. Yet, apparently, they were considered annoying rather than dangerous, except for the Black Dwarfs, which were a type of malignant elf. In the majority of Scandinavian and German folk tales, the dwarf is quite friendly to men, although sometimes complaining bitterly of human dishonesty and untrustworthiness. The erdleute (earth people) of Swiss legend were said to help farmers, to find wandering cattle, and collect fire wood and fruit to leave out for the poor children.

Many North American Indian tales concern little folk explicitly comparable to the dwarfs of European tales. The Paiutes saw all dwarfs as mischievous, but the Cherokee believed they could be good or bad—though seeing either kind was a death omen. Many Eskimo tales depict helpful, luck-bestowing dwarfs similar to those of Scandinavia.

The origins of the dwarf are obscure. Norse mythology suggests that the tiny men either came to life as dark maggots crawling from the decaying flesh of the slain primeval giant Ymir, or from the scarlet billows of the seas, which were formed from the same giant's blood. The gods granted them the wits and shape of men, and gave four of the dwarfs, Austri, Vestri, Svori, and Norori, the duty of upholding the four corners of the sky. There seems to be little evidence to suggest that any of the dwarfs themselves were ever venerated as gods.

Archeological and anthropological studies have produced evidence to justify the theory that the belief in dwarfs was based on reality rather than on imagination. Some of the first inhabitants of Western Europe were small, dark, shy people, dwelling among the dense forests which covered much of Britain, Brittany, western France, and Germany. Like the little Lapps, who inhabited the Scandinavian peninsula before the invasion of the Gothic-Scandinavian races, they were skilled in mining and smelting the metals which abounded in those regions.

Memory of an Extinct Race

From the East came strong invaders, economically and mechanically better equipped than the small natives. As these new people conquered and settled, the dominant features of their civilization became the much-hated incursions on the little people's original environment. Weaker in strength and numbers, they were forced to retreat into the swamps and islands, driven back by the clearing of their forests for the agricultural settlements of their invaders. Later came the passionately loathed church bells, as Christianity overcame the old religions. According to popular belief, the little men hated agriculture, the clearing of forests, and the ringing of church bells—anything that disturbed the peace of their underground kingdoms.

Some of these original people intermarried with their conquerors, especially the Celts, who were in their turn forced further westward by stronger Nordic groups. This mingling of races enshrined many of the very ancient crafts and beliefs of the little people, and determined that pockets of the old culture remained.

As with many minority groups throughout history, the invaders had no need to fear serious attacks from the vanquished, yet the seemingly magical practices of the defeated race gradually became the fearful superstitions of the more powerful majority. All the mysterious customs appeared to belong in the supernatural realms of some dark fairy world peopled with malevolent spirits who could use their incomprehensible knowledge of magic for the overthrow of the physically stronger overlords. Sir Walter Scott suggested that the little people's probable ability to foretell the weather from observing cloud formations and other meteorological phenomena, would have given them, in the eyes of the conquerors, another magical advantage. Thus, it was the invaders' fears, rather than the dwarf people's actual talents, which gave the relatively smaller and weaker race a curious power. Fairies, with whom dwarfs were popularly associated, were always believed to be capable of traveling quickly, and possessing the power of invisibility. Obviously, their slight stature allowed the little dark men to move swiftly, and no doubt they increased this speed in order to escape the attentions of their enemies, which would be accepted as further proof of great supernatural knowledge.

Caves in many parts of Western Europe show traces of having been inhabited from prehistoric times until as late as the fifteenth century, and it seems likely that the little people, and the descendants who shared their beliefs and magic, were forced to seek protection in caves. This may well have given rise to the widely held opinion that dwarfs were swallowed up by the earth. Right up until the seventeenth century, superstitious people claimed to have witnessed dwarfs' nocturnal revels in the vicinity of the so-called 'fairy' mounds. These were probably the barrows where once the little people had ceremonially buried their dead. Such tumuli would be considered to possess mystical and magical significance as meeting places for the secret gatherings of similar believers.

Mors Thriumphans, **Leonard Bramer (1596–1674)**

This painting depicts the god Mara, trying to disturb the Bodhisatta, just before he reached enlightenment. Mara knew Buddha was close, so he put all his efforts in trying to lure Buddha back to the world. Here is the episode where Mara drives an elephant toward Buddha.

So it may be that dwarfs are really the group memory of a long extinct race. They lived on in the minds of later generations, embellished with incredible powers, and transformed into legendary figures, characterized by the beliefs of various cultures.

SANDY SHULMAN

Evil Spirits

In the earliest beliefs, Nature's domain was peopled by elemental spirits, each having jurisdiction over a specific area of natural phenomena and supplying the motive power that induces change. The gradual evolution of elemental spirits, which were capable of both good and evil, into good spirits and bad spirits, and finally into demons and angels, was the product of ages of slow development.

There was from the beginning a tendency to regard demons as playing a somewhat ambivalent role. Although extremely powerful in their own right, they could be compelled to submit to the orders of a magician. The problem was further complicated by the fact that the gods of conquered peoples tended to be incorporated among the demons of the conquerors.

Historically, the development of a sophisticated creed of demonism, with a clear differentiation between the forces of good and evil, light and darkness, coincided with the emancipation of social institutions from subsistence economy. With the growth of the concept of gods and devils, the minor demons of earlier stages of belief tended to occupy a subordinate position in the diabolic hierarchy, at the same time retaining most of their distinctive features.

It was characteristic of demons in the East that they favoured lonely sites, particularly deserts, from which they emerged in truly terrifying hordes. The appearance of an army of demons that haunted the deserts of Assyria, said to be comprised of 'warriors, destroyers, vampires, phantoms, and ghosts', was so dreadful that when shown their own reflections in giant mirrors, placed on the walls of cities, they fled in terror from the scene.

The Master of Evil

During classical times dualism survived among the Greeks; their *daimon*, later in history to be transformed into the more familiar demon of Christian mythology, combined good and evil elements. The ancient Jews shared the general terror of the demons of darkness, which is reflected in the words of Psalm 91: 'Thou shalt not be

Mikhail Vrubel's 1899 work *The Flying Demon*. Vrubel felt that 'The Demon is misunderstood', noting that the word came from the Greek term for soul.

afraid for the terror by night; nor for the arrow that flieth by day; nor for the pestilence that walketh in darkness; nor for the destruction that wasteth at noonday.' In the earlier period of their history, before the development of the idea of Satan, the imagination of the Jews peopled the deserts with malevolent spirits; these were later reduced to a minor role as servants of the Master of Evil.

The emergence of Satan transformed demonology into a major influence in the affairs of mankind; for the preeminence allocated to the supreme Devil created the climate for the persecution of witchcraft. The Church became dominated by the conviction that Satan was intent upon making himself God's equal and that he sought ceaselessly to undermine God's kingdom by the corruption and destruction of humanity. That Satan was a truly formidable opponent is evident from the words of the eminent Johann Weyer, written in the sixteenth century: 'Satan possesses great courage, incredible cunning, superhuman wisdom, the most acute penetration, consummate prudence, an incomparable skill in veiling the most pernicious artifices under a specious disguise, and a malefic and infinite hatred toward the human race, implacable and incurable.'

The presence of a supreme spirit of evil in society's midst was a factor hardly conducive to emotional stability. Malevolent demons were held responsible for every mishap to which flesh was heir. Even the ordinary temptations of the flesh, the inevitable occupational hazard of anchorite and hermit, were laid at the door of demons who were believed to feel affronted by chastity and piety. The twelfth-century English saint Godric, after being all but seduced by a demon disguised as a naked woman, was hurled from his bed and thrashed with a stool. An unexpectedly sensitive demon, however, which attacked the Holy Man of Farne, withdrew in terror after being denounced in most vituperative terms by that sharp-tongued saint.

Even more troublesome were those agents of demonic lust, the incubi and succubi, who harassed men and women under cover of sleep. St. Augustine in his *De Civitate Dei*, written in the 5th century AD, had drawn attention to their activities in the following terms: 'It is a widespread belief that sylvans and fauns, commonly called incubi,

have frequently molested women, sought and obtained coitus from them.'

An incubus was a demon that copulated with women, while a succubus had sexual intercourse with men. It was generally admitted that there were few nunneries free of the ravages of the former, while the latter were active among communities of monks. We have it upon the authority of Albertus Magnus (1206–1280) that 'there were places in which a man can scarcely sleep at night without a succubus accosting him.' Learned theologians debated long and thoughtfully such points as how a demon, which was by definition sexless, could indulge in sexual intercourse. After earnest consideration it was decided that a demon had the power to utilize a corpse for this purpose or could create a body from the very air itself.

Demonic Specialists

There were dire physical as well as moral consequences in sleeping with incubi and succubi, for not only was the sin classed as bestiality but the offspring were likely to be monsters. Despite such dangers there was considerable interest in this specific type of demonic activity and it is said that in 1468 an enterprising brothel keeper of Bologna staffed his entire establishment with succubi. These female demons had their own separate

The Washerwomen of the Night, Jean Edouard Dargent (c.1861)

Devil's mask from Tocuaro Michoacan on display at the Museo de Arte Popular in Mexico City

organization within the satanic hierarchy under an arch-demoness, Princess Nahemah. The penalty reserved by the heavenly powers for those who trafficked with demons was an eternity in hell, a domain of fiery torments under the ministration of hordes of demons skilled in the art of inflicting perpetual pain.

Opposing the satanic host was an army of angels organized in hierarchies, who from the general state of affairs would seem to have been remarkably ineffective. As for the number and variety of demons, these grew ever more powerful as Christianity matured. Their numbers were greater than the sands of the desert, amounting to as many as 7,405,926; according to one demonologist they were divided into twelve classes whose functions were so organized as to cover all aspects of human suffering, ranging from hunger to death. According to another, demons were grouped under the headings of fire, air, earth, and water, with subterranean devils and shadows thrown in for good measure.

The demonologist Binsfeld, in 1589, compiled a list of devils to cover each of the seven deadly sins: Lucifer was the devil of pride, Mammon the devil of avarice, Asmodeus of lechery, Satan of anger, Beelzebub of gluttony, Leviathan of envy, and Belphegor of sloth. Another writer increased the number of groups to ten, divided into fates, poltergeists, incubi and succubi, marching hosts, familiars, nightmare demons, demons constructed from human semen, deceptive demons, clean demons, and those who deceived witches into the belief that they flew to the sabbath.

Demons were allocated specific territories, the north under Zimmar, the south under Gorson, the east under Amayan, and the west Goap. In addition, there was a parliament of devils and an ambassadorial court which dispatched diabolical emissaries to every land. When the army of demons went on parade, the whole earth trembled from the thunder of the march past of infernal dukes riding on the backs of griffins, winged dogs, and phantom dromedaries screaming blasphemies in Egyptian. It is on record that the chief of the demons during the course of a conversation with three monks declared: 'The strength of our army is such that if all the Alps, their rocks, and glaciers were divided among us none would have more than a pound's weight.'

Raising the Devil

Inevitably, perhaps, some people, disappointed by the inadequacies of piety and prayer, were tempted to turn to the Devil in the hope of obtaining a better guarantee of reward than that offered by the Deity. From such an attitude developed attempts to summon demons from the infernal regions with spells. Using books of magical directions called grimoires, the magician endeavoured to bind the demon temporarily to his will. There were certain rituals to which even the great Lords of Darkness, Lucifer and Beelzebub, had no alternative but to

respond. The magician, armed with a magic sword, prepared a ritual circle and uttered words of occult power. In one ritual it was necessary to utter the nine mystic names: Eheieh, Iod, Tetragrammaton Elohim, El, Elohim Gibor, Eloah Va-Daath, El Adonai Tzabaoth, Elohim Tzabaoth, and Shaddai. Following the ceremony the demon could be dismissed with the words: 'I am pleased and contented with thee, Prince Lucifer, for the moment. Leave thou in peace now, and go in quiet and without trouble. Do not forget our pact or I shall blast thee with my wand. Amen.'

The certainty that demons were always ready in waiting for the

summons of the magician is attested by the old legend describing how the actor Edward Alleyn, after invoking Mephistopheles during a seventeenth-century performance of Marlowe's *Doctor Faustus*, discovered a real devil reeking of brimstone upon the stage. This experience impelled him to abandon the theater once and for all and to embark upon good works which included the founding of Dulwich College.

The age of diabolic domination was essentially one of social disarray and general anxiety which the demonologists, whether from conscious or unconscious motives, exploited to the full. Everywhere lurked the spirits

Spirit from the Past (1999)

of evil, terrifying the more neurotic among the community. Mankind stood perpetually on guard against the attempts of demons to penetrate the human body by one of its natural orifices and to assume diabolical possession. Catholics were well aware of the dangers from the warning given by Gregory the Great, in his description of the awful situation of the nun who had absentmindedly eaten a lettuce without crossing herself. Thus exposed, she fell victim to a demon who leaped down her throat. Protestants were equally wary but sought protection more in prayer and by the rejection of impure thoughts.

Demons often opened their attacks by buffetings and beatings or by obsessing the victim with abstractions that left his soul temporarily undefended. Diabolic possession was usually manifested by writhing, foaming at the mouth, twitching, grotesque grimacing, insensitivity, and occasionally paralysis. Another remarkable feature was the tendency for the victim to answer, in French, questions addressed to him by the exorcist in Latin. These disturbing symptoms lay completely beyond the comprehension of medical men of the time and were automatically ascribed to the Devil.

Beatings and Fumigations

To drive out the unwanted demon was a task requiring the trained specialist in exorcism, although there were occasions when a gentle admonition plus a sprinkling of holy water appear to have been sufficient. There was even an exceptional seventeenth century case in which an extremely sensitive demon retreated after being sneered at by the exorcist as a 'ninny, a drunkard, and a sow'. In the main, however, demons were not so easily intimidated and every device of the exorcist's art was required to accelerate

their expulsion. It was not uncommon for a group of Protestant divines to conduct a mass prayer meeting at the bedside of the writhing demoniac, while furious arguments and lengthy dialogues took place between the indwelling demon and the exorcist, the former often revealing the most intimate details of himself and his activities, including his name. Devils were expelled by forcing the possessed man or woman to inhale some vile-smelling concoction, or by beatings with sticks. One case is on record in which a demon was drawn out of the victim through the nostrils.

In an age when the whole of society seemed beset by the forces of hell it was inevitable that the Devil's agents upon earth, the witches, should have come

> *Diabolic possession was usually manifested by writhing, foaming at the mouth, twitching, grotesque grimacing, insensitivity, and occasionally paralysis.*

under heavy attack; almost every type of natural calamity was laid at their door, particularly the onset of diseases, the sinking of ships at sea, storms, and bad harvests. It was accepted theology that a witch attained her powers by a compact with Satan; and as a penalty for forswearing her immortal soul and imperiling the human race there existed no logical alternative but to kill her. The pact with Satan became a standard charge against magical practitioners throughout Western Europe, but although it was rumoured that no less than seven popes had traded their souls for temporal delights, there is no record of their prosecution for sorcery.

Familiar Spirits

The pact, which might be negotiated by either Satan or one of his subordi-

nates, was signed in the witch's blood and ratified by the simple expedient of a bout of sexual intercourse, following which the contracted became bond slave to the Devil for the remainder of her short life. The next stage was for the witch to be supplied with a minor demon as a personal familiar; he had the dual task of keeping watch over her on Satan's behalf and carrying out the diabolical missions which she entrusted to him.

The familiar assumed all manner of guises to deceive the authorities, including that of rabbit, sparrow, cat, dog, goat, and chicken. One woman possessed as her imp a cat of brilliant blue. In the St. Osyth witch trial of 1582, the accused, Ursula Kempe, admitted to maintaining four imps, two he-cats called Titty and Jack, a black lamb called Tyffin, and a toad called Pigin. The familiar was fed with blood from the witch's supernumerary nipples, and it was the finding of these, together with certain spots on the body insensitive to pain known as Devil's marks, that so often led to the witch's downfall and death. The unfortunate animal familiar was usually burned. A case is on record in which a familiar actually claimed to be the prophet Daniel, and another in which it materialized as a bishop vomiting streams of fire. The difficulty of deciding whether such phantoms were demons or ordinary workaday ghosts was further complicated by the opinion then current that ghosts were no more than devils in disguise.

In those many cases in which the Devil assumed human shape, he commonly took the form of a man dressed in black, who from the general description might well have been a Puritan divine. One man in black was active in the educational field, trading degrees in divinity for human souls; his clients, it appeared afterward, committed suicide. In Scotland the man in black was described as 'sometimes hairy and grim and sometimes merely clad in black clothes and with cloven feet.'

The overrunning of most of Europe by hordes of men in black, witches and familiars, incubi and succubi, engaged the earnest attention of the most eminent minds of the day, including Jean Bodin, Nicholas Remy, Francesco Maria Guazzo of Milan, and Pierre de Lancre. On the other side of the argument were a few brave men who were, intellectually speaking, far in advance of their times, including Bishop Hutchinson of England, Robert Calef of New England, and, most important of all, Balthasar Bekker, a Dutch clergyman who strove to demonstrate that the idea of a personal devil was no more than an assumption. Opposition to orthodox opinion was not undertaken lightly in the witch-hunting days, since it led almost automatically to the stake, and the number of antidemonists remained pitifully small.

Indeed it was not until the eighteenth century that mankind had matured sufficiently to shake off the influence of the Devil and his hordes, and this was due as much to a general reaction against religious dogmatism as to any conversion to new ways of thought. For yet a further century Satan played a prominent role in religious doctrine, though by now he had been divested of his retinue of minor demons, and the phantom rabbits, demonic dogs, and diabolical toads were seen no more. Hell too remained long in vogue until outmoded by the greater horror of manmade warfare.

As for the victims of diabolical possession, these still remain in our midst, although the regular diagnosis of their disturbances as due to paranoiac fantasies has robbed their visions of much of their former glamour. There is very little difference in essence between the phantom cat seen by the so-called

victim of Jane Wenham, the last woman to be charged with witchcraft in England, and the modern hallucinatory experiences of elves, dwarfs, and other phantoms under the drug LSD, as described by R. E. L. Masters and Jean Houston in their book *The Varieties of Psychedelic Experience* (1967). In one case cited, a victim described how: 'Something was there all right. Something coming for me from a distant and empty horizon—and there loomed before me a devastating horror, a cosmic diamond cat. It filled the sky, it filled all space . . . '

ERIC MAPLE

FURTHER READING: S. G. F. Brandon. Man and His Destiny in the Great Religions. *(University of Toronto, 1962); N. Powell-Williams.* Ideas of the Fall and of Original Sin. *(Longmans, 1927); W. O'Flaherty.* The Origins of Evil in Hindu Mythology. *(University of California, 1977); R. C. Zaehner.* Dawn and Twilight of Zoroastrianism. *(Putnam, 1961); R. Stivers.* Evil in Modern Myth and Ritual. *(University of Georgia Press, 1982); E. Langton.* Essentials of Demonology. *(Epworth Press, 1949); Eric Maple.* The Domain of Devils. *(Barnes, 1966); Richard Cavendish.* The Black Arts. *(Putnam, 1967).*

Fairies

Belief in fairies has been explored by many people, and frequently explained, but remains one of the most mysterious and bewildering subjects that the folklorist can investigate. One reason for the mystery is the widely held belief among believers that it is unlucky to speak of fairies. Besides this, the fairies themselves are so various and the theories about their origin so diverse that it is often difficult to paint a consistent picture of them.

The word itself is perhaps a very unfortunate one. The original word

was 'fay', now so archaic as to seem hopelessly affected. It is believed to derive from the Latin *fata*, the individual fates of men, who were personified as supernatural women visiting the cradles of newly-born children. The word was used both as a noun and as an adjective, for 'fay' meant enchanted or bewitched, and 'fay-erie' (faerie) was used for both a state of enchantment and for an enchanted realm. The state became confused with the person, and 'fays' became 'fairies'. Even so, the believers in fairies did not think it wise to use the name, and the more complimentary the term could be made, the better the fairies would be pleased. The principle was the same as that by which the Greeks called the Furies 'the Kindly Ones'.

Anyone who wants to study the characteristics of fairies all over the world cannot begin better than by reading a little book, which, though nearly two centuries old, is still extremely valuable—*The Fairy Mythology* by Thomas Keightley. The subject is a wide one; this article is confined to the fairies of the British Isles, including not only those of the Arthurian legends and medieval romances, and many other types of fairies, but also pixies, hobs, goblins, gnomes, mermaids, hags, bogeys, and elementals.

Fairies vary in powers, size, character, appearance, habits, and the origins ascribed to them. When it comes to origins, there are two different lines to follow. In the first place there are the opinions of those who have actually believed in fairies, either in the past or the present—and these are by no means unanimous—and in the second there are those of the students of folklore, who have advanced a number of different theories.

Aristocrats and Commoners
Fairies are said to range from the great and potent ones of more than mortal size to the very small creatures

who are occasionally captured, and either make their escape or pine and die in captivity. Some of them can do good or ill, some are wholly wicked; even the best of them need to be treated with respect. Many a helpful brownie has turned into a malicious boggart because some fool has played a practical joke on him.

There are first the heroic or romance fairies of the Arthurian legends and medieval romances. The great example of these is the Dana o'Shee of Ireland. They are the aristocracy of fairyland, who ride and fight and hunt, and live in a beautiful land exempt from death or change, the Land of the Ever Young. These heroic fairies are associated with many tales of the Fairy Ride (or Rade) in which a procession of these lordly creatures would be seen riding in a gallant troop, headed by their king and queen. In the English tradition these fairies are generally held to be a smaller race, sometimes tiny. They have their own realm with its royal courts, they enjoy music and dancing, and wear jewelled, glittering clothes; in some parts of England they are so tiny that the whole royal dais can be caught under a man's hat.

The common people of fairyland live either in small family groups or as solitaries and some of them live in villages under the fairy knolls. There are many little fairies who ask for help in mending tiny shovels or three-legged stools, and who pay their helpers with small gifts of food, and with good luck. An example of the solitary fairy is the leprechaun, the fairy shoemaker, whose hoards of gold are much coveted by mortals. These fairies are generally small, though varying from the size of a three-year-old child to a height of a few inches.

Forgotten Gods and Guardians

In a different category are the nature fairies and forgotten gods; spirits of streams, springs, and lakes; mermaids;

Iris, John Atkinson Grimshaw (1886)

spirits of individual trees or woods; and guardians of animals, plants, and growing crops. These are rarer in Britain than in some other countries, but examples can be found even in English tradition, though more common in the Celtic parts of Britain.

Akin to these, though not identical with them, are the tutelary fairies, often guardians of one particular family, like that who gave the fairy flag to the MacLeods of Skye, or the one who watches over the Grants. Others are homely domestic spirits, brownies, lobs, cellar ghosts, down to Awd Goggie who guards the gooseberry bushes. The most tragic of these tutelary fairies are the Irish or Highland banshees, each attached to a family or clan. Banshee means 'fairy woman', but the general type has come to be applied to a special type of spirit, possibly an ancestral ghost, who is to be heard weeping before the death of any member of her special family. Lady Wilde, in her *Ancient Legends of Ireland* (1887), gives a vivid and poetic description of the banshee. In the Highlands of Scotland she is often called 'The Washer by the Ford' because she is generally seen washing the 'bloodstained garments of those about to die.

Brownies and other hobs are attached either to families or to places, but if they are offended they will move to another farm. Sometimes they follow the families to which they are attached. They have even been known to emigrate to Canada.

The fifth group consists of the bogey beasts and goblins. These are often closely linked to the homelier of the tutelary fairies. A boggart can be a brownie gone to the bad. John Rhys in *Celtic Folklore* has a rather touching story of a brownie who was driven from one farm to another, always leaving when practical jokes were played on him, until he came to a farm where there was a manservant called Moses, with whom he struck up a great friendship. He was perfectly happy and very useful until Moses went to fight for Henry VII, and was killed at Bosworth Field. Then the poor brownie went completely to the bad, and became so troublesome that he was at length caught by an awl thrust through his long, sharp nose, and kept pinned to the spot while an exorcism was read over him. Then the awl was drawn out, and a magical wind bore him away to the Red Sea.

Most of the boggarts are mischievous rather than dangerous, and Will o' the Wisps and various forms of bogey beasts are much the same. They delight in misleading travelers and playing practical jokes. A typical story is told of the bogey beast known as the Hedley Kow. He took the form of a pot of gold, and was dragged along by a delighted old woman; then he changed in quick succession into a bar of silver, a piece of iron, and a big round stone; then finally he shot up over four long legs, and leapt away like a lean colt, swishing his long tail in delight. But the old woman had the best of it after all, for she was equally delighted by every change for the worse, and finally uplifted with joy at having met the bogey beast in person, and made so bold with him.

The Hedley Kow is harmless enough, though mischievous, but some of the creatures of this class were dreaded as really evil and dangerous.

The Border Redcaps are an example. They inhabited tower houses along the Borders, where violent deeds had been done, and their red caps were dyed in the blood of the travelers they had murdered. The Highland glaistigs appeared like beautiful women, but they were vampires who sucked the blood of any human partners who would dance with them. Shellycoat, a Scottish water spirit, dressed in seaweed hung with clattering shells, sometimes played Will o' the Wisp tricks on travelers, but had been known to toss a benighted man up and down like a ball until he killed him. Water kelpies, like bogey beasts, often took the form of a horse, but their desire was always to carry their victims into the water and devour them.

The last group of fairy creatures consists of hags, giants, and monsters. Giants are always creatures of the past; the evidence for them is the great works that they have left behind,

but even the most credulous believer never expected to see a giant. The same is true of dragons, though not of all monsters. The supernatural hags, Cailleach Beurh (the blue hag) or Cally Berry, as she is called in Ulster, Black Annis of the Midlands, and a few more of the same kind are not believed in now, but were once thought to be alive and dangerous.

Fairy Ethics

The fairies have a morality of their own that does not correspond in all ways with respectable humanity. They are great lovers of cleanliness and order, and expect this to be respected by the humans whom they visit. As a rule they have few scruples about taking any mortal goods, milk, meal, or cattle, but they punish severely any mortal who steals from them. They hate miserliness above all things, and love an open, cheerful character. Perhaps because of their interest in fertility,

The Quarrel of Oberon and Titania, **Sir Joseph Noel Paton (1821–1901)**

they are rather free and wanton in their own conduct, and are friendly toward lovers. Politeness is very important in all dealings with them, though there are some that must not be thanked. They are passionate lovers of privacy, and punish spies and eavesdroppers. At the same time they are grateful for hospitality and kindness, and often repay it disproportionately.

Of all the fairy pilfering habits the most distressing to mortals is that of stealing babies out of their cradles and leaving changelings in their place. This belief has probably caused more cruelty and unhappiness than any other piece of fairy lore, for the usual way of getting rid of a changeling is to ill-treat it, though very occasionally the mother is told to take special care of it, so as to win the gratitude of the fairy mother.

Children are not the only mortals stolen by the fairies. Nursing mothers were believed to be in special danger until they were churched, and they were coveted by the fairies to serve as foster mothers for the fairy babies who did not thrive. Young men with special skills were sometimes decoyed away, and young girls, particularly those with golden hair, were carried off as brides.

The Fairy Midwife story, one of the most common and widespread, may have some connection with this. In the usual version the midwife is called out at night by an odd-looking old fellow, and taken to a cottage where a young woman is in labour. She duly delivers the child, and is given a box of ointment with which to anoint its eyes. Accidentally or on purpose she touches one of her own eyes with the

Opposite page:
Richard Dadd's masterpiece *The Fairy Feller's Master-Stroke*. Dadd worked on the painting for nine years and wrote a complementary long poem explaining each of the characters in the work.

ointment, and at once the whole scene is changed. The cottage becomes a cave, the young woman a lady of great beauty, the children round the bed are seen as hairy imps, and the old father is even uglier than before. The midwife manages to keep her surprise to herself and gets away safely, but some time later she sees the old man pilfering in the market, and accosts him. He asks which eye she sees him with, and when she points to it, immediately blinds it.

Another common fairy habit is to visit houses at night, to bathe their babies in the water left for them. The

Fairy ring of *Clitocybe nebularis* (clouded agaric), photographed near Buchenberg in the Allgäu

room must be left tidy, the hearth swept, the fire made up, and fresh water left in a pail by the fireside. The maid who attends to this will find sixpence in her shoe, which will be left after every visit as long as she keeps it secret, for fairy gifts must not be talked of. A lazy maid who neglects her duty is punished with cramps or lameness.

Fairy methods of flight and levitation are very like those practiced by witches. A ragwort stem or twig is used by a small fairy instead of a witch's broomstick. Some form of incantation is used; the antiquary John Aubrey (1626–1697) gives the operative, words as 'Horse and Hattock!' Sometimes the power of flight is given by a blue cap.

Rays of Coloured Light

The fairies vary even more in their appearance than they do in their other characteristics. The astral fairies seen by some of the modern Irish seers are described as about 7 or 8 feet in height, radiant and beautiful, with rays of coloured light streaming from them. On the other hand some fairies of the Isle of Man described by Walter Gill in *A Third Manx Scrapbook*, as seen by a friend at the beginning of this century, were little men about 18 inches high, greyish in colour, like a fungus, their bodies rather swollen in front. Their eyes and heads were clearly distinguishable, and their heads moved as they danced. The Welsh Tylwyth Teg are small but beautiful; they generally wear white, though some Welsh fairies wear striped, many-coloured clothes. Green is the most usual colour for fairies to wear, both in England and Scotland. Geoffrey Hodson, a clairvoyant who claimed to be able to see fairies, described in his book *Fairies at Work and at Play* a group of fairies about 6 inches high with oval fluttering wings, dancing in

Dancing Fairies, **August Malmström (1829–1901)**

a ring and wearing floating draperies of pale blue. This is an unusual colour for fairies. A fairy whose appearance in Perthshire is recorded in the archives of the School of Scottish Studies is described as 'a wee green man with peakit boots, with a cap like an old gramophone horn on his head.' His face was dark and furrowed.

The kings and knights of the Trooping Fairies are generally as beautiful as their ladies, but the men in the second grade of fairies are often wizened, hairy, and stunted, though their women are beautiful. Pixies have turned-up noses, red hair, and squint eyes. They generally wear green, but are occasionally naked. The tiny flower fairies are exquisite and dainty. There are any number of hideous fairy creatures, like the spriggans of Cornwall, who can be large or small at will, but are grotesque at any size. Brownies are grotesque, hairy, and ragged, and were supposed to have no noses, only nostrils, while the boggarts had long sharp noses.

Beauty and Shapeless Horror

The fairies of the British Isles have many characteristics in common, yet there is a different flavour about them in every region. The gentlest are the fairies of central England. They are often small in size, and though tricksy are not often dangerous. Their insistence on order and cleanliness, their habit of visiting houses, their influence over crops, all suggest that they were once agricultural spirits.

In the Fen Country, along the east coast of England, the traditions are grimmer. The Yarthkins of the Lincolnshire Fens were small, ugly, malicious creatures, always ready to do evil. They have gone with the draining of the Fens, and no one can regret them. Northward the picture becomes darker. Though there are still tales of little, merry fairies, there are also many boggarts and many bogey beasts, and

on the Borders we have the murderous Redcaps. In the Lowlands of Scotland there are traditions of the Fairy Rade and the fairies of the Border ballads, but on the whole the creatures are more prosaic than in Ireland. In the Highlands the Celtic imagination has again full play, but the duality of the fairy nature is strongly stressed; there are good and bad among them. Beautiful music is heard from the fairy hills, but there are traditions of monstrous creatures, blood-suckers, and water kelpies, and shapeless horrors.

The fairies assume their most beautiful form in Ireland. We hear much of their music, and of the beauty of their women and the stateliness of their men. There are also grotesque, comical fairies, and even the most beautiful of the Irish fairies are dangerous; a man goes with them at his peril, and many of them that appear beautiful are the evil host of the dead.

The early heroic legends of Ireland and the Highlands have been so well preserved in oral tradition that the fairy beliefs have retained a remarkable continuity; they have been more varied and fluctuating in England with its great admixture of races. In all countries the fairy beliefs are ancient, and probably stem back to primitive gods and religions. As has already been said, the Latin *fata* is the accepted derivation of the word 'fay', and the sophisticated fairies who were guests at Sleeping Beauty's christening are remote descendants of the Fates who appeared at Meleager's cradle and of the Norns, who were the female fates of Nordic mythology. In Greece, Italy, and other Romance countries, the nymphs and *genii* loci—spirits of the place—became fairies. In Ireland the Dana o'Shee are generally accepted as the personifications of the lost gods of the land.

In England the earliest mention of the fairies is the Anglo-Saxon charms against elf-shot, which was

Fen Fairy, Charles Prosper Sainton (1861–1914)

the infliction of disease by elf arrows; it is possible even that in the ninth-century Utrecht Psalter we have the first picture of fairies with wings, in what appears to be the representation of an elf-shot man. After the Norman Conquest, less is heard of the elves, but the twelfth and thirteenth-century chroniclers have a variety of fairy anecdotes to record. Walter Map (born c.1140) wrote a fascinating book called *De Nugis Curialium* (Courtiers' Trifles). He told an early version of the Fairy Wife tale. It comes from the Welsh borders, and is the legend of a historical character, Wild Edric, who for some time resisted the Norman

Conquest; he fell in love with a fairy and snatched her away from a fairy dance in a house in the Forest of Clun. She consented to be his wife on condition that he never reproached her with her origin. They were happily married for many years and when Edric had made submission to King William he took her to Court, where her beauty was much admired. At last, however, in an impatient moment, he asked if she had been with her sisters, and at once she vanished. The fairy house in the forest was not to be found, and he sought her in vain until he died. He was long said to ride, with his lady beside him and his train following, over the Welsh border country. The last recorded appearance was in the nineteenth century when they were seen by a girl and her father; the girl, though illiterate, correctly described their Saxon costume with the cross-gartered leggings.

An earlier ride described by Walter Map is that of Herla, who ruled over ancient Britain. One day, King Herla was visited by the King of the Fairies, a small grotesque creature riding upon a goat. He said that he was the lord of many realms and he offered to attend Herla's wedding, bringing some of his people with him, if Herla would return the compliment a year later, and honour his wedding with his presence. King Herla promised to do this, though he had no wedding in mind at that time. It happened that a match was soon arranged, however, and on the wedding day the Fairy King arrived, attended by many servants, as grotesque as himself, but all with courtly manners and loaded with gifts, food and drink, and many costly presents. They undertook the service of the banquet, and by their alacrity and good cheer they won the favour of the guests. At cockcrow they departed, the Fairy King reminding Herla of his promise.

Accordingly, in a year's time, King Herla set out, accompanied by his knights and carrying many rich gifts with him. He was royally received, and three days and nights passed in feasting and merriment. Then Herla wished to return to his young wife and his people. The Fairy King gave him many gifts, and last of all a little greyhound to sit on the king's saddle before him, and he charged them all not to dismount until the dog leapt down.

The king and his knights rode toward home, but everything was changed, and he could not find his palace. He asked the way of a peasant passing by, but he could hardly make himself understood, nor understand what the man said, for 300 years had passed since he entered fairyland, and in the meantime the Saxons had conquered Britain. When they understood this, some of Herla's knights leapt to the ground, and at once the weight of their years came upon them, and they crumbled into dust. Then Herla remembered the warning of the Fairy King and he called to his knights to ride through the centuries, waiting for the dog to leap down; it is said that he will never do this until the Day of Judgment.

Dining on Roast Frog

Another source of fairy legends is Gervase of Tilbury, author of *Otia Imperialia*, who flourished about 1210. His stories come from several parts of Europe, but he tells of the earliest tiny fairies, called Portunes in England and Neptunes in France. They were only a few inches high, with faces like wrinkled old men, and came into human houses at night, where they roasted frogs in front of the fires left burning for them. Gervase gives us the first Fairy Midwife story, complete with the fairy ointment and the blinding of the seeing eye.

The fairy references of the early chroniclers are not frequent, but they cover a surprising number of fairy types and legends. There is not such a variety in the medieval romances. Except for giants, dwarfs, and unexplained enchantments, we chiefly hear of the fairy women, with their power of enchantment. Some of these are treated as fairies, some as mortals with magical powers. In Malory's *Le Morte d'Arthur*, Morgan le Fay is a mortal, but she derives from a fairy, Fata Morgana. On the other hand, Nimue, the Lady of the Lake, seems to be thought of as a fairy, though the French author of the tale of *Lancelot du Lac* gives a determinedly matter-of-fact account of her: 'Now the story saith that the Damosel that carried Lancelot into the lake was a fay. In those days all maidens that knew enchantments and charms were called fays, and there were many of them at this time, and more in Great Britain than in other lands.'

With Chaucer begins the refrain of the passing of the fairies, which has been echoed ever since. Two centuries after Chaucer's reference to the disappearance of the elves, this thought is echoed in the words of another poet:

But now alas they all are dead
Or gone beyond the seas.

RICHARD CORBET

In the nineteenth century, Hugh Miller tells the same tale, 'The People of Peace shall never more be seen in Scotland.' Yet, in spite of this, rumours of fairies continued to run through the land, and even today there are still people who claim to see them.

Fallen Angels or Ghosts?

What is the explanation of this strange and yet recurrent body of belief? Various explanations have been given, and no single one seems to cover the whole ground. Medieval churchmen accepted St. Augustine's suggestion that the supernatural beings of the heathen were not senseless idols but fallen angels trying to usurp the place of God. The more uncompromising Puritans held that the fairies were outright devils. But a more charitable belief, still held in Ireland, is that the fairies were indeed fallen angels, ejected from heaven with the rest but not wicked enough for the depths of hell. As they were falling, the Son held up his hand, and they stopped short in flight; the most wicked, the Lucifugi, fell into the caverns below the earth, and became gnomes, kobolds, and other light-hating creatures. Some fell into the sea and became mermaids and water spirits, others into woods or flowery places, others near men's habitations, becoming brownies and hobs, whose duty was to work for man without reward.

Another equally common belief was that the fairies were the dead who had died before their appointed time, or those who were too good for hell and not good enough for heaven. In Cornwall they say that the fairies are the ghosts of the old Druids, though their stock is recruited from time to time by kidnapped mortals.

The sixteenth and seventeenth-century magicians, who had many recipes for raising fairies and putting them to use, seem sometimes to have regarded them as elementals—creatures made out of one of the four elements only: sylphs from air, undines from water, gnomes from earth, and salamanders from fire. Modern believers often regard them as nature spirits, whose special function it is to fertilize plants and look after flowers.

The theories of the students of fairy lore, who study the subject more objectively, are equally diverse. In the nineteenth century, a theory was advanced by David MacRitchie that the fairies were a conquered,

Emily's Fairies, **Emily Gertrude Thomson (1850–1929)**

pre-Celtic race; the small primitive men who inhabited these islands, forced into hiding in caves and mounds, and therefore nocturnal in their habits. They knew the ancient traditions of the land, and were thought masters of its magic. They might make shy advances to their conquerors, and do odd jobs on the farms in return for food. They would be expert pickers and stealers, and make raids on the new settlers.

Perhaps the best case of all is made out by those who think that the fairy beliefs originated in a cult of the dead. This view is ably presented by Lewis Spence in *British Fairy Origins* (1946). There is no doubt that there are many traditional connections between the fairies and the dead. In many of the Irish stories given by Lady Wilde the fairy host is explicitly stated to be the 'host of the dead'. The fairy man who advised Bessie Dunlop, one of the Scottish witches, was alleged to be a man killed at the Battle of Pinkie, in 1547, some thirty years previously. Many of the brownies and hobs are expressly described as ghosts. The Cauld Lad of Hilton is one, and in Ireland the Phooka of Kildare, though it took the form of an ass, was the ghost of an idle scullery boy, forced to work in the house, until he was considered worthy of reward. He was paid by a gift of clothing. The minute size of the tiniest of the fairies can be plausibly account- ed for by the primitive notion of man's soul being a tiny creature, in human or insect form, which comes out of his mouth when he is asleep and whose wanderings account for dreams.

Spirits of the Landscape

There are other factors, which, though not accounting for the whole body of fairy beliefs, seem to have had their share in building them. It may be taken as certain that a few of the fairies are descendants of the gods. Spirits of trees and woods seem to be

true nature spirits and not the ghosts of people sacrificed in the groves in the time of primitive nature worship. The habit of personification is natural to man, and it would be odd if trees, streams, mountains, and rocks should be left empty of personality in men's imaginations until a dead man could be found to haunt them. Animism is a primitive habit that dies hard. Certainly the foundation sacrifice beneath the hearth may become a ghost that grows into a tutelary spirit, but to what was the sacrifice made? Besides these, psychic phenomena, poltergeist activities, and so on, whatever their cause, had an obvious part in building up fairy beliefs.

A further element, still to be explored, is the symbolism of the unconscious, which everywhere produces metaphors inexplicably satisfying to the souls of men. Jung's penetrating exposition of this theme has yet to be fully examined by folklorists. He has already investigated fairy tales, but fairy beliefs may prove to be equally relevant. All these together form a fascinating complexity of beliefs and theories which merit further investigation.

K. M. BRIGGS

FURTHER READING: K. M. Briggs. An Encyclopedia of Fairies. (Pantheon, 1977). The Anatomy of Puck. (Arno, 1977). The Fairies in English Tradition and Literature. (University of Chicago Press, 1967); Robert Hunt. Popular Romances of the West. (Blom, 1968 reprint); Thomas Keightley. The Fairy Mythology. (Bohn's Antiquarian Library Series, Gale, 1975).

Faunus

Faunus was an ancient Italian nature deity who came to be identified with the Greek god, Pan. A god of forests and fields, he was associated with agriculture

and hunting. He was celebrated each year at the Lupercalia, a Roman pastoral festival held in early spring, and again on 5 December. In 1979, a number of fourth-century silver spoons engraved with his name were unearthed in Britain, evidence of how the cult was widespread across the Roman Empire. Deriving from Faunus are fauns, spirits of the woods. The statue of a dancing faun was found in a house at Pompeii.

Firebird

The legend of the Firebird, an exotic creature with glowing plumage, appears in a number of mythologies, including Russian folklore. The plumage of the bird is so bright that even a single feather shed on the ground retains its intense flamelike quality. Often, the finding of one feather is the inspiration behind the search for the elusive bird—a search that requires a journey, fraught with hazards that must be overcome. The Brothers Grimm included in their collection of fairy tales a story about a golden bird that was the object of a quest by three brothers, only one of whom was successful. The Firebird also provided the inspiration for Igor Stravinsky's ballet of the same name, first performed in 1910.

Ghosts

Belief in ghosts means to many people an unequivocal acceptance of the souls of the dead in sheets and chains, squeaking and gibbering in Gothic ruins. This caricature has grown from second-rate horror stories, films, and comic strips, and it remains current in spite of the impressive number of people who go on seeing much less melodramatic specters.

For instance, a British family were rehoused by their local authority in

1966 because of the effect on their health of strange happenings in their two-year-old council house. The father saw a man's shadow on the stairs where no man was standing; the daughter saw weird lights moving in her room. Police, clergymen, and others investigated and found nothing, but no one seemed to scoff; the council produced another house, the priest exorcized the first one, and *The Guardian* reported it all without any of the contempt that newspapers once reserved for such stories.

It may be that belief in ghosts grows out of, and is a response to, some basic and universal human need. The need, of course, is for some assurance of survival after death. In history and prehistory, ghosts were an integral part of religious belief. Religion carried the promise of immortality, which meant that the spirits of the dead had to be taken into consideration.

The Ancestral Spirits

Naturally the ghosts of a community's forebears would be the most prevalent. So ancestor worship can be said to be one of the first, perhaps *the* first, form of religious awareness that developed in man. Even the cave dwellers of the

Special placement for initiation of men in the ceremonial house of the village Apangai, Papua New Guinea. In the front one sees the clanfounder Tappoka. Behind him: female jungle-ghosts, clan-ancestors, and mythical ancestors like the creator of the yam-tuber.

Three Women and Three Wolves,
Eugene Grasset (1845–1917)

early Stone Age buried their dead with some ceremony, which suggests belief in an afterlife and worship of the dead.

Where ancestors are worshipped, they have taken on the role of gods, gaining supernatural power as they enter the supernatural world. Often they are only minor gods, perhaps divine only to their own families. But equally often the forebears can be the major gods of the community. They then become the principal overseers of the tribe's ethical and spiritual welfare.

The ancestors are viewed as protectors, interposing their power between the living and supernatural evils. More important is the negative view that if the goodwill of the ghosts is not maintained—if the offerings, praises, and so on slacken off—the ghosts punish such laxity with calamities like disease and death. If such disasters occur, the tribe concludes that someone has angered the ghosts, and a system of appeasement goes into action.

The need to propitiate ghosts is just as important in those primitive societies which do not directly worship their forebears. Some of these societies,

The Barque, Odilon Redon (1840–1916)

Doomed to Walk the Earth

The more complex primitive societies and most civilizations developed the idea of a distinct spirit world—the happy hunting ground, Elysian Fields, Valhalla, and the like. They saw ghosts as yearning for these places but being somehow balked. Thus arises the concept of the wandering ghost who infests this world while craving access to the next world and his eternal rest. Ghosts of murder victims remain to harass the living, like Hamlet's father, until vengeance is done. Ghosts remain also when their bodies have been improperly buried, or not buried at all, as with Odysseus's friend Elpenor. This idea remains strong today: Britain's famous ghost hunter, Harry Price, felt in the 1930s that the main 'haunt' of Borley Rectory would depart once Christian burial had been given to some old bones he found under the Rectory.

The association of ghosts with improper burial reveals another long-lived assumption: that there is a mystical connection after death between the corpse and the spirit. Many of the propitiations aimed at ghosts by primitives are in fact performed upon the corpse or the grave. Offerings are placed at the graveside, and all over the world the dead have been buried with food, ornaments, amulets, and weapons for the spirit to have with him after death. Of course desecration of the grave or disturbance of the bones brought instant retaliation from the ghost.

In spite of the various links between corpse and spirit, the notion of a land of the dead became of vital importance, and the corollary idea began to arise that for a ghost to be operating in this world was a clear punishment. Shades of evil-doers remained among the living because they had earned no right to eternal rest. Others, not evil in life, were trapped here if they had been murdered or inadequately buried, or if they had left something important undone. No wonder so many ghosts are supposed to be malevolent; no wonder that moans and howls and shrieks are associated with them, as they bewail their inability to go to rest. There are very few tales, past or present, in which a ghost is willing and happy to stay in this world.

Many of the foregoing primitive attitudes to ghosts and the dead remain in folklore and legend. But the old beliefs about what ghosts look like, and their nature generally, have been added to a little. Primitive ghosts are often indistinguishable from devils, and so may appear as horned giants breathing fire or as unusually large and vicious animals. Such visions do indeed still figure in old wives' tales; but a great many ghosts seen by modern man apparently take remarkably human form. This tendency has been confirmed by various societies of psychical research, which try very hard to take a scientific, clear-eyed view of ghosts. They are at pains to show that most of the more reliable and straightforward accounts of apparitions describe the figures seen as quite ordinary-looking people—three-dimensional, solid, and wholly human.

many South American jungle tribes for instance, see all spirits as vindictive and dangerous, and so requiring propitiation. It is as if the fact of death makes the spirit automatically hostile to the living, whatever its personality while alive. Sometimes the object is not appeasement so much as warding off the spirit: magic spells are set up in a house after a death in the family, to keep the ghost at a distance; or the body is buried in such a way that the ghost cannot find its way back. Ghosts are often believed to have a poor sense of direction: in fairly recent times the bodies of hanged criminals, executed witches, and so on were buried at crossroads to confuse the ghosts.

Apparitions of the Living

Many of these accounts are of apparitions of the living, which usually appear at some crisis in the life of the person who is seen. A well-known case illustrates the point: a young Englishwoman living in India in 1917 was startled to see her brother, a Royal Flying Corps pilot, standing in her living room one day. She thought he had come on a surprise visit; only when the brother disappeared did she realize she had seen an apparition. She later learned that it had materialized at the moment when her brother's aeroplane was being shot down over France. Apparitions of the dead (which are often of loved ones or close relatives) share this apparent realness; so do the many other apparitions that have been seen at the point of death of the person who appears.

Sometimes, indeed, the reality and solidity of the apparition is more than visual—as in the case of a bewhiskered ghost in a nineteenth-century Bristol vicarage, who had a nasty habit of entering bedrooms and waking people up by shaking the bed. Or the affectionate 'haunt' of a British stately home, about 1885, who awoke a maiden lady sleeping in the haunted room by bestowing a ghostly kiss. But many other apparitions lack any other aspect of a physical presence than their appearance, and so are all the more frightening. Many accounts mention that the apparition seems to 'glide' soundlessly; few apparitions have left footprints where a flesh and blood person would have done; many have seemed to float well above the ground. Odd clothing is often abnormality enough: strange figures roaming the night become all the more eerie when they are wearing authentic eighteenth-century dress. And terror would mount if they were also seen to walk through a wall or to be transparent.

One compiler of modern ghost stories tells of a company director driving through the British countryside at night, who saw what appeared to be an encampment of Roman soldiers in some woods. He assumed it was a film company on location, until he realized that he could see the trunks of trees through the soldiers' bodies. Nor was he the only person to have seen that ghostly camp. In another case, a tall clergyman was seen regularly to visit a London church to pray: quite unremarkable, thought the vicar of the church, until one day he accidentally bumped into the praying figure and walked right through it.

Apparitions often reveal their noncorporeal nature by suddenly disappearing for no obvious reason. They may also disappear if the living interfere with them. Ghosts may sometimes like to touch people or kiss them or shake their beds, but they seem to object when the living take the initiative. Try to grasp an apparition, to set traps for it, like hidden cameras or powder for possible footprints, and it will vanish. In fact, though there are hundreds of alleged photographs of apparitions, the creatures are notoriously camera-shy.

Some mention must be made of the ghostly occupants of 'haunted houses'. 'Haunts' are, above all, recurrent, walking regularly as clockwork—the same night, the same time, over the same distance. They often take little or no notice of the living (less, anyway, than most of the apparitions which appear only once), but they, too, will promptly disappear if the perceivers try to interfere with them. Haunts generally seem less lifelike than other apparitions; some authorities have described them as 'somnambulistic,' even mindless. Patrolling the same area, performing the same actions, they are like a visual record stuck in one groove.

The Sheeted Dead

For every lifelike apparition in psychical research files or in folktale—lifelike even when the illusion slips a little, as when the ghost floats or is transparent—there are at least an equal number of stories of visitations that resemble rather the inventions of horror fiction. These include the female ghost in a Norfolk manor who

Ivan the Terrible Visited by the Ghosts of Those He Murdered, **Baron Mikhail Petrovich Klodt von Jurgensburg**

A spooky church. For many, the sight of a cemetery, even in broad daylight, can produce a shiver.

had empty, fathomless hollows instead of eyes; the faceless woman who haunted a churchyard in Canewdon, Essex; and the bodiless head which in 1953 drove a series of residents from a house in Hamburg, in spite of a cruel housing shortage. Other outlandish horrors carry with them the signs of how they met their deaths, like the victim of drowning who was said to haunt a New Orleans bridge, and who was always seen dripping with spectral seaweed. Numerous cases exist of apparitions in the form of mouldering corpses, even skeletons; these are related to the appearances of ghosts in sheets (in other words the shroud or winding sheet from the grave), which provide further instances of the age-old connection of corpse with spirit.

Nor do all apparitions manifest themselves in human or even partly human form. Spectral animals are widely common, with Britain predictably leading the field; dogs figure most frequently in these tales. In many cases the animal ghosts are friendly, but more often they are semidemonic, like the Mauthe Dog that traditionally haunted a castle on the Isle of Man and the ghostly pack of hounds that made Cornwall's moors horrible with their baying. Horses occur in many ghost legends, often with a rider, just as often not; they also are seen pulling phantom coaches. So it seems legends allow inanimate objects a ghostly existence.

Prominent among such objects are various means of transport. Many are phantom ships, including the famous Flying Dutchman and the French ship La Belle Rosalie. Ghost trains also reappear to rumble through the night on their old runs, whether the railway lines still exist or not. One famous legend concerns the funeral train carrying the coffin of Abraham Lincoln, which is said to roll along a stretch of track in New York State every April, and to have on board a phantom military band playing busily, though its music cannot be heard by living ears.

Apparitions may take much less substantial and well-defined forms than the ones considered so far. For instance, a revenant (one who comes back from the dead) created by some violent death in the past may be not a full-scale haunt but instead take the form of a mere bloodstain. A nineteenth-century tavern keeper in Massachusetts murdered and robbed a traveler one night, but from then on was plagued by bloodstains in the victim's room which could not be removed. Several cases exist of ghostly manifestations in the form of clouds of mist; sometimes, though, the mist will form itself into a recognizable human shape, as happened in France in 1951 when a film writer believed he saw such a mist cloud take the form of the actress Maria Montez.

An Eerie Moving Light

Ghostly lights frequently occur when other forms of apparition are absent, and often contribute to haunted-house legends, as with the flickering lights repeatedly seen round the notorious Borley Rectory during its several uninhabited periods.

It is obvious that an empty house could easily have temporary tenants, such as tramps, exploring children, or vandals, who might light their way with flickering candles or matches. Yet the legends go on, related to the notion that spirits sometimes glow in the dark. So, in America, the ghost of a North Carolina railway conductor haunts a particular trestle bridge in the form of an eerie moving light: he had been decapitated near that spot, and the light is said to be his head on an eternal and forlorn search for its body.

With phantoms formed of mist and light must be reckoned the phantoms associated with smoke. Even the smell of smoke can apparently breed ghost legends, as in the story of the seventeenth-century American girl who was burned to death for no good reason, and whose ghostly presence is recognizable by its accompanying pungent odour of smoke. Visible smoke led to another ghost tale being added to the lore of the Tower of London. In 1954 a sentry left his post in pursuit of a smoke cloud that moved as if of its own volition, changed its shape, but did not seem to diffuse or drift like ordinary smoke—until it disappeared with alarming suddenness.

Setting aside apparitions, of whatever shape or form, there is an immense variety of nonvisual ghostly happenings. Many of these must be ascribed to the poltergeist: church bells ringing themselves, pianos or organs being played by invisible fingers, weird laughter or screams or footsteps echoing through empty corridors.

Less overtly poltergeist ghosts would include those invisible manifestations that lay their cold hands on people or touch them in other ways, like the kissing ghost mentioned earlier. In Sheffield in 1956 an invisible phantom made itself known to an elderly lady by lying down on the bed beside her, making the mattress sink and the springs creak.

Somewhat closer to the traditional poltergeist, perhaps, is the invisible ghost of a former Bank of England cashier who now tends playfully to disarm the guards; and the Bavarian ghost first heard of in 1949 who gained the name 'Gus the Nazi' when he persecuted women who fraternized with Allied Occupation troops. He was said to have cropped the hair of one girl, with scissors held by his invisible hand, in full view of her parents.

A 'creepy feeling'—a nonphysical awareness of some presence—occurs to a great many people in quite ordinary circumstances.

A Sense of Evil

Last of all the categories of ghosts are the totally intangible phenomena which can loosely be described as 'eerie feelings'. In a large majority of cases of clearly seen or heard ghosts, those who have experienced such phenomena have reported a definite sensation of cold, a feature that occurs as often in well-attested psychical research files as in the annals of folklore. But sometimes this chill that has no physical cause can occur entirely on its own, or can occur before the apparition is seen, usually giving the percipient an almost instinctive feeling that something evil or fearful is present.

Animals, particularly dogs, are believed by occultists to be specially attuned to supernatural manifestations; many sensible people have told psychical investigators of their pets'

unexplained fear of something that apparently only the animal could see. Dogs, for instance, were often frightened round Borley Rectory, even in broad daylight; and Dennis Bardens relates the story of a modern visitor to Compton Castle near Torquay, whose pet greyhound was riveted to the spot in utter terror of something only it could perceive.

Sometimes such presences make themselves felt without the aid of chills or whatever special senses dogs may have. A 'creepy feeling'—a nonphysical awareness of some presence—occurs to a great many people in quite ordinary circumstances. It often happens that someone enters unfamiliar but quite ordinary surroundings (like an empty house or flat visited during a house-hunting excursion) and has a definite feeling of oppression, depression or similar 'atmospheric' reaction from the place. Nor need this reaction be due to any perceptible physical factors, such as poor lighting, dank overshadowing trees, rising damp, atrocious wallpaper, or bad smells. Many people have admitted their personal experience of this unpleasant sensation in an apparently ideal dwelling, as if there were some sort of 'psychic emanation' from the very walls of the place reminiscent of past horrors that took place there.

The forms and habits of ghosts may be incredibly varied, but their reasons for returning, the basic purposes behind their presence among us, tend according to folklore to be fairly limited. Many of the reasons for ghosts returning suggested by past and primitive societies can still be found in modern legend. So ghosts can return apparently out of sheer malevolence. Vampires, a special kind of revenant, return solely for evil purposes as, in many tales, do the ghosts of executed witches.

Apparition of the Monstrous Cat, Utagawa Kuniyoshi (1797–1861)

Haunting ghosts seem to return to re-enact some crisis scene from their former lives—usually their death. Ghosts in modern lore, as in the past, have been said to return to seek vengeance on their slayers, to punish the living for crimes against them or against their descendants, to seek proper burial, to complete some task left undone or merely to continue one.

The ghost of an American farmer returned for the specific purpose of informing his heirs where he had hidden his will; another American ghost returned to claim what it felt to be rightfully its own. This was the deceased wife of a thrifty New England farmer, whose husband had removed her rings before the funeral, eventually to pass them on to his next wife. But the second wife awoke in terror one night to find the apparition of her predecessor angrily pulling the rings off her fingers.

Quite a number of ghosts have appeared to announce their own deaths, in the 'point of death' form of apparition met so often in psychical research.

> The 'creepy feeling' mentioned before in connection with specific houses might be ascribable to a collection of possibly unconscious impresssion—signs of decay or odours and the like . . .

But others are said to appear as harbingers of someone else's imminent death. The spirit of a deceased loved one might appear to a person, perhaps beckoning; Josephine's ghost apparently came to Napoleon in this way, some days before he died. Or some ancestral figure might appear to the title-holder of a noble family, heralding his death, as a spectral Black Friar was supposed to visit members of Byron's family.

Some stories exist of ghosts appearing because the person has, before death, promised to return in order to indicate the continuance of life 'on the other side'. Dennis Bardens gives several accounts of such promises that were apparently kept, including that of the nineteenth century Lord Brougham, who materialized in the presence of a friend. Predictably, several people whose lives were devoted to psychical research are said to have returned, or at least to have sent messages backlike the 'spirit writings'

transcribed by a medium that were asserted to be from the great pioneer of British psychical research, F. W. H. Myers.

Tricks of the Senses?

The foregoing must of course be taken as only a broad sample of what people have believed regarding ghosts, their nature and habits. To make some sense of it, we must look at some of the answers that experts have given to the question of the reasons behind this universal belief.

The short answer that is often given is, obviously, that people who see ghosts experience nothing except a temporary derangement of their senses. It is true that our senses do often play tricks on us, when we are in an excitable or suggestible state, or when we are drunk, ill, or half asleep.

Certainly quite a few accounts of ghosts can be dismissed on this account. The 'creepy feeling' mentioned before in connection with specific houses might be ascribable to a collection of possibly unconscious impressions—signs of decay or odours and the like, not consciously perceived but nonetheless affecting our reactions.

At the very least, no occultist has yet come up with a convincing explanation of why certain tragedies in certain houses should breed these ghostly emanations, or should produce haunts, while others do not; yet there must be a great many houses quite happily occupied today that have tragic or horrific histories. In the same way, one tends to mistrust sightings of ghosts that are traditionally in residence in particular buildings. Too often people see what they expect to see.

Many psychologists tend instantly to dismiss accounts of ghost sightings as the 'product of a disturbed mind.' But for a few men in this field the easy answer does not satisfy. Freud searched for explanations among the repressed relics from our primitive past, the ancient ghost fears of primeval man now hidden within the unconscious mind, but sometimes slithering into conscious awareness. Jung looked for answers in his theory of the collective unconscious, the contents of which can in his view take on almost an autonomous life of their own, being projected or manifested as seemingly outer occurrences.

Both Freud and Jung made it clear that these views should not be taken as complete answers, but more as avenues of approach for psychoanalytic researchers. Other theorists depart from these standpoints, but still share with the two great psychological pioneers the idea that phenomena like ghosts are at least worth the time and effort of study. As the American psychologist William James put it, 'it is bad method to ignore them'. James himself produced one of the more interesting

Entrance of the Ghosts of Venice, Alexandre Serebriakoff (1907–1994)

Tyrrell, offered the idea that the other minds telepathically affect the sensory apparatus (like the optic nerve) of the percipient, so that the brain receives the message that a ghost is standing there.

Psychons and Astral Bodies

None of these theories accepts the possibility that something with objective reality might indeed be standing there. For these experts, apparitions are hallucinations, however caused. Other theories tend to grow a trifle more fanciful. Students of the occult who recall the many hundreds of accounts of 'astral traveling'—when a person's astral self seems to detach itself from his body and move about, fully conscious and supernaturally mobile—often relate these astral selves to ghosts.

An explanation of haunting has been offered on the basis of psychic emissions analogous to the photons, gluons and other theoretical elements that are supposed to effect the exchange of energy in particle physics; these psychic particles have been called psychons, and the theory suggests that they remain in a house, carrying an imprint of a particular scene in some form of psychic energy, which becomes perceptible to certain minds in certain circumstances. Alternatively, there is the suggestion that every piece of matter—whether a person, a dog, or even a train—has an 'etheric' nonmaterial counterpart that exists in 'psychic space', which sometimes interpenetrates physical space and so becomes visible to a percipient.

Most of these theories, acceptable in terms of the frequently occurring 'phantasms of the living', raise difficulties when applied to apparitions of the dead. For if we accept the possibility of telepathically projected apparitions, or astral bodies, or etheric selves, we must

theories concerning apparitions, based on the idea of spontaneously produced hallucinations. Like other psychical researchers after him, he turned to extra-sensory perception—telepathy, clairvoyance, and so on—as the possible cause of these hallucinations.

However, even after years of concentrated research into ESP very few conclusions about ghosts have been drawn or could have been, in spite of the mountains of statistics amassed from years of experimentation. So to the layman at least, explaining ghosts in terms of telepathy is of only abstract interest. Nonetheless, it is interest-

ing to find William James describing apparitions as products of our own unconscious minds when they are being stimulated by other minds. This telepathic contact, he says, produces an 'objective' hallucination (as opposed to the subjective kind that our minds can produce by themselves, without help from an outside agency).

F. W. H. Myers had a comparable idea that the other minds did not stimulate our minds directly, but tinkered with part of the environment we were looking at to produce the hallucinatory apparition. Another great British student of the paranormal, G. N. M.

Opposite page:
The Poet Dainagon Sees an Apparition,
Utagawa Kuniyoshi (1798–1861)

accept that these transmissions can also come from the dead; that, in short, a person's mind and psychic qualities can cross the barrier of death.

That means that we must accept the idea of the survival of the individual personality after death. Or, if we balk at that, we must accept the idea of a striking time-lag in the case of post-mortem apparitions—that the telepathy or other emanation came from a living agent, perhaps at the point of death but no later, and did not reach a percipient's mind until sometime after the agent's death.

None of these explanations is wholly satisfactory, for none seems applicable to the whole range of ghost lore. It seems likely that the question will remain open until, somehow, man is able to discover what, if anything, transpires after death.

Meanwhile, for whatever reason or amalgam of reasons, people will go on seeing things or have experiences which tradition teaches them to call ghostly. These experiences can apparently happen to anyone, however rationalistic, nerveless, phlegmatic or hard-headed he thinks he is. And hardly anyone has been able to hang on to his total disbelief in such phenomena after having had such an experience, in any form. There is a mystery here which man is no nearer solving than he was when he strung amulets round his hut to keep out the spirits.

DOUGLAS HILL

FURTHER READING: R. C. Finucane. Appearances of the Dead: a Cultural History of Ghosts. *(Prometheus Books, 1984); C. Green.* Apparitions. *(Hamilton, 1975); A. Jaffe.* Apparitions. *(University of Dallas/Spring Publications, 1978); A. MacKenzie.* Apparitions and Ghosts. *(Barker, 1971); Gwen Risedorf.* Ghosts and Ghouls. *(Raintree, 1977); Eric Maple.* The Realm of Ghosts. *(A. S. Barnes 1964).*

Giants

The belief in the former existence of a race of giants is world-wide. They feature in the mythologies of most peoples, in local legends and in folktales. The evidence relating to them is as complex as their appearance is ubiquitous, but from the collected mythologies of the world it is possible to trace their development. The evidence suggests that descending from their original status as 'sons of heaven', the

giants finally came to feature as grisly monsters and demons.

The deepest and most ancient significance of the myth of giants lies in the cosmogonic cycles (cycles of creation myths) of many peoples. These allude to the existence of an immense primordial being who, in order to make possible the creation of the universe, and in particular of the earth, had to sacrifice himself. The first beings on this earth were creatures that manifested qualities and powers akin to those of this one mythical being.

Jack and the Giants, Richard Doyle (1824–1883)

The Demon Kumbhakarna Is Defeated by Rama and Lakshmana. **According to the Ramayana, Kumbhakarna, the terrifying giant and brother of Ravana, was causing great damage to the monkey army when Rama and Lakshmana entered the battle. Using magical arrows of great power, Rama severed Kumbhakarna's limbs and filled his mouth with pointed steel shafts. The pathos of the demon's defeat is emphasized by his dismembered body parts being carried away by the bear and monkey warriors. Compared to the Mughal depiction** *The Awakening of the Demon Kumbhakarna,* **which shows the giant sleeping, this Malwa portrayal focuses on his violent and bloody demise**

Seen in relation to man, giants are personifications of the overwhelming manifestations of the natural universe. Similarly, on a psychological level, they may be seen to represent man collectively as a species asserting himself on this planet, or they may be regarded as symbolizing all those forces in man which he is unable to control.

In nearly all traditions the giants appear as miraculous and ominous manifestations, that is, they represent all that surpasses human stature and achievement. But often giants exhibit inferior qualities such as stupidity and helplessness, which render them subordinate to man. According to traditions preserved in mythology and folklore, giants died out because they came into conflict with either gods or heroes. Essentially, the giant is a symbol of dissatisfaction, in that he either aims at dethroning the gods or destroying the work of man. The hero's deed is to

restore the equilibrium that had been upset by the giants' overturning of the universal order.

Goliath of Gath

Their mythological or early legendary character is clearly in evidence in the giants mentioned in the Old Testament. Biblical sources make only very scanty reference to what was probably a much larger body of current local folklore, which entered literature more extensively in the apocryphal writings. There is a passage in Genesis chapter 6, which speaks of a race of giants that sprang from a union of angels—called the 'sons of God,' the 'Watchers' of the apocryphal writings—and women or the 'daughters of men.' This passage appears to be a short fragment of a myth accounting to the Hebrew mind for those giants that were already known to common folklore. The contest of the giants with God appears first in the Apocrypha (Ecclesiasticus 16.7) and is developed greatly in later writings. In the other biblical references to giants the terms Nephilim and Rephaim, among others, are used to signify a race of giants who inhabited Palestine as the predecessors of the Canaanites. 'Rephaim,' incidentally, is connected with the word meaning 'shade' or 'ghost' and thus fits the mythological references to the extinct races which were supposed to have inhabited the land. In general, Hebrew legend attributes long life and abnormal stature to prehistoric races. In these ancient myths, referred to in Genesis 6. 1–4, we find the origin of the idea of angels of high estate who fell from the grace of God. This idea was perpetuated through the millennia, finding its personification later in the figure of Satan in the New Testament, as well as in the figure of the dragon. It came to be widely expressed in Christian literature, as for example in Milton's poem *Paradise Lost.*

More realistic descriptions are

The Assault on Heaven

Another account speaks of how certain tall and terrible giants, the Gigantes, with long locks and beards and serpents for feet, plotted an assault on heaven. They were enraged because Zeus, the successor of Cronus, had confined their brothers the Titans to Tartarus. Without warning they seized rocks and firebrands and hurled them upward from the mountain tops against Olympus, disdaining the lightning of Zeus. An oracle had declared that the gods could not conquer them except with the assistance of a mortal. The hero Hercules was called to the aid of the gods and he slew the most formidable of the giants. The remainder perished by the hands of the gods or fled. Local legend explains those places noted for volcanic eruptions, as for instance the islands of Cos and Sicily, as being the spots where the giants were buried. The Gigantomachia, or War of the Giants, is also referred to by the Roman poet Ovid at the beginning of his *Metamorphoses*.

In revenge for this destruction, Gaia lay with Tartarus and brought forth her youngest child Typhon, the largest monster ever born. 'From the thighs downward he was nothing but coiled serpents, and his arms which, when he spread them out, reached a hundred leagues in either direction, had countless serpents' heads instead of hands. His brutish ass-head touched the stars, his vast wings darkened the sun, fire flashed from his eyes, and flaming rocks hurtled from his mouth. When he came rushing toward Olympus, the gods fled in terror to Egypt, where they disguised themselves as animals.'

The human hero in all mythologies takes part in the battle with the giants. In his *Odyssey* Homer related how Odysseus intoxicated and outwitted the one-eyed, human-eating giant Polyphemus who lived on Sicily.

Tradition holds universally that before the close of the mythical Golden

Nearly every culture features giants of some sort in their myths, almost certainly as a menace.

found in relation to the giants Og and Goliath. In Deuteronomy chapter 3 we are told of the former: 'For only Og the king of Bashan was left of the remnant of the Rephaim; behold, his bedstead was a bedstead of iron; is it not in Rabbah of the Ammonites? Nine cubits was its length, and four cubits its breadth, according to the common cubit.' Of Goliath of Gath, the champion of the Philistines who was slain by David, it is said that his bronze coat of mail weighed 5,000 shekels, which is 208 pounds; about his weapon we are told 'the shaft of his spear was like a weaver's beam, and his spear's head weighed 600 shekels of iron' (approximately 25 pounds).

In Greek mythology there are various accounts of the birth and the subsequent fate of giants; always they are closely related to the pantheon of gods. Hesiod speaks of their origin in his *Theogony*, written in about the 8th century BC.

Uranus (sky) begot immense beings, the Titans and the Cyclopes, with Gaia (earth) and then shut his offspring in the depths of Tartarus. But Gaia in revenge incited the Titans to attack their father. This they did, led by Uranus's youngest son Cronus. Armed with a sickle Cronus castrated his father. The Titans then released the Cyclopes from Tartarus and awarded to Cronus the sovereignty over the earth; however, no sooner did Cronus find himself in supreme command than he confined the Cyclopes again to Tartarus.

Age, people had been much taller and much stronger. Survivals of such beliefs are found in the mythologies of many peoples, and references to them are frequent, especially in Inuit, North American Indian, Mexican, and Persian legends and stories. All the Greek and Latin poets and historians shared the opinion that they and their contemporaries were dwarfs compared with their ancestors.

Immense Stone Figures

The fact that ancient peoples have possessed a belief in giants is further evinced by the vast images of their gods and their colossal monuments in sculpture and architecture. Examples of such edifices and statues abound and survive from civilizations all over the world. The Colossus of Rhodes, one of the Seven Wonders of the World, exemplifies the ancient taste for the vast human figure. Grecian temples in general portray the gods and goddesses as being of superhuman size.

In front of the portals of the palace at Karnak in Egypt are placed gigantic human statues, and in one of the courts there are erected twelve immense stone figures, each of a height of about 52 feet. Similarly, at the outer gate of the Temple of Longevity at Canton were four gigantic figures. Many more examples of this kind could be cited. The various ancient representations of huge human forms were the corporeal shapes of those gigantic mythical figures which still existed in the imagination of our ancestors and which, having been perpetuated in this way in stone, served to continue the early belief in giants.

Norse and Germanic mythology assign an important place to giants. Our knowledge of northern mythology is derived mostly from the *Prose Edda* of Snorri Sturluson, which he wrote in the thirteenth century. The Icelandic scholar relates in it that according to Norse mythology there were in the

beginning two regions: the South, full of brightness and fire, and the North, a world of snow and ice. Between them there stretched a great void. When the heat and the cold met in the midst of this expanse, a living creature appeared in the melting ice: he was Ymir, a great giant. From under his left arm grew the first man and woman, while from his legs the clan of frost giants was begotten. Ymir was thus the ancestor of all the giants. When he was slain the earth formed under his body. There is also mention in Nordic creation legends of the giant Bergelmir who escaped in his boat from the flood caused by the blood of Ymir which overwhelmed the world. Having escaped, he then founded a new race.

Subsequently the giants of the Edda feature either as companions of the gods or as their adversaries, as in the following account.

One day the god Thor and Loki, a giant's son, set out to the land of giants. Toward evening they came to a huge building with an opening to one side. They groped their way in and spent the night there. But as there was a deafening noise coming from outside, and as the building shook with a continuous earthquake, they sat up most of the night in terror. At daybreak they discovered that not far from this building there lay a giant. He was Skrymir, who when he rose picked up what Thor and Loki had taken for a building, but which was in fact his glove. The passage in which they had spent the night proved to be its thumb.

The giants slain by Thor are characterized by their enormous size, power and greed and by being particularly jealous of the possessions of the gods. Gods and giants intermarry. Born from such a union was Loki, who was handsome to look at but was evil in his ways. He was a cunning schemer who

both helped and hindered the gods in their work. He was the father of the wolf Fenris, the World Serpent, and Hel, the ruler of death.

Legends universally ascribe the numerous stone structures of a former age to the work of giants. These stone structures are found particularly in Palestine, Greece, and Central Europe, and are almost exclusively associated with buildings known as *cyclopean*. Apart from these edifices there are very numerous megalithic structures, both above and below ground. These cairns, heaps of stones akin to dolmens, known as *Riesengraber* in Germany, are found throughout Europe.

Gargantua, engraving by Gustave Dore' (1832–1883) for *Gargantua and Pantagruel* by Francois Rabelais (1494–1553)

Local legend frequently pictures giants as throwing rocks about by way of trying each others' strength. According to a Dorsetshire legend, two giants once stood on a hill contending as to which of them could hurl a rock the longer distance across the valley to another hill. He whose stone fell short was so mortified by his failure that he died of vexation; he was buried beneath the mound which has since been known as the Giant's Grave. Similar legends are often attached to blocks of stone which occur naturally, and which appear strewn about, as it were, by some giants in an antediluvian game.

Finds of huge skeletons and bones all over the world have frequently led to the belief in a former gigantic tribe of men. Pliny relates that in the time of Claudius Caesar there was a man named Gabbaras, brought by the emperor from Arabia to Rome, who was 9 feet 9 inches high, 'the tallest man that has been seen in our times'. The Emperor Maximus, so the story goes,

Opposite page:
The Goblins in the Gold-Mine,
Heinrich Schlitt (1849–1923)

was about 8 or 9 feet tall and of great bulk. He was in the habit of using his wife's bracelet for a thumb-ring. His shoe was a foot longer than that of any other man and his strength was so great that he was able to draw a carriage which two oxen could not move. He could strike out a horse's teeth with one blow of his fist and break its thigh with a kick. He generally ate 40 pounds of meat every day and drank 6 gallons of wine.

Folk tradition uses the term giant in connection with a supposed race of mortals of immense size who inhabited the world in early times. In most European folktales giants appear as cruel and stupid savages, often one-eyed and given to cannibalism; sometimes they are akin to monsters. The hero of the follktale, like the English Jack the Giant-killer and Grimm's Valiant Tailor, always emerges victorious from a battle with them. Kindly giants occur only in a few stories, as in the legends of Rubezahl, the giant of the Bohemian forest. The majority of them, however, were feared and hated, although marriage between their daughters and the hero of the story was not impossible. Jonathan Swift invented a race of benevolent giants in the second part of his satire *Gulliver's Travels.*

The figure of the superman in the ancient myths, legends and tales speaks of man's inherent tendency to magnify real occurrences, to idealize them and present them in the imagery of dreams. The human hero is a being of more than life-size ability and physique, who is presented as conquering giants, demons, and dragons; thus the giants gradually come to embody almost exclusively negative qualities.

Man's love-hate relationship with the abnormal and the extraordinary, the violent idealization or rejection of the giant-hero, is apparent too in contemporary myth-making. The giant and the hero overlap. The negative giant, the master villain and the

hero's enemy, embodies those qualities that are rejected by the current code of values or the ideology of a given community. The hero-giants may be cosmonauts, secret agents, political figures or other popular heroes always winning against odds and excelling in power and intelligence.

MARIA-GABRIELE WOSIEN

FURTHER READING: M. Grumley. There Are Giants in the Earth. (Doubleday, 1974); R. Norvill. Giants. (Aquarian Press, 1979).

Gnomes

Name invented by Paracelsus for the elementals of the earth; dwarfish spirits which live underground and guard buried treasures: Paracelsus said that they move through the earth as easily as we move through the air.

Goblins

Or hobgoblins, mischievous, and sometimes dangerous fairies or imps: descriptions of their behaviour in a house, rapping on walls, breaking crockery, clattering pots and pans, whisking bedclothes off sleepers, frequently resemble accounts of poltergeist phenomena: a way of getting rid of one is to sprinkle flaxseed on the floor.

Gog and Magog

The names of two mythical giants, statues of which now stand in the Guildhall, London: according to legend, Gog and Magog were the last survivors of a race of British giants overcome by Brutus, who had them taken to London where they were compelled to work as porters at the gates of the royal palace: in the Bible,

Gog is described as a terrible ruler living in the north, and in the Apocalypse the terms Gog and Magog stand for all the enemies of the kingdom of God.

Golem

A golem is a creature, especially a human being, created artificially by magic. In the late Jewish form of the legend, as told by Jakob Grimm in his *Journal for Hermits* (1808), the golem is the figure of a man, made of clay or mud, and brought to life when the miraculous name of God is pronounced over it. The golem is dumb (though other versions of the legend do credit it with the power of speech) but it can understand orders and is used as a servant to do the housework. It must never be allowed to leave the house. On its forehead is written the word *emeth* (truth). With every day that goes by, the golem gains weight and it gradually becomes bigger and stronger than anyone in the house, until they become afraid of it. They then rub out the first letter of the word on its forehead, altering it to *meth* (he is dead). The golem immediately collapses and turns back into clay again.

One man's golem, according to Grimm, grew so tall that its forehead was too high to reach. Its owner ordered the golem to take off its boots, so that when it bent down he would be able to reach its forehead. The golem did as it was told, and the owner succeeded in erasing the first letter but the mass of dead clay fell on top of him and crushed him.

The Hebrew word *golem* occurs once in the Old Testament (Psalm 139. 16), where it means a human being which is not yet fully formed, an embryo. In the Talmud (the oldest extant code of Jewish law) the word is used once for Adam's body during the first hours of its existence but before it was fully endowed with life and consciousness. Elsewhere in the Talmud the word is used to denote an uncultured, boorish man. In medieval Hebrew the word was used as a technical philosophical term equivalent to the Greek hyle, that is, hylic matter, matter without form. Only at a much later stage was the word golem associated with magical traditions about the possibility of creating human and other beings by means of formulae, divine names, and permutations and combinations of Hebrew letters.

Act of Creation

The idea that it is possible to create living beings or to endow lifeless images or statues with life by magical means is widespread. In classical antiquity it was frequently associated with the alleged imparting of the power of speech to idols and statues. The Talmud too contains evidence that legends about such magical feats were current among Jews. One rabbi is said to have 'created a man' and sent him to a colleague. When the latter spoke to the messenger but received no reply, he recognized his true character and commanded him, 'Return to your dust'. Two other rabbis are reported to 'have made a calf for themselves' on the eve of every Sabbath and to have eaten it. They produced this calf by busying themselves with the book *Yetsirah*.

The reference to the *Sefer Yetsirah* (the Book of Creation) indicates the range of ideas and concepts underlying the theory of the magical creation of living beings. There is no way of knowing whether the *Sefer Yetsirah* (or *Hilkhoth Yetsirah*) of the Talmudic legend is or is not identical with, or similar to, the extant book bearing that name. According to this book which came to be highly regarded in later Jewish mysticism, the world is derived from thirty-two elements which are the first ten numbers and the twenty-two letters of the Hebrew alphabet. All reality is a reality of the letters, the elements of which the cosmos is formed.

These ideas, which go back in part to Talmudic notions concerning the creative power of the letters of the

Opposite page: Statue of clay golem depicting Golem of Prague

name of God or of the Hebrew letters in general (because all combinations of these were held to be mystical names of God), obviously lent themselves to magical interpretation and application. Whereas the idea of creating living beings by magical means was associated in Greek and Arab magic with astrology, the emphasis in the Jewish tradition is on letter mysticism. These concepts were developed in the commentaries on the *Sefer Yetsirah* that were composed from the twelfth century onward. In these commentaries the word golem also begins to appear as a technical term for a being artificially created by applying the mysteries of the Sefer Yetsirah.

In the circle of Jewish mystics of the twelfth to thirteenth centuries known as the 'Hasidim of Germany' these conceptions gave rise to a mystical rite of creating a golem. There is little doubt that this ritual, in spite of its magical character, did not serve any materialist purpose (such as creating a robot servant) but was essentially a spiritual experience fraught with symbolic meaning. At the conclusion of their studies of the *Sefer Yetsirah* and similar texts, these mystics would perform a ritual 'act of creation' symbolizing their level of spiritual achievement. In this ritual the participants would take earth from virgin soil and shape it into a golem, or, according to another version, bury a golem made from clay in the earth, and bring it to life by walking round it and using the appropriate combination of letters and mystical 'names of God'. By the act of walking in the opposite direction and reciting the magic formulae in reverse order, the golem would again become lifeless.

Rebellious Servant

What was essentially a mystic-symbolic ritual in the circles of the German Hasidim soon became a subject for popular folklore and legend. Concurrently the golem too became an actual creature serving his master and fulfilling menial and other tasks laid upon him. Legends of this kind were fairly widespread among German Jews after the fifteenth century and came also to be known among non-Jews; Goethe's *Sorcerers Apprentice* is indebted to the golem legend.

Earlier legends implying the possibility of resurrecting the dead by putting a piece of parchment with the name of God into the mouth or on the arm, were transferred to the golem, which it was believed could be made lifeless again by removing or inverting the mystical formula. The idea of a golem also linked up with the alchemists' notion of an artificial man produced by alchemical means (the homunculus of Paracelsus). As in the *Sorcerers Apprentice*, the idea that the golem could get out of hand and his creator might no longer control or master him became a major feature of popular legend. The golem would grow to giant size, and become a serious threat to others, even to his master or members of his household. To reduce this Frankenstein's monster to dust again it would be necessary to remove the parchment with the mystic formula from his forehead. The golem's giant size made such an attempt very hazardous.

The best known form of the golem legend is associated with Rabbi Judah Loew of Prague (sixteenth century) but without any historical foundation whatever. As a result of this association, which seems to date from the end of the eighteenth century, most current forms and versions of the golem legend, popular as well as literary are connected with the history of the ghetto and the old synagogues of Prague. The first legendary biography describing a rabbi as the creator and master of a golem servant appeared in connection with Rabbi Elijah of Chelm (died 1583), and its substance was later transferred to Rabbi Judah Loew of Prague. In the later versions the golem is credited not only with enormous strength but also with uncanny instincts which enabled him to serve the Rabbi and the Jews of Prague by discovering plots against the Jews—especially accusations of ritual murder—and preventing their execution. Many stories relating to Rabbi Judah Loew and the golem are meant to 'explain' special liturgical practices of the congregation of Prague.

In the nineteenth century the golem legend became a favourite literary subject both with Jews and non-Jews. First in German literature, and later in Hebrew and Yiddish, the legends were expanded and interpreted in diverse ways. The verses emphasizing the golem's function in preventing libellous accusations and their consequent dangers to the Jewish community were probably composed after the resurgence of accusations of ritual murder in the 1890s. Among the best known works inspired by the legend are the mystic-occultist novel *Der Golem* (1915) by Gustav Meyrink, published in an English translation as *The Golem* (1964) and the Yiddish drama Der Golem by H. Leivick.

R. J. ZWI WERBLOWSKY

FURTHER READING: G. Meyer-Meyrink. The Golem, *trans., by Madge Pemberton (Ungas, N.Y., 1964). See also chapter 5 of Gershom G. Scholem,* On the Kabbalah and its Symbolism, *(Routledge & Kegan Paul, 1965).*

Gorgons

The Greeks applied the name Gorgo or, less commonly, Gorgon to female monsters which are a favourite subject in their extant art, sometimes terrifying but sometimes, to all appearances, humorous. In mythology, the Gorgons figure chiefly in the story of Perseus. The ancient lore concerning them

them is most fully summed up in Apollodorus's *Library of Mythology*, in Ovid's *Metamorphoses* and in Lucan's *Pharsalia*. These accounts written between the 2nd century BC and the 1st century AD, are all late versions of the myth of Perseus, and depend on much older poetry, which has been lost. It is not known that there was ever a complete epic that described the adventures of Perseus in his quest for Medusa.

The scattered references to the Gorgon or Gorgons in earlier poetry and poetical fragments known to us are usually to the terrifying aspect of the Gorgon's head, as for instance in the *Odyssey* (Book II) where Odysseus fears that Persephone may send up the Gorgon's head to confront him if he stays longer by the entrance of Hades. In Hesiod's poem *Shield of Hercules* the Gorgons are said to be represented on the shield pursuing Perseus as he flies away carrying the head of Medusa, which is so large that it covers all his back. After him rush Medusa's sisters, the other Gorgons, 'not to be approached and not to be described, eager to seize him. The shield rang sharp and shrill with a loud din as they trod on the pale adamant, on their belts were two serpents writhing and arching their necks and darting out their tongues and furiously gnashing their teeth as they savagely glared. And over the terrible heads of the Gorgons a great Dread quivered.'

The Three Sisters

This is the earliest continuous piece of poetry dealing with the Gorgons (except for the summary account of their origin and dwelling in Hesiod's *Theogony*). In the common versions of the myth of Perseus, at least in those which became accepted by such writers as Apollodorus, there were three Gorgon sisters, daughters of the ancient sea gods, Phorcys and Ceto, namely Stheno and Euryale, who

Rabbi Löw statue, Prague, Czechoslovakia

were immortal, and Medusa who was mortal. According to most writers, they lived on the Atlantic shores of Africa, which seems to link them with the underworld, which was likewise placed in the far west. According to the philologists, the name Gorgons should once have denoted a terrible roaring or bellowing. But in Greek usage the name always suggests their glaring eyes.

Perseus, son of Zeus and Danae, grew up on the island of Seriphos, whose king Polydectes conceived a passion for Danae, while Perseus protected her. To get Perseus out of the way, Polydectes sent him to fetch

the Gorgon's head, an enterprise which would, he hoped, lead him to his death. But Perseus was helped by Hermes and Athena. The nymphs gave Perseus the winged sandals of Hermes, the *kibisis*, apparently a large sack or wallet, and the cap of Hades which made its wearer invisible. Hermes also gave him the sickle (*harpe*), a special curved sword with which he was able to cut off the head of Medusa.

Once Famous for Her Beauty

Perseus flew to the home of the monsters where he found the three Gorgons asleep, their heads covered with snakes instead of hair, and their

Fragment of an Etruscan gorgon statue from the sixth century BC

the class called 'the harrowing of hell' to which the similar expedition of Hercules to Hades to fetch up Cerberus certainly belongs.

If the origins of the Gorgons are sought outside Greece, the most likely source is the Near East, Anatolia, Phoenicia, or Mesopotamia, where religious art abounds in monsters. It has been plausibly suggested that the origin of the Gorgon face is in the Anatolian and Syrian sculptures of open-mouthed lions with lolling tongues which were attendant on the gods. Perseus has a connection with Joppa in Phoenicia, where he delivers Andromeda from the sea monster. His sickle-shaped sword, like that used by Cronus to castrate Uranus, is of Near Eastern origin.

FURTHER READING: Apollodorus. Library of Mythology. *(Loeb edn.); K. Schefold.* Myth and Legend in Early Greek Art. *(Thames & Hudson, 1966).*

Gremlin

Mischievous air spirit believed to cause mishaps to airplanes; the name is said to have been coined by a British bomber squadron in India, not long before the Second World War, by amalgamating Grimm's *Fairy Tales* with Fremlin's *Elephant Ales*; the gremlin has now largely disappeared from British and American airmen's lore.

Griffin

The Griffin or Gryphon was a fabulous beast with the head, shoulders and feet of an eagle and the body of a lion,

mouths armed with great tusks like those of boars. Their gaze turned to stone all who beheld them. As they slept, Perseus stood over them, Athena guiding his hand, and looked away at a polished shield while he cut off the head of Medusa. From her as she died sprang forth the winged horse Pegasus. Perseus put the head into the sack and set off homeward, pursued by the other two Gorgons, who could not see him but tracked him by smell. They failed to catch him. On his way back he made use of the Gorgon's head against his enemies, and when he arrived at Seriphos he turned Polydectes and his followers to stone. He returned the sandals and other gifts to the nymphs and finally gave the head of Medusa to Athena to adorn her goatskin shield.

Though in Ovid and other writers Medusa is said to have been once famous for her beauty, she was grotesquely ugly when she had taken on the nature of a Gorgon. In art, particularly on vases and architectural ornaments, the Gorgons are shown in human form but with wings and very wide faces to contain their immense tusked mouths and thick lolling tongues. Their great eyes glare in an inhuman manner, sometimes like those of wild beasts and sometimes those of cuttlefish. Their pursuit of Perseus, as described in Hesiod, is often shown with the details that he gives. The gorgoneion, or gorgon-face, was one of many demon-faces that existed in archaic Greek art. One of its purposes as a magical object was to frighten away evil beings. It seems likely that the Gorgons have a special connection with the underworld because they are so lethal. If so, the expedition of Perseus might fall within

Opposite page:
Small sculpture of a griffin, the heraldic animal of Malmö, Sweden

making it a combination of the two most powerful of all creatures. Only the females had wings—the males were armed with protruding spikes in their place. Described by the Greek poet Aeschylus as 'the hounds of Zeus, who never bark, with beaks like birds', Griffins were the enemies of horses whose chief role was as fierce guardians against the theft of hidden treasures. According to the Roman historian Herodotus Griffins even made their nests of gold.

In his *Natural History* the Roman author Pliny the Elder describes the ongoing battle between the Griffins, who guarded the Scythian and Indian gold mines, and the one-eyed Arimaspi from Schythia. The poet Milton visualizes the scene in *Paradise Lost* in which the Arimaspi succeed in their mission:

> *As when a gryphon through*
> *the wilderness*
> *With winged course, o'er hill*
> *or moory dale,*
> *Pursues the Arimaspian, who*
> *by stealth*
> *Had from his wakeful*
> *custody purloin'd*
> *The guarded gold.*

In the Graeco-Roman world, the Griffin was the emblem of Apollo, the sun god, and associated with both Athene, the goddess of wisdom, and with the avenging god Nemesis. They were thought to draw the chariot of the sun, occupied by Zeus, across the sky. In the early days of Christianity it represented the combined human and divine nature of Christ. The notion of the Griffin probably originated, however, from Indo-Iranian mythology.

Since the sixteenth century the Griffin has been the emblem of the Society of Grays Inn, one of the four Inns of Court in London. It also appears in the art of Greece, as in the Minoan palaces of Crete where it has a protective function, and a pair of griffins adorn the helmet of Athena Parthenos, atop a 38-foot statue in the Parthenon in Athens.

Harpy

Like the sirens, the Furies, and the Gorgons, the Harpies were female monsters of Greek legend. They were depicted in art and literature as winged women, or as birds with women's faces and long, hooked claws, and their peculiar activity was to swoop upon human beings, or at least upon their food; their victims were carried off to unknown places. The origin and nature of the Harpies are in dispute, but

Hittite Griffin in Istanbul Archaeological Museum

they seem to have a definite connection with the underworld, having some of the characteristics of ghosts.

Wind and spirit were closely allied in ancient thought, and the Harpies are linked in literature with storms, whirlwinds, or sudden squalls such as are very dangerous at sea and damaging on land. They appear first in Homer, where the Harpy Podarge (swift-foot) is mentioned in the *Iliad* as mating with the wind Zephyrus, and giving birth to the two supernatural horses of Achilles, Xanthus and Balius.

In the *Odyssey* (Book 1) Telemachus says that Odysseus has been away so long that he must have been carried off by the Harpies 'with no tidings, out of sight'. So too, in her grief, Odysseus's wife Penelope wishes that she had been carried away to the mouths of Ocean by a storm such as swept off the orphan daughters of Pandareus. A legend relates that the goddess Aphrodite, who had been protecting these girls, left them unattended for a period while she interceded for them on Olympus. The Harpies then swept

them off and 'gave them as servants to the hateful Erinyes'. Since the Erinyes or Furies belonged to the underworld, the Harpies must have brought the maidens alive to dwell among the dead. This was the fate which Odysseus's family and friends imagined had overtaken the hero.

Harpies are commonly described as birds with the faces of women, and this is how they are depicted on the Tomb of the Harpies in Asia Minor: they appear to be carrying away evildoers for punishment by the Furies. With their habit of carrying off people and food, the Harpies are associated with whirlwinds and sudden squalls: they 'keep pace with the blasts of the winds on their swift wings, for they swoop high aloft'.

When the Harpies appear, they chase them away through the air with drawn swords; they catch them . . . and are about to kill them when Iris flies down . . .

Snatching at Table

Persecution by the Harpies was one of the punishments sent by the gods on Phineus the blind king who indiscreetly used his gift of prophecy to reveal secret plans of the gods. In Aeschylus's play *Phineus* they appear with ravening jaws and snatching hands, and wearing ankle-boots and stout socks, to seize food from Phineus's table. In one of the fragmentary plays by Sophocles also called *Phineus*, the Harpies are called snatchers; in the other they are compared to locusts.

The Harpies belong particularly to the Argonautic legend, in which the Argonauts visit Phineus on their way eastward to Colchis to find the Golden Fleece, and the fullest account of them, which has become tradi-

tional, appears in the *Argonautica* of Apollonius Rhodius, written in the 3rd century BC. The Argonauts arrive at the palace of Phineus on the west coast of the Black Sea, and are welcomed by him because they will deliver him from the Harpies. Phineus had accepted the gift of prophecy, even at the price of blindness and a long old age, but had misused it and offended the gods. As his heavenly punishment, the Harpies were sent to swoop down upon his table at every meal, carrying off nearly all the food but leaving enough to keep him alive and miserable, and leaving also a disgusting stench which could be smelt for some distance.

A Chase Through the Air

Fortunately, among the Argonauts are the winged Boreades, Zetes and Calais (sons of the north wind), who promise to rid Phineus of the Harpies if this is permitted by the gods. When the Harpies appear, they chase them away through the air with drawn swords; they catch them by the Plotae islands and are about to kill them when Iris flies down from Olympus to forbid it, promising that the Harpies will never return to plague Phineus. The Boreades turn back at the islands, now to be renamed the Strophades or Turning Points, and the Harpies dive into a cavern on Crete.

In a fragment from Apollodorus is another version of this legend, where the Harpies Nicothoe (victorious speed) or Aellopus (wind-foot) and Ocypete are pursued by the sons of the north wind. Nicothoe falls into the River Tigris in the Peloponnese (called Harpyes after her), and Ocypete flees to the Strophades; these islands were not originally localized but were later placed west of the Peloponnese.

Later poets, including the Latins, add little more information about the Harpies. Virgil, however, in the *Aeneid*

(Book 3) makes the Harpies sweep down on Aeneas and his Trojans as they try to spread a banquet on the beach of one of the Strophades Islands. The Harpies behave as they do in the account in the Argonautica but they are not driven off successfully; one of them warns Aeneas that his men will suffer hunger before they found a new city.

Ancient poets, commentators and lexicographers were inclined to derive the name 'Harpies' (Greek Harpyiai or sometimes Arepyiai) from the root of the Greek verb *harpazein* meaning 'to seize' or 'to snatch'. Modern philologists, concentrating on the form Arepyiai, tend to interpret the name as meaning 'tearers' or 'sheers'.

Homunculus

The man-made man of ancient and medieval alchemy, the homunculus, is the forerunner of the test-tube baby of modern scientific experiment and speculation. The first recorded dream of an artificial man appears in the work of the alchemical writer Zosimus, an Alexandrian Greek of the 3rd or 4th centuries AD, who describes a vision he had of the transmutation of metals, in which a homunculus changed successively from copper, to silver and then to gold, the process being helped by burning the blood and bones of a dragon. At about the same time, a Christian writer accused the 'arch-heretic and sorcerer' Simon Magus of making an artificial man with an instrument resembling a cupping glass. Here again, the homunculus passed through several stages, the spirit taken from the body of a dead boy being changed successively to air, water, blood and finally flesh. Simon also had the power of changing the homunculus back to air.

It is possible that the medieval alchemists knew something of these ancient traditions. One of the first to

In Goethe's *Faust*, the title character creates, through alchemy, a homunculous of his own.

have the manufacture of a homunculus attributed to him was Arnold of Villanova (c. 1238–1313), a famous alchemist, astrologer, and court physician in his own day. If Arnold really did make any experiments in this direction, they may have been linked with his long search for a medicine which would rejuvenate man in body and soul, and with his belief that the aim of alchemy was to transform the natural elements into something more spiritual and more divine.

The most detailed instructions for the manufacture of a homunculus are to be found in the writings of Paracelsus (1493–1541), a life-long student of magic and the supernatural, whose researches led him into anthropology, medicine, and alchemy. In his recipe for a homunculus, Paracelsus says that a man's semen must be put into a hermetically-sealed retort, buried in

horse manure for forty days, and 'magnetized'. During this time, it begins to live and move, and at the end of the forty days it resembles a human form, but is transparent and without a body.

The homunculus must now be fed daily with the arcanum (hidden mystery) of human blood, and be maintained at the constant temperature of a mare's womb for a period of forty weeks, and it will grow into a human child, with all its limbs developed, as normal as any child born of woman, except that it will be much smaller. 'It may be raised and educated like any other child,' Paracelsus adds, 'until it grows older and is able to look after itself.' The secret of how to make the homunculus was known to the ancient philosophers or miracle men, some of whom were themselves said to have been begotten by the process, but this is 'one of the greatest secrets, and will remain a secret until the end of days, when everything will be made known.'

It is likely that it was not mere morbid curiosity which prompted these experiments of Paracelsus, as the semen and blood mentioned were regarded as carriers of the *pneuma* or soul-substance, and as such represented the *materia prima*, or elemental matter of which, in alchemical theory, all substances were ultimately composed.

Similar experiments were reported by one of Louis XIV's physicians, Borel, who also conjured a human form, which emitted bloody rays of light, from distilled blood. The physician and mystical philosopher Robert Fludd also distilled blood, and claimed to have removed a human head, complete with face, eyes, nose, and hair, from the retort after he had heard a frightful noise coming from it.

A story which, through various film versions, has become known to a wide public is Mary Wollstonecraft Shelley's *Frankenstein* (1818), 'an adolescent's version of the eternal story of Man's attempt to create human life' (as Richard Church characterizes the novel). This owed its immediate inspiration to a conversation between the poets Byron and Shelley about the experiments of Dr. Erasmus Darwin (grandfather of the author of *The Origin of Species*). Darwin had preserved a piece of vermicelli in a glass case until it began to move of its own accord. 'Perhaps,' wrote Mary Shelley in the introduction to her story, 'a corpse would be re-animated . . . perhaps the component parts of a creature might be manufactured, brought together and endued with vital warmth.' The Dr. Frankenstein of the story developed his own interest in natural science through his reading of Paracelsus and other alchemists.

In 1873, Dr. Emil Besetzny published an elaborate account of ten homunculi generated in bottles by a certain John Ferdinand, Count of Kuf-

stein in the Tyrol, in 1775, with the aid of an Italian mystic and Rosicrucian, the Abbe Geloni. This account purported to be based on a collection of Masonic manuscripts and on the diary of the Count's butler. Whether stories of this sort were circulating in Europe at the time Mary Shelley wrote her Gothic novel (in Switzerland) and whether she also heard them cannot be known for certain, but it seems not unlikely.

The homunculus belonged, by the beginning of the nineteenth century, to a double tradition: the literary one partly based on folktales and the pseudoscientific one based on alchemy. In our own time, these two strands are represented by science fiction and horror films on the one hand, and test-tube fertilization and genetic experimentation on the other. The homunculus, it seems, has a future even more interesting than its curious past.

Hydra

The many-headed water snake Hydra infested the marshy plain of Lerna in Argolis, where the mysteries of Dionysus, the Greek god of wine were cele-

Lernaean Hydra, California Palace of the Legion of Honor, San Francisco

Burlesque Feast, **Jan Mandyn (c. 1500–1559)**

brated. The foul and poisonous breath that emanated from each of its many mouths was deadly to both man and beast. This infamous creature, when it emerged from the swamp, attacked herds of cattle and local villagers and terrorized the area so much that the Dionysan rituals were forced to cease. Hydra was the offspring of Typhon, the monster associated with the winds and volcanoes, and Echidna who was half woman, half serpent. It was raised by Hera, the wife and sister of Zeus. The number of its heads vary in different accounts, from 100 to fifty to the nine of the Herculean legend.

In the second of his twelve labours, the hero Hercules was instructed to kill the Hydra. His task was complicated by the fact that of the nine heads, the middle one was immortal, while the rest systematically regenerated themselves each time Hercules lunged them at them with his sword, with two heads appearing for each one that was severed. Eventually Iolaus, Hercules' cousin, charioteer and companion, lit a huge fire from which he ignited a series of brands, using them to burn the roots of the outer heads before Hercules cut off and buried the central one. Finally he dipped the tips of his arrows into the gall of the monster and into the mouths of the now lifeless heads, rendering his weapons poisonous for future use.

In the course of his battle with the beast Hercules succeeded in crushing under his heel a giant crab that had come to assist the Hydra. Legend has it that subsequently Hera placed the two together amongst the stars to form the constellations Hydra and Cancer.

Imp

An imp is a small demon, usually malignant, though at least one magician in London will provide an invisible but allegedly helpful imp that lives in an empty wine bottle. The bottle is corked and sealed with red sealing-wax. Around it is a piece of paper bearing magical signs and numbers in pencil and green crayon. The imp's chief duty is to prevent papers from going astray.

Paracelsus was supposed to keep a small demon shut up in the crystal pommel of his sword but the most indefatigable demon-bottler of history was a Frenchman named Alexis Vincent Charles Berbiguier, who died in 1851. For the first nine years of his life he was crippled and he early decided that demons were persecuting him. His room was full of ox-hearts stuck with pins and the aroma of antidemonic soups, and his clothes and bed were riddled with pins, each of which transfixed the body of a wriggling imp. He stupefied the imps with tobacco and shut them up in bottles, 'where they would later awaken to grin and gibber at their conqueror.'

An eighteenth century French grimoire, Secret des Secrets, has a formula for conjuring a demon into a bottle. It is summoned by God, by Jesus, by the Holy Trinity, by the virginity of the Holy Virgin, by the four sacred words spoken to Moses by God (Io, Zati, Zata, Abata) and by the nine heavens, 'to appear Visibly and without delay in a fair human form, not terrifying, without or within this phial, which holds water prepared to receive thee.'

FURTHER READING: for Berbiguier see E. J. Dingwall, Some Human Oddities, *(Home & Van Thal, 1947).*

An Incantation Scene, **Frans II Francken the Younger (1581–1642)**

Kelpies

Water spirits or fairies of Scottish folklore, who often took the form of a horse; usually mischievous, they were thought to graze on the banks of rivers and lakes; having enticed travelers to mount them, they tossed them into the water and devoured them; to see a kelpie was said to be a sure portent of drowning.

Kraken

'Amongst the many things which are in the ocean and concealed from our eyes or only presented to our view for a few minutes is the Kraken . . .' The sea monster described here by Erik Pontoppidan, Bishop of Bergen, in his *Natural History of Norway* (1752), was reputed to be the largest in the world. Also known as the *kraxen, krabben* or sea *korven*, it was so elusive as to be dismissed by ancient and modern skeptics as nothing more than a sailor's myth.

Throughout history, however, a few writers have mentioned a giant sea creature with characteristics similar to those of the kraken. Pliny wrote of a monster in the Straits of Gibraltar which blocked the entrance to ships; other experts on sea life referred to a mammoth starfish that had been found in the waters around Sicily.

It seems likely that the kraken was a kind of giant polyp or cuttlefish, per-haps a survival of some almost extinct prehistoric sea creature. Bishop Pon-toppidan, who wrote quite extensively about this inhabitant of Norwegian waters, had a theory that the floating islands which suddenly appeared or disappeared in Northern seas, were in fact kraken; and also that the medusa or jellyfish might be its ovum.

Another bishop, cited by Pontoppi-dan as a reliable witness, claimed that

For centuries, sailors lived in constant fear of the terrible wrath of the Kraken, a giant squid-like creature that could drag large ships down to the depths of the ocean.

in 1680 the remains of a young kraken were found putrefying when the crea-ture got wedged among some rocks in a fjord. Apparently, the monster was not particularly dangerous, except be-cause of its size. Any ship, even one as large as a man-of-war, that was caught up in the swell of a submerging or surfacing kraken would be wrecked.

The creature only appeared on hot

summer days when the sea was calm. Norwegian fishermen, who rowed out several miles to where they reckoned the sea should be at least 480 to 600 feet deep, would suddenly find a depth of only 120 to 150 feet, and the water teeming with shoals of cod and ling. This they took to be a sign that a kraken was present. If the water began growing shallower they stopped fishing immediately, and rowed some distance away, for it meant that the monster was about to emerge.

Owing to its enormous size, the whole body was never visible; an entire kraken could be observed only when it was young. The back of a fully grown monster was estimated to be 1½ miles in circumference, and at first sight the creature looked like a number of small bumpy islands, surrounded by fronds of floating seaweed, with fish leaping about the shallows. After a time, huge tentacles were said to appear, with which the kraken propelled itself along, and gathered food.

The kraken only remained on the surface for a short while. Its descent into the ocean was a treacherous time, for it churned the waters around it into a whirlpool and drew everything into its depths.

A Pungent Sea
The creature lived according to a definite rhythm. For some months it was seen only to eat, and at others solely to excrete. During the latter period the sea's surface became thick and disturbed and gave off a pungent aroma. The smell and muddiness attracted the shoals which gathered to feed, and the kraken then opened up its tentacles and drew in all the fish, which were converted into bait for the creature's next feeding period.

Whether the kraken was merely a legendary sea monster, or the remains of some primeval sea creature, or the over-dramatized account given by lonely sailors of an extremely large

cuttle-fish, Bishop Pontoppidan's own words seem particularly apt in describing all those monsters which the modern world has not glimpsed: 'In the ocean many things are hidden.'

Leprechauns

Fairy shoemakers of Irish folklore; they own buried hoards of gold which are much coveted by human beings; if caught, a leprechaun can be forced to reveal where his treasure is hidden, but he will vanish if you take your eyes off him; leprechauns live alone and vary in stature from a height of a few inches to the size of a three-year-old child.

ELLIC HOWE

Leprechaun Crossing sign at Killarney National Park, Killarney, County Kerry, Republic of Ireland

Leviathan

When they cast their spells the cabalists, practitioners of the ancient secret lore, deem as most powerful the one they used to summon up Leviathan, the great fish or monster of the waters. This fearsome beast, a monster of the deep, is described in the Bible's Book of Job: 'Out of his mouth go burning lamps, and sparks of fire leap out . . . He maketh the deep [sea] boil like a pot'. So evil is this beast that only on the Day of Judgement will he meet his end when 'his flesh will be food for the righteous.' There are various other Biblical references. In Psalm 74 God is said to 'break the heads of Leviathan in pieces' before giving his flesh to the

people of the wilderness while Isaiah describes it as the 'wriggling serpent' who will be killed at the end of time.

Various animal identities have been ascribed to Leviathan, including crocodile, whale and sea serpent. Its name comes from the Hebrew lawo, meaning to twist or to writhe. In the Jewish tradition, Leviathan had dual incarnations of its serpentine form. As a male it was deemed responsible for seducing Eve, and in its female form for having the same effect upon Adam.

Little People

Respectful and often affectionate term for fairies: believers in fairies frequently preferred not to name them directly for fear of summoning them, and instead used vague, preferably complimentary, terms like 'the little people' or 'the people of peace'; despite the term, not all fairies are believed to be diminutive creatures.

The Loch Ness Monster and Other Lake Creatures

The murky waters of Loch Ness, a fresh water lake in the remote Scottish Highlands nearly 23 miles long and more than 750 feet deep at one point, provide a suitably atmospheric setting for the location of one of the most renowned and mysterious creatures—the Loch Ness Monster. More than any other legendary lake dweller, the Monster, familiarly known as 'Nessie', has attracted sustained popular and scientific interest over the past eighty years as well as being the subject of media hype and hoaxes.

The earliest account of a water monster in the area can be found in the seventh century *Life of St. Columba* describing how in AD 565,

Monster hunters constantly look for any sign of a creature. Are these simply ripples on the water of Loch Ness in this photo, or something more?

Loch Ness in Scotland, which is famed for its mythical monster (c. 1930)

the saint was at the northern end of the Loch on the banks of the outflowing River Ness when he saw a burial party digging a grave for a man who had been killed by a monster in the river. Columba told one of his companions to swim across the river whereupon the monster appeared and started to follow him. Columba commanded the monster to stop and the creature halted abruptly and disappeared, much to the astonishment of those present.

An account exists of a sighting in the 1870s of an 'enormous and extraordinary animal', which startled a group of children as they picnicked by the shores of the Loch. The creature came down off the hillside to make its way to the water where it was rapidly lost to view. The children's experience was dismissed as make believe but the description of the event has features in common with that given by George Spicer and his wife when the possible existence of the Loch Ness Monster first came to the notice of the press. In July 1933 Mr. and Mrs. Spicer were motoring by the side of the Loch and saw ahead of them an extraordinary creature crossing the road from the hillside. It had a neck resembling an elephant's trunk and a

huge body with what appeared to be a fleshy protuberance at the junction of the neck and the body. It was clearly a terrifying phenomenon, being described as 'a loathsome sight', resembling a 'huge snail with a long neck'. Five months later a photograph was taken from the shore of a strange object in the Loch two hundred feet away, an object of 'great size' as the photographer said. Its shape was interpreted by some as being very similar to the creature seen by the Spicers.

There was enormous media interest in the Monster with a circus even offering a reward of $32,000 for the animal's capture. But even at this early date Nessie was susceptible to pranksters. A photograph taken the following year showing what looked like an elephant's trunk emerging from the surface of the water, supposedly the neck of the creature, turned out to be a fake. Whatever the scepticism of the scientific community about the existence of the Monster, the accounts had gained sufficient credibility by the late 1930s for the Inverness County Police Chief to write to a government minister that 'the preservation of the Monster was desired'.

One account of an odd incident at Loch Ness involved a stag that was being pursued in a hunt. The animal came down to the shore of the Loch and started swimming away but suddenly the water began to churn up. The stag came back to the shore and it was observed to have lost a leg in the water.

Numbers of dedicated 'Nessie watchers' spent hours at Loch Ness scanning the surface of the water for evidence of activity. Over the years there have been a large number of sightings including swiftly moving strange shapes in the Loch and a detailed description of the creature's head and neck. A 1960 film of a sighting was analysed by a specialist department in Britain's Ministry of Defence who concluded that it probably showed 'an animate object' although they could not give a more precise identification. There have also been several systematic and scientific investigations that have attempted to determine the truth. One team using satellite navigation equipment and sonar beams conducted an intensive search of the Loch but could find no evidence for the Monster's existence. One idea put forward is that the creature has now died but never-

theless the legend persists. Theories of the origin of the Monster include a prehistoric plesiosaur, turbulence as a result of gas escapes from faults in the Loch bed, and seismic activity.

The Loch Ness Monster has been beneficial to the entertainment industry appearing in many fictional—and often bizarre—contexts including an episode of *The Simpsons* where Mr Burns takes Homer and others to find the Monster. They drain the Loch, capture the Monster and take it back to the USA. Mr Burns gives it a job in a casino. A cult film made in 2004—*Napoleon Dynamite*—relates a story of Japanese scientists blowing Nessie out of the Loch with explosive detonators.

Stories of mysterious lake-dwelling creatures, however, are not unique either to Loch Ness or to Scotland but occur across the world. A number of Scottish Highland lochs are home to mythical beings including the Mhorag of Loch Morar, who is able to assume different forms one of which is a beautiful mermaid-like creature that entices young men to their deaths. Recent sightings of a mysterious creature in the loch include descriptions similar to Nessie's long neck and humped outline. Loch Maree is reputed to contain a monster known as the Muc-sheilch.

There are many reports of an aquatic creature living in Okanagan Lake in British Columbia, a legend which is believed to originate from native Indian folklore. Known by the name of the Ogopogo, typically the creature is dark green, with a sinuous snakelike body and the ability to move very fast. One account mentions the animal's 'dignified demeanour'. Similarly, Lake Manitoba contains at least one mysterious animal that has defied identification, as does the reptilian inhabitant of Lake Tahoe.

In contrast, the legend of Lake Superior focuses on a catlike creature, an aquatic panther with scales and spines along its back, that was held to be the most powerful being in the underworld, and was chief of all water creatures.

A report from Eastern Siberia described a sighting of a huge creature on Lake Vorota that progressed across the surface of the water looping its body. In the same region, at Lake Labynkyr, there are stories of a mysterious and malevolent creature known locally as a 'Devil'. One theory is that this monster could be a dinosaur survivor. Stories of a monster living in Lake Storsjön in Sweden also report the existence of a reptilian creature originating according to one legend from a concoction cooked up by two trolls. Sightings of this creature most often seem to occur in the summer, and it has a formidable turn of speed. Lake Ikeda in Japan is the focus for a legend of a large aquatic creature, originally a white horse whose foal was stolen by a samurai. The horse jumped into the lake where she became transformed into a reptilelike animal forever searching for her offspring and breaking the surface of the water in her endeavours.

Lycanthropy

From Greek words meaning 'wolf' and 'man,' the transformation of a human being into some other carnivorous animal, especially a wolf but alternatively a bear, tiger, leopard or, in South America, a jaguar: form of insanity in which the sufferer believes he is the animal and behaves accordingly.

Maenads

Or Bacchae, frenzied women devotees of the Greek god Dionysus; armed with ivy-twined staffs tipped with a pine cone, and clothed in animal skins,

Dancing maenads, fragment of a relief

Opposite page:
Sweden has its own water monster, complete with tour boats proving an opportunity for a glimpse

Opposite page:
**Dancing maenad on vase. Detail from a
Paestan red-figure skyphos (c. 330–320 BC)**

they roamed the mountains celebrating the cult of Dionysus with ecstatic dance and song: they tore live beasts apart and devoured the flesh, probably as a rite of communion with the god.

Manticore

The Manticore was a fearsome human-headed creature possessing three rows of interlocking teeth, the body of a lion complete with sharp claws and the tail of a scorpion or dragon that could sting. It had a strong preference for human flesh and was renowned for consuming its victims whole leaving not a trace behind. The Manticore was believed to originate from India and was first mentioned by the 5th century BC Greek writer, Ctesias, in his history of Persia; its name derives from the Persian for 'man-eater'. The Manticore also appeared in medieval bestiaries which describe its formidable speed and strength, and its powerful voice.

Mermaids and Mermen

The mermaid, a beautiful girl to her waist but a fish from there down, and her male counterpart, the merman, are still among the most popular of legendary creatures. The mermaid of tradition is a seductive and dangerous enchantress, who personifies the beauty and treachery of the sea, and especially of the shoals and rocks of the coastline. She is also closely associated with the moon (the ruler of the tides), which is represented by the mirror she holds in her hand. Her long hair is said to be composed of green seaweed,

or perhaps of the rays of the sun as they fall upon the water. In folklore this fatal green-haired spirit appears constantly in legends of lake, river and sea, and for a sailor to see a mermaid is almost always a portent of disaster.

Among the predecessors of the medieval and modern mermaid are the Sirens, who lured sailors to destruction, though exactly when and why they changed from bird-women to fish-women is uncertain.

The mer-people were supposed to dwell in an underwater world of great splendour, to which the mermaids lured their victims and where they kept their souls close prisoner in the kingdom beneath the waves. This theme occurs again and again in the lore of the sea, with a constant emphasis on the presence of a mermaid as foreshadowing some calamity—storm, shipwreck, drowning.

Merman, St. James Kastelaz, Tyrol, Italy

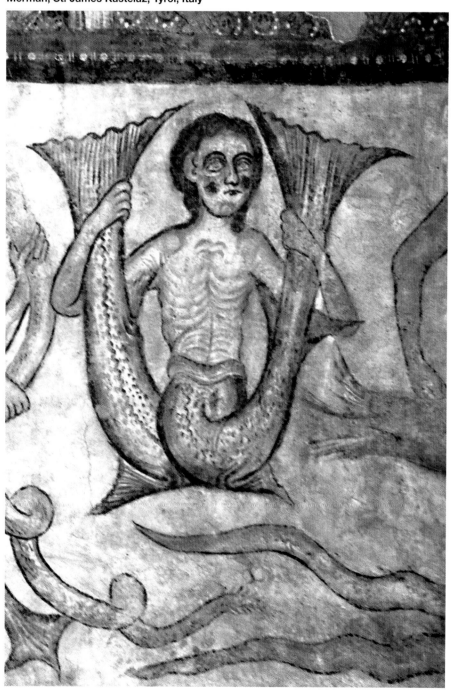

On the other hand, power over a mermaid could always be obtained by possession of her cap or belt. There are many tales in which a human being brings a mermaid on shore to be his wife. In *The Little Mermaid* by Hans Christian Andersen, a mermaid takes human shape so as to acquire a soul, to be near the man she loves for all eternity. There are also many stories of marriages between mermen and human women.

In the Gironde, in France, mermaids had two tails. In Brittany, the Morgan's or sea women were extremely dangerous to men. The fisher folk of the Channel Islands believed in a strange sea creature called the King of the Auxcrinier, whose presence was feared as the forerunner of storm. In Norse folklore the Havemand is a merman with a black beard and green hair.

The Estonian Nakk is someone who has drowned, and may appear as man, woman, child, or even animal. His lovely singing entrances people and he swallows them in his giant mouth. A Nakk maiden is very pretty, combs her long locks with a golden comb and only sometimes has the tail of a fish. The Nakki of Finland are very similar, and their women have gleaming white bodies, and breasts so long that they can throw them over their shoulders.

The nixes or nixies of Germanic lore are spirits of fresh water. Green-haired and lovely, they can transform themselves into old women, in which form they venture on land on market days. They lure humans to drown in treacherous waters, and must have at least one victim each year.

In 1403, it is said, a mermaid was found becalmed in shallow water at Edam in Holland. She became accustomed to life on land but never learned to speak. She lived for some fifteen years after her capture, and was given Christian burial.

In 1560 several supposed mermaids were caught by fishermen in Ceylon. They were dissected, and it was reported that they possessed organs like those of human beings. An early seventeenth-century tale from America reported an attack on a canoe by a fierce merman whose arm had to be severed with a hatchet because he would not release his grip. The famous explorer Henry Hudson reported a sighting of mermaids in 1608, near Novaya Zemlya in the Arctic Ocean north of Russia. He described one of them as being 'as big as one of us, her skin very white and long hair hanging down behind, of colour black. In her going down they saw her tail which

> *. . . her skin very white and long hair hanging down behind, of colour black . . . her tail which was like the tail of a porpoise, speckled like a mackerel . . .*

was like the tail of a porpoise, speckled like a mackerel . . .' and 'from the navel upward her back and breasts were like a woman's.'

The Sea-Maid's Music

Among many curious legends once current in the British Isles is the tale of the mermaid who swam up a subterranean channel from the River Mersey at sunrise, seated herself on a church bell and began to sing. In Cornwall, the mermaid of Zennor lured a lovelorn youth into the sea by the charm of her voice, and for years afterward his voice could be heard singing from deep beneath the waves.

However, according to John Shaw, the author of *Speculum Mundi* (1635), the song of the mermaid was not as tuneful as was popularly supposed. 'But above all the Mermaids and Menfish seem to me the most strange fish in the waters. Some have supposed them to be devils or spirits in regard to their whooping noise that they make.'

There is a tradition that the people of Machaire in Ireland are the descendants of mermaids. The Irish thought that mermaids were originally pagan women, transformed into mermaids by St. Patrick, then banished from the Emerald Isle forever.

If Ireland managed to dispose of its mermaids, as well as its snakes, Scotland did not. Till the close of the eighteenth century it was a common belief in Aberdeenshire that mermaids inhabited the caves of the rocky coastline. As late as the 1890s a mermaid was said to have appeared on two occasions in the Orkneys.

The Scots also populated their inland waters with spirits. It was a certain portent of drowning to see a kelpie, a mischievous and evil creature which lived in a stream or a lake and appeared in the form of a horse. He would lure people to climb on his back, and then drown them in the water. The Welsh equivalent is the ceffyl, or water horse. In northern England many lakes and ponds were said to be tenanted by a sinister siren known as Jenny Green Teeth, a green-haired monster with a taste for drowning young children who ventured too close to her domain.

With the passing of the age of magic, dedicated rationalists attempted to discover in natural history the true source of the mermaid legend. Manatees and dugongs have been considered likely candidates. Both are sea mammals (of the order *Sirenia*, found in coastal waters of the Atlantic and Indian oceans) and they suckle their young, holding them with their flippers in the manner of a woman with a baby. The walrus and the seal are other candidates. One naturalist commented: 'I have seen many plain women but never yet one quite so plain as the face of a dugong.'

Fifteenth-century carving of a mermaid with comb and mirror at the southern pier of the chancel arch, Clonfert Cathedral, Clonfert, County Galway, Ireland

The Roman writer Pliny, the first naturalist to discuss mermaids at length, would have been intrigued by the amount of evidence for the existence of mermaids which came to light in Europe from the sixteenth century onward, in the shape of fish-tailed sub-humans, most of whom found their way into fairground booths or were exhibited at inns. In 1830 a mermaid was on show at the Egyptian Hall in London, and in the 1870s Phineas Barnum's 'Greatest Show on Earth' included a mermaid. Until London's Royal College of Surgeons was bombed in the Second World War, two stuffed mermaids were preserved in a showcase in its museum.

Sightings of mermaids, of one sort or another, have still not ceased.

In June 1857 the *Shipping Gazette* reported the appearance off Britain of a mermaid with 'full breast, dark complexion, and comely face.' In 1937 a mermaid was reported in the Far East; and in 1956 at Accra in Africa, a bank cashier was persuaded to hand over more than $800 from his till to a confidence trickster disguised as a mermaid, who offered to double his money for him.

ERIC MAPLE

Minotaur

In Greek mythology, the monster with a human body and a bull's head who was the offspring of Queen Pasiphae of Crete by a bull; he was kept in the labyrinth at Cnossus and, every nine years, seven young men and seven maidens were sent from Athens to be his prey; he was killed by the hero Theseus.

Naiads

A naiad was a water nymph of Greek mythology, associated with streams and fresh-water sources, but separately identified from river deities. The legend of Daphnis, the shepherd boy, who was the focus of a naiad's affection but who was blinded by her, demonstrates how they could be seen as unpredictable and dangerous. In western art, naiads are depicted as beautiful and seductive young women. The idea of spirits of place associated with bodies of water was common throughout Europe, and local cults often developed at individual sites. Water spirits are also found in native North American folklore.

Opposite page:
The sea nymph, *Galatee*, by Gustsve Moreau (1826-1898)

Nymphs

Generally regarded as goddesses of subordinate status, nymphs are personifications of human feminine youth, invested with magical charm, beauty and dread, and often, of course, with superhuman power. They belong to the oldest and deepest layers of Greek popular religion, mythology and folklore, populating seas, rivers and springs, caves, trees and mountains, in fact Nature in all its aspects. In Greek 'nymph' means simply a young girl, a bride (and, in a secondary sense, a nurse).

The Oceanides, nymphs of the ocean, were looked upon as daughters of Ocean himself. A band of them forms the chorus of Aeschylus's *Prometheus Bound*. After he has been

These are the divine counterparts of the human girls who regularly purified themselves at such places before religious ceremonies

chained to the rock, Prometheus invokes all the forces of Nature. He hears strange sounds in the distance:

A faint sound, a fragrance, is floating about me.
Is it god or man? Who is it that seeks me out,
Visiting this desolate edge of earth,
Spectator of my agony? It must be so.
Then see imprisoned here an ill-starred god—The detested of Zeus, the rejected of all who walk in
The heavenly courtyards, one that held mankind too dear! Ah!
Yet again that murmur! The air is a stir with
The whisper of hurrying wings. How fearful is all that approaches!
The chorus of ocean nymphs then

enters, performing a dance as if riding sea-horses. They address the tormented Prometheus:
You need not fear us, we are friends.
Our father said no, but
We pleaded, then in haste took to the air,
Breathlessly beating long wings,
And on and on raced with the wind,
Riding the crests of the mountain breezes.
We heard the dull strokes of a hammer through the sea-caves,
And we leapt a horse without time to remember manners,
Each foot in the stirrup without a sandal.

They are still with him, impulsively sympathetic and loyal, at the end of the play, when Prometheus, refusing to disclose his secret, is caught up in the earthquake of Zeus. 'No, no, we refuse to desert him, we stay at his side to the end; for of all vile things in the world the worst is a traitor.' The young nymphs as it were counterpoise the most generous and tender impulses of Nature against anger and violence directed against the weak and vulnerable.

The Nereids were the daughters of Nereus, the wise old man of the sea. Traditionally, there were fifty of these marine nymphs of the Mediterranean, dwelling with their father in the depths of the sea, lovely young goddesses, kindly to sailors. One of their number was Thetis, the mother of Achilles, who also befriended both Dionysus and Hephaestus. Brought up by Hera, she was obliged by Zeus and Hera to marry Peleus, a mortal. The story of the marriage illustrates a common folktale motif of the fairy or nymph won through guile and struggle, at least for a period of time. Thetis, like other sea creatures, had the power of self-transformation, but Peleus, instructed by Chiron, the wise old centaur, held her fast until she promised to marry him.

After the birth of Achilles, Thetis returned to the sea, but emerged again from time to time to give him comfort and succor. At the end of the *Odyssey*, the ghost of Agamemnon tells how Thetis came up from the sea with the other Nereids to join in the morning at the funeral of Achilles, and brought a golden urn for his bones, a gift from Dionysus, made by the smith god, Hephaestus.

Different from the nymphs of the broad ocean and the sea were the Naiads, the nymphs of running water, of rivers and springs. These are the divine counterparts of the human girls who regularly purified themselves at such places before religious ceremonies or who, as brides, bathed before their weddings in rivers or in water brought from them. There were also the Oreads or Orestiads, special mountain nymphs, and the Dryads and Hamadryads, who were closely involved with trees and tree cults.

As M. P. Nilsson pointed out (in *Greek Popular Religion*), Artemis is a great goddess very similar to the nymphs, and is traditionally accompanied by nymphs. She haunts mountains and meadows, and is connected with the tree cult, with springs and rivers. She protects women in childbirth and watches over little children. She was leader of the nymphs; small wonder that she was a popular goddess, nymph incarnate. She took the young of all creatures under her care and a choral passage in the *Agamemnon* of Aeschylus portrays her anger at the sight of two eagles tearing a hare with her unborn litter in the womb.

Artemis was known as a bear goddess in various parts of the ancient world in a ritual associated with initiation and marriage. In Arcadia, the mother of Arcas, after whom the district was named, was changed into a bear shortly before he was born.

The mother's name was that of the nymph Callisto, properly an epithet of Artemis. Artemis Brauronia had her temple at Brauron in Attica. Here girls, dressed in saffron, performed a bear dance before they were married.

It has been reasonably argued that the bear goddess belonged to the ancient Pelasgians, who brought her to Arcadia from Attica, to Attica from Lemnos, and ultimately from the shores of the Black Sea, reaching the Aegean by way of the Propontis, now known as the Sea of Marmara, which connects the Black Sea with the Aegean. It has been argued that she was identified with Artemis because of the influence of the Ephesian fertility goddess.

Evidence which has come to light in recent years has further suggested the possibility that the Cretans perpetuated a similar association in the neighbourhood of the peninsula of Akrotiri, northeast of Canea, now the island's capital city. A local myth implies a ritual involving a sacred bear, a cult of a divine nursing-mother in a cave, whose worshippers were pre-Dorian. The myth and the ritual could be associated with the cave on Akrotiri called Arkoudia, 'Cave of the She-bear,' described under that name by travelers for several centuries.

The old traditional sphere of the nymphs was to look after mortals in the days of their youth. They were mothers and nurses of heroes and they were also said to look after infant gods. As Homer says in his *Hymn to Dionysus*:

I will begin my song about Dionysus,
the ivy-crowned,
Loudly-clamoring god, the glorious
son of Zeus and of
Far-famed Semele, who was received
in their arms by long-haired
Nymphs from his father, their lord,
and they fostered and cherished

him tenderly
In the valleys of Nysa . . .

The infant Zeus was also tenderly nurtured and legends of his childhood show the close relationship between nymphs and wild creatures. After his birth in a Cretan cave, it was said, the baby Zeus was fed by a pig or by doves or by bees or a goat. Two nymphs, Melissa and Amalthea, supposedly the daughters of Melisseus, King of Crete, reared the infant on the milk of a goat. Amalthea made him a golden ball and put him to sleep in a golden cradle.

Tradition said that in Crete there was a cave sacred to bees, where Rhea gave birth to Zeus, which neither god nor man might enter. The cave was occupied by sacred bees, nurses of Zeus, and the god fed on honey. It is possible to argue that this story was replaced later by the legend of the nymphs, who retained the title melissai, bees.

R. F. WILLETTS

Ogre

Legends of grotesque, humanoid creatures who prey on and consume human beings, very often children or young women, appear in different mythologies across the world. These monsters may also be giants. In the

A mask representing Tsonoqa, a giantess in Kwakwaka'wakw mythology who carried away children in order to eat them

The epic poem *Beowulf* describes a battle between Beowulf and a terrible monster called Grendel, an ogre by all accounts. Henrietta Elizabeth Marshall (1867–1941)

Pegasus

In classical Greek mythology, Pegasus was a winged horse sired by Poseidon and created, according to one legend, from the blood of the snake-haired Medusa when she was beheaded by Perseus. Pegasus was caught and tamed by Bellerophon, who rode him when he was carrying out the series of challenges set by King Iobates of Lycia. These included the destruction of the Chimera, a fire-breathing monster with the head of a lion, the body of a goat, and a dragon's tail. Pegasus flew above the monster enabling Bellerophon to stay out of range of its lethal breath and kill it. Pegasus is also associated with the creation of a spring, Hippocrene, on Mt. Helicon the home of the muses, when he was ordered by Poseidon to strike the Mount with his hoof causing water to gush out. Pegasus was eventually elevated to the heavens by Zeus to become a constellation.

Stories of supernatural horses occur in many cultures including the eight-legged horse, Sleipner, of Norse mythology, and the seven-headed Hindu horse, Uchaishravas. The patron saint of England, St. George, rode a white horse when he destroyed the dragon. In nineteenth-century America, reports of a legendary horse were widespread—a superb white mustang that evaded all attempts at capture and was never seen to tire.

Pegasus is well represented in art from classical times through the medieval period and the Renaissance, right up to the present day. A Greek drinking cup from the 5th century BC shows a battle scene with an infantry soldier whose shield bears an image of Pegasus. In recent historical times, Pegasus also acquired military significance when an image of Bellerophon riding Pegasus was used in 1941 by the newly formed British Parachute Regiment as their insignia. The airborne troops'

classic tale of 'Jack and the Beanstalk', typically the giant is able to detect the presence of the young boy by smell and begins to hunt for him saying, 'Fee, fi, fo, fum, I smell the blood of an Englishman'. The word 'ogre' probably originated with Charles Perrault, the author of a collection of moralistic fairytales in late seventeenth century France and was possibly derived from the name of a Roman god of the underworld, Orcus.

In one folktale from Egypt, the hero is sent to the country of ogres to search for a ram; in order to ensure his protection, he is instructed to suckle the breast of a female ogre and thus be adopted as her son and so avoid being devoured by her. In a Japanese legend describing the activities of demonic beings that abduct and eat young women, the cannibalistic feasts are recounted in graphic detail. Another tale by Perrault is of a young woman who marries a man who may be described as an ogre, Bluebeard, and discovers the bodies of his murdered wives in the dungeon of the castle.

capture of a key objective in the 1944 Normandy Invasion has been commemorated ever since in the name given to a bridge on the Caen Canal—Pegasus Bridge.

Phoenix

For a mythical creature, the phoenix is familiar enough; it is used in everyday life as a trademark, it rises from stylized flames on heraldic bearings, it enriches the poet's language, and appears briefly in history. What its legend is and means, on the other hand, has largely been forgotten as the symbol gains wider and wider currency.

The phoenix, according to the most developed forms of the story, is a bird about the size of an eagle, brilliantly coloured in plumage; it is either purple with a golden collar, or a dazzling mixture of red, gold, and blue. It is the only one of its kind, and lives in Arabia; at the end of an epoch, as it feels death drawing near, it builds a pyre of the sweetest spices, on which it then sits, singing a song of rare beauty. The rays of the sun ignite the nest, and both this and the bird are consumed to ashes. From the ashes there arises a worm, which eventually grows into a new phoenix. The bird's first task is to gather the remains of its parent and, accompanied by a throng of other birds, to fly to Heliopolis (the City of the Sun) on the Nile. Here the priests of the sun receive it with great ceremony; it buries its parent in the temple, and returns to Arabia.

The roots of this story first appear in ancient Greek literature, in Herodotus's account of Egypt (c. 430 BC). When he was at Heliopolis, he was shown the bird in pictures; and its very name may be due to his confusing it with the date palm on which it is often depicted, which is also phoenix in Greek. It was a red-gold bird about the size of an eagle, and the priests said

The Phoenix, Friedrich Johann Justin Bertuch (1747–1822)

that it arrived there every 500 years bearing its predecessor embalmed in a ball of myrrh, which it buried in the temple of the sun. Later writers give other details, such as the bird's rebirth as a worm from its dead parent's body, and the accompanying flight of birds. There was, however, some doubt as to the length of the true interval between the arrival of two phoenixes: Aelian (c. 170–235 AD) mocks the priests who do not know when it will arrive and 'have to confess that they devote their time "to putting the sun to rest with their talk", but do not know as much as birds'. Tacitus reports: 'Regarding the length of its life, accounts vary. The commonest view favours 500 years. But some estimate that it appears every 1,461 years . . .' The particular phoenix which had come to his attention as a historian was that said to have arrived in the reign of Tiberius; but since the previous one had been welcomed at Heliopolis under Ptolemy III, and 'as between Ptolemy and Tiberius there were less than 250 years some have denied the authenticity of the Tiberian phoenix, which did not, they say, come from Arabia or perform the traditionally attested actions.' Pliny rejects it out of hand; although it was displayed in public, 'nobody would doubt that this phoenix is a fabrication'.

It is only in the 4th century AD that the idea of a fiery death is to be found, in two complete poems on the phoe-

nix, by Claudian and Lactantius. This description of the bird's death is taken from Claudian, in Henry Vaughan's translation:

> He knows his time is out! and
> doth provide
> New principles of life; herbs he
> brings dried
> From the hot hills, and with rich
> spices frames
> A Pile shall burn, and Hatch him
> with his flames.
> On this the weakling sits; salutes
> the Sun
> With pleasant noise, and prays and
> begs for some
> Of his own fire, that quickly
> may restore
> The youth and vigor, which he
> had before.
> Whom soon as Phoebus spyes,
> stopping his rayns
> He makes a stand, and thus allayes
> his pains . . .
> He shakes his locks, and from his
> golden head,
> Shoots one bright beam, which smites
> with vital fire
> The willing bird; to burn is
> his desire,
> That he may live again; he's proud
> in death,
> And goes in haste to gain a
> better breath.
> The spicie heap fir'd with
> celestial rays
> Doth burn the aged Phoenix, when
> strait stays
> The Chariot of th'amazed Moon;
> the pole
> Resists the wheeling, swift Orbs,
> and the whole
> Fabric of Nature at a stand remains,
> Till the old bird a new, young
> being gains.

With this description of the death of the phoenix, our picture of the legend is complete. Where did such a tale come from, and are its details part of the clues as to its origin or mere decoration? Herodotus's account of the phoenix as a sacred bird at Heliopolis sets us in the right direction: for in the Egyptian mythological texts, such as the Book of the Dead, which are concerned with the soul's safety in the otherworld and are often magical, the bird benu or bennu appears, with many of the attributes of the phoenix. This creature is a prime mover of the world: prototype of the individual soul, it arises from the Isle of Fire in the underworld and flies to Heliopolis to announce the new epoch, in which the sun is renewed. Because the sun, too, had been envisaged as a bird which made its daily journey from east to west, so the bennu came to be identified with Khepera (Khepri) himself, the rising sun.

Companion of the Sun

The texts on the bennu itself fall into three groups: those concerned with

. . . Baruch is shown by an angel the sun as it sets out on its daily journey, accompanied by the phoenix, 'a bird as large as nine mountains' . . .

resurrection, those identifying it with Re, Osiris and the rites of the dead, and those identifying it with the planet Venus. The three groups are linked by the solar theme, and a new idea of the bennu appears, as a bird accompanying the sun on its daily journey. In the *Apocalypse of Baruch* (2nd century AD), Baruch is shown by an angel the sun as it sets out on its daily journey, accompanied by the phoenix, 'a bird as large as nine mountains'; and at twilight the same procession returns. The phoenix is weary, 'Because he holds back the rays of the sun, because of the fire and heat which last throughout the day . . . if his wings did not form a screen against the rays of the sun, no living being would survive.' This legend reappears in a slightly different form in the story of the bird called heliodromos or 'sun-runner', and other variations linger in the medieval descriptions of the phoenix.

A Fenghuang or Chinese phoenix on the roof of the Main Hall of the Mengjia Longshan Temple in Taipei, Taiwan

Phoenixes by Paulownia Trees, Kano Tan'yu (1602–1674)

In the Egyptian texts, the bennu is shown as a heronlike creature, which does not correspond to the eaglelike bird described by Herodotus; but it is possible that the original bennu was a falconlike creature which was only later confused with the heron. Its colouring, gold, red, pink and blue, is that of the phoenix. Among the few details of its habits, we learn of the flight of birds which escort it at a respectful distance; perhaps a simile for the stars following Venus at eventide. A sarcophagus bears the inscription 'I am the bennu who begets himself and gives incense to Osiris.' The identification with Osiris, the god of resurrection, which is found elsewhere, strengthens the idea of the bennu as self-reviving. Finally, the bennu is associated with the new epoch or great year in the same way as the phoenix. The cycle of 1,461 days (Tacitus's 'years' is an error) is exactly the length of four solar years including Leap Year day. All in all, there can be little doubt that the phoenix of Herodotus and tradition is indeed the same creature as the bennu of Egyptian myth.

Yet even the bennu's solar associations are not quite enough to account for the strange phenomenon of the phoenix's fiery end. Here a modern naturalist comes to our aid: Dr. Maurice Burton, in his researches into the habit of 'anting' has pointed

out the parallel between this and the resurrection in flames of the phoenix. In 'anting', which is common among various species including rooks, the bird performs a series of almost ritual movements, often involving glowing cinders or actual flaming twigs, which give the impression that it is using fire and smoke to drive ants out of its feathers. Closer investigation shows that this is not the case, and the real reason for this behaviour is unknown.

However, a bird emerging from the flames in this way might easily suggest revival by fire. The only weakness in this theory is that the habit has not so far been observed in any of the proto-types of the bennu and phoenix: eagle, heron, and falcon.

Death in a Nest of Spice

The legend of the phoenix was widespread in the Middle Ages: but medieval curiosity about the natural world was limited. Accepted authority was preferred, and the authority on bird and animal lore was the work known as the *Physiologus* or *Naturalist*. This small collection of descriptions was steadily enlarged between the sixth and thirteenth centuries and became known as the bestiary or *Book of Beasts*. The most important change was that the original text was turned into a moral tract by the addition of an explanation in theological terms of the natural events. The entry for the phoenix reminds us of the Resurrection. First the version by which it meets a fiery end is given, and is used as an argument for the truth of the scriptural account of the Passion: 'If the Phoenix has the power to die and rise again, why, silly man, are you scandalized at the word of God . . .?' The alternative is given (ignoring the contradiction), according to which the bird's body decays in a nest of spices and a worm emerges to grow into a new phoenix.

The bestiary was very popular, and many variations developed, both orthodox and unorthodox. In one version, the phoenix is confused with the eagle, but the most interesting is that of the bestiary of the heretical Waldensian sect that flourished in France and Italy in the twelfth century. This revives an aspect of the legend which was rarely touched on: the phoenix's sweet song on its pyre, which was taken to symbolize man's duty to praise God. Although this fable is very like that of the swan that sang so beautifully before it died, it is a very old attribute of the phoenix, and found in Roman writers. In the most unusual of all the bestiaries, the 'Lovers' Book of Beasts', the phoenix masquerades as a salamander, and can only be identified by the illustration, which shows it as a bird.

From theology, the phoenix migrates to literature. The cold sceptical eye of the seventeenth century ejected it from the canon of natural history, but poets seized on it as an exotic symbol of the unique—which quickly became debased to the merely rare—and phoenixes abound in their eulogies of monarchs and other great men of the world, and in the lines inspired by the great beauties of the day. In this century, W. B. Yeats, thinking of his love Maud Gonne, could revive the myth's magic as he scorned 'a score of duchesses surpassing womankind' for her sake, saying 'I knew a phoenix in my youth, so let them have their

day.' Florian, the eighteenth century French writer of fables, gave the myth a new charm by placing it in a homely setting. One day the phoenix appears in the forests of France, where all the birds are overcome with envy and admiration—all, that is, save the turtledove; she sighs as she gazes at the phoenix, and when her mate asks her the reason for this, answers: 'I can only pity him; he is the only one of his kind.' On a more complex and subtle plane are two symbolic recreations of the legend in poems by Sidney Keyes and Herbert Read. In Keyes' poem, the phoenix stands for corrupting pride, while in sharp contrast Read sees it as an archetype of life's continuation.

Outside this Western tradition there is the Asian phoenix. As with the bennu bird, the equation between feng-hwang and phoenix is not absolute. The feng-hwang is not unique: feng is the male bird, hwang the female. But in other respects it resembles the Western phoenix. It is renowned for its sweet song and is accompanied by crowds of birds. It is a heavenly emissary which appears when the land enjoys the gods' favour, and is not seen in times of war, just as in Roman Egypt the phoenix was a good omen. The idea of the rarity of the bird is complicated by reports that if you play the flute, almost invariably the creature will appear to accompany you, and when friends gather in a garden in the cool of the evening to play music together, it will often join them. The feng-hwang, however, is really part of the otherworld, as one of the four spiritual creatures, symbol of the empress and of the element fire. It bears on its body the characters for virtue, righteousness, humanity, sincerity, and integrity; it will eat no living thing, not even grass; and of all four spiritual creatures—tortoise, ki-lin (unicorn), dragon, and feng-hwang—it is the feng-hwang which is the most exalted.

RICHARD BARBER

Satyrs

Partly human, partly bestial, the satyrs were minor rustic gods or demons, traditional companions of the god Dionysus, lewd and lascivious by nature. Their ultimate origin is puzzling and it may be that their association with Dionysus began in Attica and Ionia. They were commonly represented with bristly hair, round and upturned noses, and pointed animallike ears, with small horns growing from the tops of their foreheads and with tails like those of horses. Dressed in animal skins, wearing wreaths of ivy, vine, or fir, bibulous, sensual, and pleasure-loving, they lie sleeping, play musical instruments, or join in wild dances with the nymphs.

Their chief prototype is Silenus himself, that ancient Falstaff, bald, jovial, and rotund, carrying a wine bag, usually so tipsy that he rides around on an ass or has to be propped up by other satyrs. A dancer and flute player, he was also regarded as a prophet.

To make any sense of this odd jumble of characteristics we must bear in mind the nature of the god with whom the satyrs were closely associated. As E. R. Dodds has pointed out, in the introduction to his edition of the *Bacchae of Euripides*, to the Greeks of the classical age Dionysus was not solely, or even mainly, the god of wine. His cult titles identify him as the power in the tree, the blossom-bringer, the abundance of life, his domain the liquid fire in the grape, the sap thrusting in a young tree, the blood pounding in the veins of a young animal, all the mysterious and uncontrollable tides that ebb and flow in the life of Nature. It may well be that his association with certain wild plants, such as the fir and ivy, and with certain animals, is in fact older than his association with the vine.

Dionysos and satyrs. Attic red-figured cup interior (c. 480 BC)

'It was the Alexandrines,' adds Dodds, 'and above all the Romans—with their tidy functionalism and their cheerful obtuseness in matters of the spirit—who departmentalized Dionysus as "jolly Bacchus" the wine-god with his riotous crew of nymphs and satyrs. As such he was taken over from the Romans by Renaissance painters and poets; and it was they in turn who shaped the image in which the modern world pictures him.'

Links with the Birth of Zeus

The Greeks in the time of Euripides were beginning to bring other Nature-spirits of other cults into association with the satyrs. Thus the chorus in the Bacchae tells the myth of the origin of the kettledrum; how it was invented in a Cretan cave by Curetes or Corybantes to drown the cries of the baby Zeus, then presented to Rhea, his mother; and how the satyrs obtained it and introduced it into Dionysiac ritual.

The Curetes of Crete were guardians of the infant god and attendants on the mother goddess. Hesiod tells us that they were lovers of sport and

Bust of a satyr. Marble with traces of polychromy, Roman artwork of the Imperial era (c. 1st or 2nd centuries AD). Copy of a Hellenistic type

whole performance. A satyr-play was similar to a tragedy in structure, but was shorter. It was a kind of burlesque and its chorus was always composed of a group of satyrs, who had a typical dance, called the sikinnis. Its themes were taken from the same sources as those of tragedy—epic and mythological.

The only two satyr-plays that have survived are the *Ichneutai* of Sophocles and the *Cyclops* of Euripides, which is a medley composed of the Polyphemus episode from the ninth book of the *Odyssey* and the legend of the capture of Dionysus by Lydian pirates. We know too that the satyr-play that accompanied the *Oresteia* of Aeschylus was called *Proteus*. Apparently this play, in lighter vein, counterbalanced the story of Agamemnon's homecoming with the adventure of Menelaus, his brother, on his return from the Trojan War.

R. F. WILLETTS

FURTHER READING: E. R. Dodds ed. The Bacchae. (Oxford Univ. Press, 2nd edn, 1960); William Arrowsmith ed. 'The Bacchae' in Complete Greek Tragedies. (Chicago Univ. Press, vol. 4, 1958)

Shape-Shifting

The idea that it is possible, in certain circumstances, for men to change their natural bodily form and assume, for a time, that of an animal or a bird or some other nonhuman creature, is very old and was once practically worldwide. The gods of many regions were credited with the power of transforming themselves at will into anything, animate or inanimate, that they chose. Sorcerers also, and some great heroes, were believed to have

dancing; and they are compared by Strabo with similar bands, such as Corybantes, Cabiri, Dactyls, and Telchines. It was sometimes considered likely that Curetes and Corybantes were the same, namely unmarried Kouroi, 'youths' chosen for the war dance connected with the rituals of the mother of the gods, known also as Corybantes because they walked with a butting of their heads, in dancing style.

To Strabo, Tityroi (a name connected with the satyrs) were like the Corybantes. They belonged to that cycle of Cretan-Phrygian tradition which was bound up with the sacred rites of the rearing of the child Zeus in Crete, which were held in honour of the mother of the gods in Phrygia and in the region of the Trojan Ida. In Crete, such rites were performed with orgiastic worship and with such ministers as served Dionysus—the satyrs. These the Cretans called Curetes, the armed young men who danced the story of the birth of Zeus.

The Satyr-Play
Greek drama developed out of Dionysiac ritual. Competitors in the dramatic festival submitted four plays, consisting of three tragedies and a 'satyr' play. It seems that tragedy and 'satyr' had an independent growth out of the ritual, until it became the custom to add a satyr-play to the tragic trilogy as a conventional part of the

Opposite page:
Werewolf gargoyle at Moulins Cathedral, France

Legendary Creatures and Monsters

the same power, by virtue of magical knowledge or some innate quality; and so, though more rarely, were a few otherwise ordinary people who acquired the gift through possession of a charm or the performance of a ritual act. The medieval Icelandic historian Snorri Sturluson, in Ynglinga Saga, says that Odin often changed into a bird, or a wild beast, or a fish, or a dragon, and traveled thus to far-off places in the twinkling of an eye. Zeus, in the course of his frequent amorous adventures, became a swan, a bull, a ram, a serpent, a dove, an eagle, and a shower of gold.

Similar tales of self-transformation are told of various Celtic, Hindu, and Egyptian deities, and of spirits, heroes, sorcerers, and magicians in the Far East, Polynesia, and throughout the Americas.

Man into Wild Beast

A widespread story with many variants is that of an individual, human or divine, who changes in quick succession into a number of different shapes during a fight, or in order to escape from some peril or difficulty. Homer relates in the *Odyssey* how the soothsayer Proteus was seized, as he lay asleep, by Menelaus, who had come to him seeking guidance. But Proteus would never give of his wisdom unless he was forced to do so, and now he instantly turned himself, first into a bearded lion, and then into a snake, a leopard, a bear, running water, and a tree. Through all these changes, Menelaus held on firmly, until at last Proteus resumed his true form and consented to answer his adversary's questions.

In the Welsh legend of Taliesin's birth, Gwion Bach, flying from Ceridwen's anger, changed himself into a hare, and she pursued him as a greyhound. Then he became a fish in the river, but she turned into an otter

and swam after him there. Hard-pressed, he became a bird, and found her hovering above him as a hawk. As she stooped upon him, he fell headlong into a heap of winnowed wheat on a barn floor and turned into one of the grains. That was the end of the contest (though not of the story), for Ceridwen transformed herself into a black hen which found and swallowed that grain. There are other tales of this kind in which the hero's changes of form are not of his own choosing, but are imposed upon him by outside magic. In the Scots ballad Tarn Lin, when Janet plans to rescue her lover from fairyland, he warns her that the fairies will change him in her arms into a variety of fearsome creatures. She must, he tells

Nevertheless, many did believe that shape-shifting was possible, as an effect of magic, or a curse, or by the help of Satan who was himself a shape-changer. . .

her, 'hold me fast and fear me not' until he becomes a burning coal, and that she must instantly douse in well-water. In the end, if her courage does not fail her, he will be freed from enchantment and become himself again.

The commonest form of the shape-shifting tradition was not, however, concerned with multiple change, but with transformation, voluntary or by compulsion, into one particular type of wild creature. The belief that this could and did happen was very long-lived, and is the basis of countless legends of European werewolves and were-bears, of Indian were-tigers, and of leopard-men or hyena-men in Africa. It was well known in the ancient world. Pliny mentions it in his *Natural History*, though he thought it a 'mere

fable', and he quotes Euanthes' curious account of the Antaei in Arcadia.

On the feast of Zeus Lykaios, a member of that family was chosen by lot and conducted by his kinsmen to the shore of a certain lake. His clothes were taken from him and hung upon an oak tree, after which he plunged into the water, swam across to the other side, and disappeared into the forest. There he became a wolf and ran wild with other wolves for nine years; but if, during that time, he managed to refrain from eating human flesh, he could then return to the oak tree, put on the clothes that hung upon it, and become a man again.

Herodotus, in the 5th century BC, reported that all the men of the Neuri, a Scythian tribe, became wolves for a few days in every year, and then resumed their human form. He found this very hard to believe, but he observed that the Neurians themselves constantly asserted that it was true, and were prepared to do so upon oath. It seems likely that here we have a record of a ritual transformation connected with an animal cult, in which the men concerned 'became' wolves for the time being by ceremonially putting on the skin or mask of a wolf, or by some similar rite.

A straightforward werewolf story of the time of Nero occurs in Petronius's account of Trimalchio's feast, in the Satyricon. Niceros, who was present at the feast, related how he went one night to visit Melissa, and persuaded an acquaintance to go with him for part of the way. As they came by some tombs, he was astonished to see his companion take off his clothes, lay them on the roadside, and make water round them. He then turned suddenly into a wolf and ran off, howling, into the woods. When Niceros went to collect the clothes, he found them changed into stone. Much alarmed, he hurried on to Melissa's house, and was told on arrival that a fierce wolf had been there before him. It had attacked the livestock, but luckily it had been driven off by a slave who had wounded it in the neck with a spear. Next morning, on his way home, he saw that the petrified clothes had disappeared, but the ground on which they had lain was stained with blood; and ongoing later to inquire for his companion of the previous night, he found him in bed, being treated by a surgeon for a severe wound in his neck.

That injuries suffered in the animal body were reproduced in the human body was a very persistent belief. Gervase of Tilbury remarks in *Otia Imperiala* (c. 1211) that 'women have been seen and wounded in the shape of cats by persons who were secretly on the watch, and . . . the next day the women have shown wounds and loss of limbs'. Five centuries later, in 1718, the same idea appeared in evidence given at an enquiry held in Caithness. A certain William Montgomery, enraged and terrified by the nocturnal yowling of cats which he believed to be witches, rushed out with a sword and a hatchet, killed two of the cats, and injured others. Soon afterward, two local women were found to have died very suddenly, and a third, Margaret Nin-Gilbert, was so badly wounded in the leg that the limb subsequently withered and dropped off. Even as late as the nineteenth century, the guilt of women suspected of turning into hares was often 'proved' when a hare was shot, and a woman was later seen to have some injury in the corresponding part of her body.

Werewolves with Human Speech

How, and for what reason, men were thus transformed was the subject of earnest debate in the Middle Ages.

Many learned men rejected the whole idea of metamorphosis, and declared that any person thinking himself changed was really the victim of delusions inspired by demons.

The unknown author of the *Canon Episcopi*, a document first recorded by Regino de Prum in the early tenth century, stated clearly that even to believe a man could turn, or be turned, into a creature of another species was impious, since only God could alter that which he had created. Nevertheless, many did believe that shape-shifting was possible, as an effect of magic, or a curse, or by the help of Satan who was himself a shape-changer, or simply through kinship between man and beast.

St. Natalis is said to have cursed all the people of Ossory so that, two by two, they were forced to become wolves for seven years at a time. In *Topographica Hibernica*, Giraldus Cambrensis describes how a priest met a wolf who was one of the saint's victims. The animal addressed him in human speech imploring him to come and shrive his dying wife, who also lay under the curse and was now a wolf.

A folktale from Ireland relates the power of changing oneself into a wolf to the ancient concept of the animal ancestor. A hunter took shelter during a storm in the house of an old man previously unknown to him. While he was there, two wolves entered and went into an inner room; soon after, two young men emerged and sat down by the hearth. The old man said they were his sons, and that he and they, being descended from wolves, could assume that form whenever it pleased them to do so.

The actual change was commonly supposed to be effected by the use of magical salves, or by spells and incantations, or by putting on the skin of a wolf or a bear, or a girdle made from such pelts, or from human

skin. Bjorn, in *Hrolfs Saga Kraba*, was struck by his stepmother with a pair of wolfskin gloves, and thereafter became a bear by day, though he was a man at night. In *Volsunga Saga*, Sigmund and Sinfjolti found two men sleeping in a cabin, with wolfskins hanging on the wall above them. Sigmund and his son put on the pelts, and found they could not get them off again. They became wolves, and killed many men while the enchantment lasted, but when the day came round on which they could doff the skins, they burned them, to prevent further evil.

These tales, and others like them, reflect the most usual form of the European tradition, in which actual bodily transformation occurred. The shape-shifter, voluntarily or otherwise, cast off his human attributes and appearance and, for the time being, really became an animal or a bird, though he sometimes retained his human eyes.

There was, however, another type of belief, better known in Asia than in Europe, but found in both continents, where no physical change took place. The man's soul passed into the body of an existing wild creature, while his own lay in a sort of cataleptic fit, sometimes quite still and lifeless, and sometimes tossing and violently moving in correspondence with the movements of the beast that temporarily contained his soul. Odin's shape-shifting seems to have been of this kind, for Snorri says that while he passed through the world in many different forms, 'his body then lay as if sleeping or dead'.

CHRISTINA HOLE

Sirens

Female beings connected with the underworld, the Sirens were particularly dangerous to men; it is hard to find any story in which women suffered at their hands. They first appear in the *Odyssey* (Book 12) as beautiful females who sit in a meadow by the sea, enchanting passing sailors with their song so that they swim ashore, or land, and perish miserably. Round them is a great heap of bones which come from the rotting corpses of men.

Odysseus was advised by the enchantress Circe, when she warned him of the Sirens, to stop the ears of his rowers with wax as the ship passed them; and she told him that, if he wished to hear their song himself, he should make his men bind him to the mast and not release him however much he might implore them. A mysterious calm fell as the ship passed their island, so that it depended entirely on rowing to make headway. The Sirens sang to Odys-

Ulysses and the Sirens, John William Waterhouse (1849–1917)

seus that they knew of all his deeds and sufferings at Troy. In Homer they are mentioned in the dual number, so that he recognized no more than two. Their names are not given, and their physical form is not described. Like other such beings in the *Odyssey* they are not located in known or normal geography.

For the historical period corresponding to the heroic age, it is of some interest that tablets inscribed in the script known as *Linear B* from Mycenean Pylos seem to refer to decorations on furniture as sere-mokaraoi and seremokaraapi which has been interpreted as 'siren-headed'. If this is so, the word serem, in that form with M not yet changed to N, already existed in Mycenean Greek, and the Sirens were known in myth in some form. What form the Mycenean 'siren-headed' decorations had is not known.

In later periods poets and mythographers continued to write of Sirens, revealing more of their nature. Hesiod in a fragment of his *Eoiai* called

Theopompus and Nicophon, mention the abundant feasting of the Sirens and their taunting of the hungry wanderer Odysseus. This association with fabulous plenty is difficult to explain, even given the food-loving conventions of comedy.

'Barren Nightingales'

In Apollonius the island of the Sirens is Anthemoessa and they are the daughters of the river Achelous and Terpsichore, the Muse of choral dance and song. They once attended Persephone before she was carried off to Hades and they were then formed partly like birds and partly like maidens. The Argonauts would have been drawn into their power as they passed, but Orpheus with his lyre drowned the sound of their voices. Only Butes swam toward the shore, but Aphrodite snatched him up and set him on the height of Lilybaeum. In Apollonius the Sirens are placed on the coast of the Tyrrhenian Sea, as is usual in post-Homeric poetry. But the river Achelous belongs in Aetolia in northwest Greece, which may have been their original home in Greek legend. The tradition of this location is preserved later by Lucian and others, particularly by another Alexandrian poet, Lycophron, author of the poem *Alexandra*, in which Cassandra prophesies the future wanderings of the Greek chiefs, including Odysseus, on their return from Troy.

Lycophron calls the Sirens 'barren nightingales and slayers of the centaurs', because the centaurs were so charmed with their song that they forgot to eat. Later he says that Odysseus will be the death of the Sirens, who will hurl themselves from the cliff-top into the Tyrrhenian Sea. One will be washed ashore by the towering Phalerus (Naples) and the river Glanis (Clanius) where the inhabitants will build a tomb for her as the bird goddess Parthenope, and honour her

From about 300 BC, the Siren of Canosa, half woman and half bird

their island Anthemoessa and named them Thelxiope, Molpe, and Aglaophonus, daughters of Phorcys the sea god, saying also that they calmed the winds. In the 7th century BC the lyric poet Alcman spoke of the Muse 'the clear-voiced Siren' as if Siren and Muse were the same, and elsewhere mentions the Sirenides, but only for their music. A fragment of Sophocles makes them daughters of Phorcys and 'singers of songs of Hades'. The comic poet Epicharmus makes the Sirens try to attract Odysseus by descriptions of the food and drink that they enjoyed and which he might share; plump anchovies, sucking pigs, cuttlefish, and sweet wine. When they begin to speak of their evening meal Odysseus cries 'Alas for my miseries'. Other comic poets, with yearly sacrifices. Leucosia will be cast ashore by the strand of Enipeus (Posidon), that is, at Posidonia or Paestum. Ligeia will come ashore at Tereina and will be buried with honour in the stony beach. The tone of this passage shows that in Italianate Greek belief, on the coast of Campania and further south, the Sirens were regarded as beneficent beings, at least after their death. Their cult here and its centres, particularly on the Sorrentine peninsula south of Naples and its neighbouring islands, are also described by Strabo. This region became their regular location in myth, and this is where they had a temple. This lore, like most of the legends about Odysseus in Italy, was spread by the Greek colonists from Euboea who reached Italy by passing northwest Greece.

In later tradition Parthenope is presented by the medieval Cronaca di Partenope as a princess of Sicily who sailed into Naples Bay and died of the plague. She was buried there and became a sort of local saint who was consulted as an oracle. At some time in the Middle Ages the Sirens lost their bird form and acquired fishes' tails so that they became a form of mermaid. Earlier Greek art shows them always in the form of birds or birdlike women. One reason for locating the Sirens on or near the Sorrentine peninsula, while their character was still conceived as in the *Odyssey*, is the appearance of a cave on the coast. In this is a great mass of prehistoric bones preserved under transparent breccia (composite rock consisting of fragments of stone cemented together). The bones are in fact the remains of game that was killed and eaten by Paleolithic hunters. They must have been seen by generations of Myccnean and later Greek voyagers who thought they were human bones.

E. D. PHILLIPS

Siren, detail of Romanesque frescos (1210) at St. James church in Kastelaz, Tyrol

Sleeping Beauty, Viktor M. Vasnetsov (1848–1926)

Sleepers

A curious account of an attempted robbery in County Meath appeared in the *Observer* of 16 January 1831. A group of thieves, who had entered a house without any attempt at concealing themselves, were discovered by the household and fled. The men supposed, wrongly, that a magic charm they had brought with them would act as a protection by casting a spell over the occupants. The charm, well known in Europe centuries ago, was called the Hand of Glory: that is, a hand cut from the body of a man who had been hanged. Dried and pickled, it was used as a holder for a candle made from the fat of a hanged man, or sometimes the fingers themselves were set on fire. When this charm was carried into a

house and set alight, everyone inside would fall into deep sleep from which they would only wake if milk was used to extinguish it.

Sleep and death are obviously closely linked here and the logic behind the charm may have been that, just as the dead sleep in their graves, so portions of a dead body may be used to induce a similar condition. The Hand of Glory was specifically a European charm but related objects have been used both in Europe and in other parts of the world, again chiefly by burglars, to induce a similar condition. Among the southern Slavs the thief threw a human bone over the roof, saying: 'As this bone will weaken, so may these people waken', the significance of the spell lying of course in the fact that a bone remains as it is, an immutable object. In Java the thief strewed earth

from a grave right round the house. Hindus placed ashes from a funeral pyre in front of the door, and Peruvian Indians also used charred human remains. The left arm stolen from the corpse of a woman who had died in her first childbirth was used by Mexican Indians. With this they struck the ground in front of the house to be burgled. In Indonesia, when a young man wanted to visit his girlfriend at night, he threw soil taken from a grave over her parents' room. This was to prevent them from waking and disturbing the young couple. All these charms served the same purpose: to throw the householder and his family into a trance.

Methods for inducing magic sleep make an interesting comparison, and in some cases they are perhaps suggestive of a rudimentary knowledge of hypnosis. Combing the hair is one method occurring in certain fairy tales. Another is the sung or chanted verse, sometimes so reminiscent of a lullaby or sleep charm that one might assume this to be its origin.

A tale from Bengal, 'The Story of the Rakshasas', describes how a beautiful girl is placed in a deathlike trance by means of a silver stick, and revived with a gold one. Slumber is produced by a spindle in the well-known story of 'The Sleeping Beauty', the princess who lies in enchanted sleep for 100 years until a prince arrives and revives her with a kiss. Opera-goers are familiar with Richard Wagner's treatment of Germanic legend in *The Ring of the Nibeltings*: Wotan lays Brunhild down on the mountain and causes a magic fire to blaze around her. Only a hero brave enough to pass through the flames can rouse her from this charmed slumber. Eventually it is Siegfried who awakens her with a kiss.

The converse of this idea occurs in the widespread legend of sleeping heroes, such as Sir Francis Drake in Henry Newbolt's poem *Drake's Drum*:

*Drake he's in his hammock till
the great Armadas come
(Capten, art tha sleepin' there
below?),
Slung atween the round shot, listenin'
for the drum,
An' dreamin' arl the time o'
Plymouth Hoe.
Call him on the deep sea, call him
up the Sound,
Call him when ye sail to meet the foe.
Where the old trades plyin' an' the old
flag flyin'
They shall find him ware an' wakin',
as they found him long ago!*

Inevitably human psychology plays its part. Popular leaders are not readily forgotten by the people from whom they sprang. They live on in the memory of the folk, and in times of peril and national emergency it is good to feel that they are there, waiting to be called upon. This expresses partly that basic human unwillingness to face up to unpleasant facts, and partly that dependency upon another greater than oneself, represented in its simplest form by the child who wants his parents to live forever, and never die. The hero fulfills such a need. Bridging the gap between deity and man, he represents an image of transition, the pre-Christian version of a saint.

According to many accounts, King Arthur is not dead but living, sunk in magic sleep and waiting to be roused. One of the best known is from Yorkshire, where Arthur and his host are believed to sleep beneath the ruins of Richmond Castle. Once, so it is said, a man called Potter Thompson was taken to an underground vault where they all slumbered. He was told to unsheathe a sword and blow a horn,

Budhanilkantha (sleeping Vishnu)

but though he tried to do so, he grew timid before the task was completed; the sleeping figures had begun to stir. As he left, a voice cried:

Potter Thompson, Potter Thompson,
If thou hadst either drawn
The sword or wound the horn
Thou hadst been the luckiest man
That ever yet was born.

Parallel stories of slumbering heroes appear all over Europe: King Wenzel and his knights below Blanik mountain in Bohemia; Frederick Barbarossa with his men beneath the Kyffhäuserberg, a peak in Thuringia; King Marko sleeping in the mountain Urvina with his horse Sharatz, according to Serbian legend; Dobocz, the Carpathian robber chief; the founders of the Swiss Federation; Olaf Tryggvason; Ogier the Dane, one of Charlemagne's paladins; Charlemagne himself, and Don Sebastian of Portugal. There are many others.

Sometimes there are references to treasure: King Arthur dreams in the Vale of Neath beneath the Craig-y-Ddinas (Castle Rock) with his warriors and a quantity of gold. Of course, important leaders often possessed great riches during their lives, so the idea of the hero and his treasure is easily understandable. But it has also been suggested that such wealth was originally linked to the Nature spirit of the site, an idea perhaps associated with the ancient custom of killing a man so that his shade could guard buried treasure.

Slumbering Heroes

Certainly in many of these legends the hero sleeps, not in a distant land of the imagination, but literally underneath the ground, which could represent some earlier stage of folk belief and an identification with local earth deities. Legendary heroes exhibit a tendency to sink from the fortresses in which they lived to the clefts and caverns below. Norse tradition holds that aged heroes, dissatisfied with the world, shut themselves up in a hill. The subterranean location of the sites is of interest since a characteristic theme in mythology is removal: disappearance or translation to another sphere. A usual method is enclosure within the earth, which opens for the purpose.

Popular belief sometimes places the world of souls underground, and there the hero is secluded with his company. This suggests a possible association of ideas between the sleeping army and the host of the dead. Or there may

'Germany awake!' was the Nazi's favourite slogan. It was inscribed on their banners, which were designed by the Fuehrer himself.

be a memory here of the custom of slaughtering a man's retinue to keep him company and maintain him in his customary state in the afterlife. Such sleeping warriors occur in two examples from the Isle of Man and Rathlin Island, County Antrim. The first describes a hole called Devil's Den at the base of a mountain: one man brave enough to go in found a group of sleeping giants and, on a stone table in the midst, a bugle. He blew a blast, which woke the giants, and he fled in terror. On Rathlin Island, one of the traditional sites of Robert the Bruce's escape in a cave, where he was inspired by the spider and its web, there is a ruin called Bruce's Castle. Below it, in a grotto, the Bruce and his men lie in enchanted sleep. A man who ventured in found a group of slumbering men dressed in armour, and a sabre, partial-ly sheathed, in the ground. When he tried to draw the sabre, the warriors woke and he ran away.

A Christianized sleepers myth, well known in the early centuries of this era, is the story of the Seven Sleepers of Ephesus. It appears in many versions and Mohammed used it in the Koran. According to *The Golden Legend*, a medieval collection of lives of the saints, seven Christians—Maximian, Malchus, Marcian, Dionysus, John, Serapion, and Constantine—were living in Ephesus during the persecution by Emperor Decius in 250 AD. This group of Christian heroes, refusing to abandon their faith, hid in a cave on Mt. Celion and fell asleep. Hearing a rumor to this effect, Decius caused the entrance to be blocked with stones. Several centuries later during the reign of Theodosius II, a workman chanced to remove the obstruction and the sleepers awoke. They were hungry so Malchus was sent to buy bread. Shopkeepers in the city, amazed at the ancient money with which he tried to pay, took him before the authorities and accused him of stealing treasure. The bishop agreed to go to Mt. Celion and see the cave where the others were waiting. At that time there was a heresy in Ephesus denying the resurrection of the dead. The seven martyrs who were shown to Emperor Theodosius declared: 'God has resuscitated us before the great resurrection day, in order that you may believe firmly in the resurrection of the dead.' This said, they bowed their heads and died. The day commemorating the event is still venerated by the Eastern Church, and people suffering from insomnia ask the seven martyrs for assistance.

The timely appearance of these religious heroes when the Church was threatened with heresy resembles the sleeping patriots waiting to come when their country is in peril. These ideas may seem remote from us today, but are they really so? Siegfried, hero of the Nibelungenlied, traditionally slumbers in the mountain of Geroldseck, ready to fight for the fatherland; and, because the imagination of Hitler was fired by these old legends, the motif of the slumbering hero played a prominent role in Nazi ideology—the sleeper is Germany itself.

Rage! Rage! Rage!
The alarm bells sound from tower
*   to tower . . .*
The sleepers call from their
*   chambers . . .*
The dead call from their graves
Germany awake! . . .
Woe to the people that today
*   dreams on!*
Germany awake!

The refrain of the first Nazi party anthem—'Germany awake!'—was the Nazis' favourite slogan. It was inscribed on their banners, which were designed by the Fuehrer himself, and it was also the title of the volume which commemorated their seizure of power.

VENETIA NEWALL

FURTHER READING: E. S. Hartland. The Science of Fairy Tales. *(Gale, 1968); Sabine Baring-Gould.* Curious Myths of the Middle Ages. *(Oxford University Press, 1978).*

Subterranean Races

An ancient Peruvian legend relates that four brothers and four sisters emerged from the cavern of Pacari-Tambo, east of Cuzco, the ancient city that became the capital of the Inca Empire. The eldest brother climbed a mountain and, throwing stones to the four cardinal points, took possession of the land. The youngest brother, Ayar Uchu Topa, contrived to dispose of his elders, married the sisters, and subdued the surrounding peoples, founding Cuzco and many other cities.

The great Mammoth Cave in Edmondson County, Kentucky, was discovered only in 1809. Bodies of an unknown race reputed to antedate the Indians were found in its recesses with reed torches beside them, but all crumbled to powder when touched.

There is a belief that a low type of subterranean being sometimes appears in astral form on the earth's

Early Native Americans mined for minerals in Mammoth Cave, Kentucky

surface, attracted by manifestations of the human sex-force. For example, in *Real Ghost Stories*, W. T. Stead tells of an apparition seen by a woman in an English suburb: 'I saw this light develop into a head and face of yellowish-green light, with a mass of matted hair above it. The face was very wide and broad, larger than ours in all respects, very large eyes of green which, not being distinctly outlined, appeared to merge into the yellow of the cheeks; no hair whatever on the lower part of the face. The expression was diabolically malignant.'

One of the most interesting accounts of subterranean people, which purports in one sense to be factual, is by the Theosophist C. W. Leadbeater. Although he claimed to have up-to-date confirmation of some of the facts, his story is allegedly a report of the experience of two Indian youths, which took place in 10,402 BC and was recovered from the 'memory of Nature' (the record of history supposed to exist on the astral plane).

Both young men had some psychic faculty, and one heard a voice, from time to time, which guided him and suggested interesting enterprises. On the instructions of this invisible guide,

> *Birds fan the air with their wings, and it was therefore supposed that storms and tempests were caused by huge winged creatures*

who demanded a pledge of secrecy, they set out to a certain mountain area where they ultimately found a cave entrance. They prepared food packages to last several weeks and bundles of torches and, with some trepidation, entered.

After a long, fairly level, penetration into the mountain, they reached a sloping rugged downward fissure, which they descended perilously for some days. Finally they reached an immense cavity in the earth. Their torches were unnecessary there, because the air around them was charged with a strange luminosity.

They found underground rivers, several varieties of vegetation (which lacked the green of the upper earth), semi-reptilian animals and, to their astonishment, naked humans. These were of less than normal stature, but broad and stocky, and their skin had a repulsive leaden hue. They had no culture and no shelters, catching the reptiles to eat raw. They also fed on an abundant huge fungus.

The youths declined the reptile flesh, but found the fungus good and invigorating. After a week or so their unseen guide directed them to walk

Pukapukara in Peru was a former Incan fortress checkpoint and administrative centre.

away from the wall where they had entered. After some hours, they came upon a different type of people, of higher intelligence. Although ignorant of fire, like the primitives already seen, they availed themselves of hot springs to cook the flesh of turtles and goatlike animals that they kept, and drank the animals' milk. They lived in chambers hollowed out in the rock, and wove a kind of matting and string from reeds. Both sexes smeared themselves with rose, green, and yellow mud from the edges of the hot springs.

They were able to draw, and incised meaningful sets of marks on the rocks. These were mainly cup-markings, rounded hollows ground on the surface and arranged in patterns, each pattern having a meaning—in other words, they were ideographs. A certain number of these in a straight line had one meaning, a set making an angle had another. The two young explorers eventually found their way back to the entrance of the cave.

C. NELSON STEWART

Thunderbird

In the past it was widely believed that birds were connected with the sun, wind, thunder, and lightning. As aerial creatures seen ascending into the heavens, they were associated with the celestial powers and particularly with those controlling the weather. For this reason birds were often regarded as in various ways responsible for rain and the conditions which make life possible for man and the plants and animals on which he depends.

Since in many parts of the world outside the tropics migratory birds appear in spring, it was assumed that they were in some way responsible for the increasing warmth and fertility or, at least, in league with the powers responsible for favourable weather. The mysterious appearances and disap-

Kwakwaka'wakw big house and thunderbird totem pole British Columbia, Canada

pearances of migrating birds stirred the primitive imagination, and mythical birds were endowed with powers beyond those of any known species; commonly these birds were thought to be gigantic. Birds fan the air with their wings, and it was therefore supposed that storms and tempests were caused by huge winged creatures. And as some make drumming, booming, and clattering noises with their wings, voices or bills, primitive folk supposed that thunder was caused in some such way by invisible, supernatural, monstrous birds.

Thus belief in a thunderbird, sometimes also conceived as a firebird, lightning bird or storm bird, became widespread. Such birds could be regarded as beneficent because fire is useful to man and thunder showers foster fertility, but they could also be viewed with fear and awe because lightning can be destructive, killing men, shattering trees, and setting forests on fire. Moreover, as giant birds were thought to act as the steeds of the gods, some of whom were not always friendly to man, their nature and activities might have an important bearing on human welfare.

The Flapping of Great Wings

In North America the thunderbird was pictured differently by various tribes. The Hareskin Indians spoke of a huge bird which spent the winter in the land of the dead with other migratory birds and beasts, returning with the warm weather. When it shook its tail thunder was heard, and lightning was the flashing of its eyes. At Eneti, in Washington state, a face said to represent the thunderbird was carved on a rock; the Indians believed that rain could be caused by shaking the rock and so arousing the anger of the thunderbird. According to the Dakotas, it was the parent thunderbird which made thunder; it was wise and did no harm, but the young were irresponsible and might cause destruction. These Indians claimed to have killed a thunderbird, and to have discovered that it had a man's face with a nose like an eagle's beak.

On the northwest coast the thunderbird was thought of as an eagle with an extra head on its abdomen; it was huge enough to be able to carry off whales. A story told how two hunters saw an enormous bird rise from a lake with the sound of thunder and then sink back with a terrific roar. An early traveler recorded that the Hurons regarded thunder as a large bird because a similar noise, on a smaller scale, was made by a bird like a swallow. In British Columbia the Indians likened the thunderbird to the ruby-throated hummingbird. The sound made by the hummingbird's wings probably suggested the connection with thunder, while its red throat feathers associated it with lightning.

In West Africa the spirit of lightning, So, is a flying being partaking of the nature of a god. Thunder is caused by the flapping of his wings and he casts lightning from the dark clouds. The image of the Nigerian thunder god is placed between two poles, on which are placed representations of birds. Among many Bantu tribes an image of a bird is placed on huts to ward off lightning; its form may vary from that of a flamingo to that of a bird of prey. Stone effigies of birds found at the ancient town of Zimbabwe have a crocodile or serpent carved at the base, suggesting that the powers of heaven and earth respectively were symbolized, as in some Asian cultures. In southern Africa the lightning is said to be a bird, brown or white-necked like the fish eagle. Persons struck by lightning are said to have been scratched by its claws. The Luyia in Kenya say that a huge, red cock lives up in the clouds. He sends lightning when he shakes his wings and thunder is the sound of his crowing.

In Asia the thunderbird is widely associated with rain. The forest Tungus of northeast Asia say that thunder is caused by the rustling of a mighty bird's wings. Ancient Chinese literature reveals belief in thunderbirds: the pheasant is prominent in these traditions, probably because pheasants

make a thudding noise when they flap their wings, and carry red markings on their heads. Young people in China used to perform springtime dances, in the course of which they imitated pheasants and flapped their arms to induce rain to fall. The connection between the bird and fertility also appears from the fact that in Chinese the word or character representing the sounds made by a pheasant also signified the noise of thunder and the 'agitation of a woman as she becomes pregnant'.

The Chinese thunder god, Lei Kung, is thought to have been originally a bird, possibly an owl. He is represented with a man's body, blue and hideous; he has a beak, wings, and talons, and carries a wooden mallet, with which he beats a number of drums hung around him. He may carry a dagger or be shown shooting the arrows of lightning. The Japanese thunder god is also shown festooned with drums. In northern Asia tribal drums are painted with pictures of birds and frogs; as in other areas the drums are beaten, imitating thunder, to induce rain to fall.

The diver is associated with rain in Europe, Asia, and North America because of its close connection with water. Its cry is said to foretell rain and the Thompson Indians of British Columbia therefore imitate its call to make the rain fall. Belief in the efficacy of imitative magic extends to Mexico, where the Tarahumare Indians perform dances imitating the courtship antics of the turkey: they assume that as the gods grant the

Imitative rain magic was also performed in Europe: near Dorpat in Estonia a man would climb a tree and rattle on a kettle, simulating the noise of a woodpecker drumming on a branch.

prayers of the bird, expressed in its dances, by sending rains, so they too must dance like the turkey to bring fertility to the countryside.

Imitative rain magic was also performed in Europe: near Dorpat in Estonia a man would climb a tree and rattle on a kettle, simulating the noise of a woodpecker drumming on a branch. The drumming noise which the bird makes with its bill as it hammers on a tree has been regarded from ancient times as rain magic, mimicry of thunder in order to create thunder and cause a downpour, a belief which still survives.

Enemy of Snakes

In southern Asia the thunderbird belief appears to be superseded or obscured by the concept of a solar bird dominating a creature of the waters. The Hindu god Vishnu, who sometimes appears as a solar deity, rides the Garuda bird which is itself a solar divinity. In the art of Indo-China, Garuda is represented in immense stone sculptures as a winged and beaked human figure holding a snake in its taloned feet. This is interpreted as symbolizing the sun drying up the waters, represented by the Naga snakes, Garuda's traditional enemies. The Brahmanic god of the waters, celestial and terrestrial, Varuna, is depicted mounted on a monster, half bird, half reptile. Other gods also ride birds: Kama, the god of love, rides a parrot, Sarasvati, goddess of eloquence, a peacock. The immense birds of Near Eastern mythology such as the Simurgh and the Roc, and even the huge birds of Irish legend, appear to have some affinity with the mythical birds further east.

The concept of opposing powers, celestial and terrestrial, is also found in Europe where the design of an eagle holding a snake or perched on an aquatic creature appears in ancient art. In Greece Zeus, the Thunderer, was symbolized by an eagle, and he disguised himself as an eagle in order to abduct Ganymede, the son of King Tros. The myth of celestial and terrestrial powers in conflict is very ancient. Among the Hittites there was a story describing the conflict between the weather god and the dragon. In various forms this myth is represented in many cultures, including our own, for the legend of St. George and the Dragon may be regarded as a variant.

E. A. ARMSTRONG

Troll

This elemental spirit of northern European mythology belongs to that supernatural fairy community which was once assumed to exercise dominion over Nature, a class of spirit regarded with considerable apprehension since all elementals were known to be capricious, treacherous, and frequently hostile. Elementals were in the main associated with particular sites, in the case of trolls, mountain caverns from which they emerged after nightfall. Broadly speaking, there were two classes of trolls: the giant and the dwarf, both of which were reported to steal women, exchange human children for their own hideous offspring and indulge in a good deal of petty theft. It has been generally assumed that all trolls were originally of giant stature but that, especially in areas like Denmark and Finland, they became gradually reduced in size. Giant trolls, however, abounded in mountainous countries such as Norway and Sweden, where they were the spirits of the mountains, and were in the main dull-witted cannibals with huge noses for smelling out the blood of their human prey. An allied species, the trow, haunted the Orkneys and Shetlands, frequenting both land and sea.

An Old Mountain Troll, John Bauer (1882–1918)

The dwarf trolls in their own particular way were quite as hideous as their giant counterparts and were recognizable by their humped backs and red caps. They were good mechanics and clever dancers, and they possessed beautiful wives but, unlike the giants, they seem to have been extremely sharp-witted although their cunning was of a low order. One species at least must have been extremely small, hence the words of an old Danish ballad: 'Out then spoke the tiny troll, no bigger than an emmet'.

Scandinavian folklore contains a great deal of interesting information about the habits and idiosyncrasies of the troll population. All trolls hated noise, an aversion they acquired in the days of old when the Teutonic god Thor dedicated much of his time to hurling his hammer in their direction. Their instinctive hostility to

the Christian faith led to an intense loathing of church bells, the sound of which could reduce the most powerful troll to a heap of pebbles. As creatures of darkness, trolls were terrified of sunlight, which could petrify them.

Giant trolls were frequently credited with building mighty structures like castles, bridges, and churches, and legends abound describing how they were cheated of their wages (usually human souls) by their sharper-witted clients. At the root of this tradition lay the belief that some kind of payment was due to the owner of the soil when land was set aside for building or cultivation, the landlord, in this case, being an earth elemental demanding his rent in blood or souls.

Anyone who managed to learn a troll's name had the power to destroy him by repeating it. There is a famous Norse legend about a troll named

The Troll and the Boy, John Bauer (1882–1918)

Wind and Weather, who contracted to build a church in return for which he was to receive as wages the sun and moon. Alas, his client, the saintly King Olaf, discovered his name by accident, and cried out: 'Hold, O Wind and Weather, you've set the spire askew', and the troll crashed to the ground, being reduced to a large heap of flints.

Despite the useful work performed by church-building trolls, a pronounced antipathy existed between mankind and trolls in general, due largely to the trolls' deplorable habit of stealing babies and seducing wives. Trolls could be kept at bay, however, by attaching sprigs of mistletoe to crib and byre and bedroom ceiling, and by lighting huge bonfires known as Baldur's Bale Fires at crossroads on St. John's Eve, using nine varieties of wood, and at the same time hurling toadstools into the flames. In Sweden fires were lit at Eastertide, the peasants firing warning shots in all directions.

A rapid degradation in the status of the troll followed the advance of Christianity into northern Europe which had the effect of transforming all Teutonic elementals into what can only be described as Christianized devils. Among the seventeenth-century evil spirits referred to by Burton in his Anatomy of Melancholy were 'Robin Goodfellows, trolls etc., which as they are most conversant with men do them the most harm'. Many of the basic characteristics of the troll are clearly discernible in the attributes of devils, the troll wife-stealer becoming in time the demon lover, the incubus seducing women in their sleep.

With the departure of devils from the modern mythological scene, troll-lore has undergone an encouraging revival, largely in the interests of the Scandinavian tourist industry. Toy trolls, huge, long-nosed and hairy, often brandishing flint axes, are now available in Norwegian shops and the traveler is carefully reminded that trolls wearing their traditional red caps can

Statues of the trolls from the movie *The Hobbit* on the exhibit floor at the 2012 Comic-Con in San Diego

occasionally be seen at night in the proximity of hills and mounds. Fortunately, modern trolls have developed more sophisticated appetites than their ancestors for, according to the last vagary of folklore, they no longer demand tribute in the form of souls but request heaped platefuls of bananas and cream.

ERIC MAPLE

Unicorn

A fabulous beast born of man's imagination, the unicorn plays a leading role in some of his most ancient myths and legends. Its form and function are as variable as the minds and religions of men; but whatever its shape—and it has been described as an ox, ram, goat, bull, antelope, wild ass, horse, rhinoceros, serpent, or fish, and as a monster in which the characteristics of several of these animals are combined—a one-horned beast was always a symbol of supreme power, connected with gods and kings. It concentrates into a single horn the vigour and virility associated with the two horns of real animals.

An early distinction was made between the caprine unicorn, a gigantic one-horned goat, and the equine unicorn, in the form of a horse. The latter, the unicorn par excellence, was gracefully adapted by the College of Heralds as a symbol of 'the very parfit gentil knight'.

The first to mention the unicorn in the West was Ctesias of Cnidos, a Greek historian and doctor who was court physician to the kings of Persia for some seventeen years. A fragment of his book on India, written about 398 BC, is the most important Western document concerning the unicorn: 'There are in India,' wrote Ctesias, 'certain wild asses, which are as large

as horses, and larger. Their bodies are white, their heads dark red, and their eyes dark blue. They have a horn on the forehead which is about a foot and a half in length. The dust filed from this horn is administered in a potion as a protection against deadly drugs. The base of this horn is pure white, the upper part is sharp and of a vivid crimson; and the remainder or middle portion is black. Those who drink out of these horns made into drinking vessels are not subject, they say, to convulsions or the holy disease. Indeed they are immune even to poisons if, either before or after swallowing such, they drink wine, water, or anything else from these beakers . . .'

Pliny emphasized the fact that unicorns could not be captured by men, and Aelian their love of solitude and their indomitability.

The Ctesian unicorn is a compound of three animals: rhinoceros, wild ass, and a rare, fierce Himalayan antelope which, in profile, appears to have one horn. This confusion of the attributes of different animals, and the inability to distinguish between the artificial and the natural, is a perpetual stumbling-block in the complex history of the unicorn; but it was inevitable in a time when travelers' tales were the only sources of information. Ctesias had never seen a rhinoceros, but it is assumed that he saw a cup made from rhinoceros horn, which had been brought from India where these were commonly used as drinking vessels by potentates and princes, and often decorated with bands of colour—white, black, and red. These are of course the colours on the horn of the Ctesian unicorn.

The Great Re'em

Aristotle (384–322 BC) mentions two kinds of unicorn, the Indian ass and the oryx, a kind of antelope that is single-horned in profile; and the Roman writers Pliny (23–79 AD) and Aelian (170–235 AD) between them muster seven different kinds, the most important being the rhinoceros, though, like Ctesias, neither realized they were describing that beast. Pliny emphasized the fact that unicorns could not be captured by men, and Aelian their love of solitude and their indomitability.

The most momentous thing that happened to the Western unicorn was a mistake. The Greek translators of the Old Testament rendered the word Re'em as monoceros, 'single-horned' or unicorn. This magnificent error conferred on the unicorn a lifespan far exceeding that of the rest of the mythical menagerie and lasting well into the eighteenth century. Through this mistranslation the unicorn became part of the Bible and to doubt its existence was to question the inspired word of God. The battle over the true identity of the Re'em was long and complex, but it was eventually identified as *bos primigenius*, the giant aurochs, a species of wild buffalo that was extinct in Mesopotamia by about 500 BC.

Sir Austen Layard identified the aurochs with the superbly sculptured 'bulls of Nineveh', dating from the time of Nebuchadnezzar (6th century BC) which were seen by the Jews at the time of their captivity. The beasts are shown in conventional profile and therefore look single-horned. However, as Odell Shepard points out in *The Lore of the Unicorn*, there is little in the Hebrew text of the Bible to suggest that the Jews themselves thought of the Re'em as anything but two-horned, since the word for 'horn' is almost invariably in the plural.

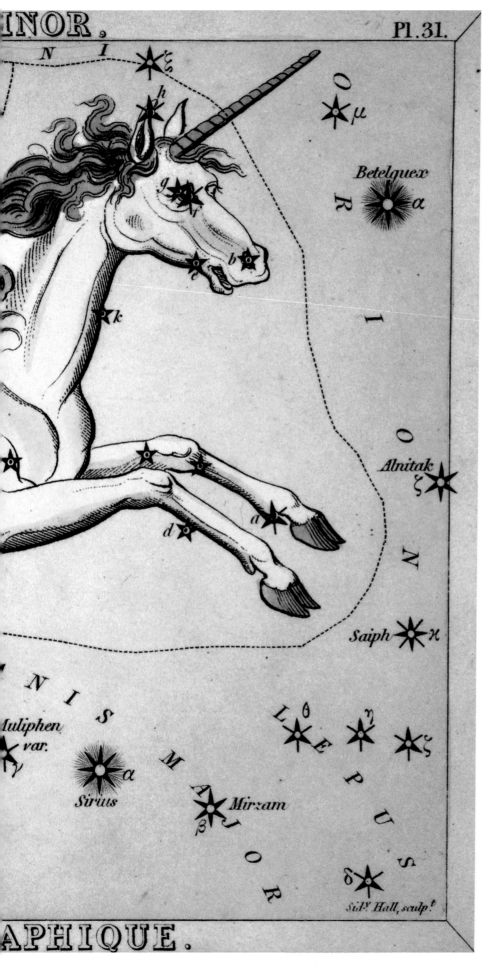

Later Jewish commentators exaggerated the Re'em out of all proportion. A young unicorn becomes as large as Mt. Tabor and as high as the sky. Because it could not fit into Noah's ark, the unicorn had to be towed by a rope attached to its horn; and another tradition states that it perished in the waters. Talmudic texts link the unicorn firmly with the lion: 'And in our land there is also the unicorn, which has a great horn on its forehead. And there are also many lions. And when the lion sees a unicorn it draws him against a tree, and the horn pierces so deep into the tree it cannot pull it out again, and then the lion comes and kills the unicorn—but sometimes the matter is reversed . . .'

Bestiaries, collections of moral tales about real or fabulous animals, were very popular all through the Middle Ages. Texts varied according to local and religious influences, but all recounted the most famous of all legends about the unicorn—its capture by a virgin. According to this tale, the unicorn, a small kidlike beast armed with a sharp pointed horn, is too fleet and fierce to be taken by hunters. Only a virgin seated alone under a tree in a forest can capture it; because it is irresistibly attracted by the odours of virtue, the unicorn approaches, head in her lap, and permits itself to be caressed into sleep. She breaks its horn, the dogs leap, the huntsman pounces, and the unicorn is taken to the palace of the king.

Details vary, vividly, from text to text; in some the unicorn indulges in familiarities remarkably unsuited to virginal virtue, and in others the virgin is a boy in disguise. Although this legend, of unknown provenance, is transparently

Detail from Urania's Mirror, plate 31: Monoceros, Canis Minor, and Atelier Typographique, Sydney Hall

The Mystic Hunt of the Unicorn Representing Annunciation, Martin Schongauer (1450–1491)

erotic, it was tortured into ill-fitting Christian significance. The treacherous virgin was identified with the Mother of God, and the unicorn with Christ and also, despite its dubious familiarities, with purity. The single horn was said to symbolize the unity of Father and Son, and also the 'horn' of the cross, the upright beam projecting above the transverse. The huntsman became the Holy Spirit acting through the angel Gabriel, and the king's palace was heaven. The dogs represented truth, justice, mercy, and peace, despite the fact that their function was to tear the unicorn

to pieces; they were said to couple at the beast's death, signifying that, though seemingly irreconcilable, truth, justice, mercy, and peace were now one.

Another famous legend concerns the virtues of the alicorn, the beast's horn, as an antidote to poison. The animals gather at sunset to quench their thirst, and find the 'great water' poisoned with venom discharged by a serpent. Unable to drink, they await the unicorn. The beast approaches, makes the sign of the cross over the water with its horn and instantly the water is cleansed. The horn symbolizes the cross, the serpent the

Devil, and the poisoned water stands for the sins of the world.

As a result of this legend, drinking cups made from horn were commonly found on the banqueting tables of the Middle Ages and the Renaissance, as a defence against death by poisoning, a common hazard besetting those in high places. The horn was said to sweat in the presence of poison. Alicorns, bought and sold at formidable prices, were rated among the most precious items of princely and papal treasure. For the rich there were cups made from alicorn or pieces of it; while for the poor there were scrapings of horn or l'eau a la licorne, water into which the horn had been dipped. Apothecaries kept an alicorn chained to their counters, for it was considered to be the most effective panacea for a variety of evils; finally, it was claimed to raise the dead.

A veritable library of learning has been built up in search of the beast providing the 'true alicorn', and it is sad to reduce that quarry of forgotten lore to a brief citation of the main providers: rhinoceros, antelope, mammoth tusk, and the tusk of narwhal, a marine mammal. Practically all the pictures in ancient books show a horn based on the last of these. By 1600 Europe boasted at least nineteen famous alicorns.

Unicorns held a high place in the religion and sacred writing of Persia: '. . . the three-legged ass . . . stands amid the wide-formed ocean . . . its feet are three, eyes six, mouths nine, ears two, and horn one. Body white, food spiritual and it is righteous . . . The horn is as it were of pure gold and hollow . . . With that horn it will vanquish and dissipate all the vile corruption due to the efforts of noxious creatures . . .' However, the one-horned ass is frequently thought to have been imported from an older culture; it is thought that the one-horned beast that haunts the high snows of the Himalayas has the most ancient tradition, and many authorities cite Tibet as the most likely source of unicorn legends, though there was a time when the Mountains of the Moon, heaving high over Ethiopia, held pride of place. The tradition was long and strong, and four brazen unicorns dominated the court of the Ethiopian kings.

In Tibet, antelope horns were used for magical and ritual purposes for centuries, particularly the horn of a fierce fleet antelope known as *Anthlops Hodgsoni*, named for a

nineteenth century British resident of Nepal who identified its horn. In profile, the beast looks single-horned. The unicorn is frequently depicted in the paintings and sculptures of Buddhist temples; the circle containing the body of a dead lama was drawn with the horn of the sacred antelope. From Tibet the unicorn is assumed to have spread into China.

The Chinese unicorn does not have the fierceness of its counterpart further west; it is so gentle that it will not tread on so much as a blade of grass, and its backward sweeping horn is fleshy-tipped, indicating that it was not used for attack. Called the *ki-lin*,

the Chinese unicorn was believed to appear at the start of a beneficent reign or the birth of a man equal to an emperor in stature; traditionally it announced the birth and death of Confucius. But there is more to the unicorn than that. The 'key' to the beast lies hidden in its Chinese name, *ki*, 'male', *lin*, 'female'.

The unicorn's most vital function has been as a symbol, whether of power or virility, or purity, or the combination of opposites, of the male horn and the female body. Many modern interpreters regard this last role as the crucial one and relate it to the symbolism of the soul as the

Unicorn statue, Buckingham Palace, London, England

spark of divine light in the darkness of matter and evil, the body, and to the concept of the hermaphrodite as the perfect union of opposites.

This explains the unicorn's place in the symbolism of alchemy. The 'great work' of alchemy was an attempt to liberate the divine spirit of light from its prison of darkness by transforming base metal into gold by means of the Philosophers' Stone, and by transforming the alchemist himself into the psychic equivalent of gold, a being who was spiritually purified, who had liberated the god within himself. Mercury, the 'male-female', the *androgyne*, was an essential element in the work, and the personification of Mercury as the precursor of triumph, proclaiming victory over darkness was the unicorn.

The moment for which every alchemist laboured is illustrated in *The Book of Lambspring* (1625) by a picture which shows a deer and a unicorn meeting in a forest, with the text: 'In the forest (body) there is a soul (deer) and spirit (unicorn) . . . He that knows how to tame and master them by art, and couple them together, may justly be called a master, for we judge rightly that he has obtained the golden flesh.' Another of the many symbols of Mercury as androgynous god and precursor to triumph was the green lion wounded in the lap of the virgin. Because both were figures for Mercury, green lion and unicorn were often considered one, and certainly the image echoes with familiar resonances for those acquainted with the legend of the 'virgin capture'.

The French scientist, Baron Cuvier (1769–1832) dealt the final blow to man's belief in unicorns as an actual species when he declared that beasts with cloven hooves had cloven skulls, and that no horn could grow in the cleft. Although Dr. Dove, an American biologist, proved Cuvier wrong in 1933 when he transplanted the horn buds of an Ayrshire calf into its

skull cleft, and produced a synthetic unicorn, this did nothing to resurrect belief in the beast.

JUNE GRIMBLE

FURTHER READING: N. Hathaway. The Unicorn. *(Viking, 1980); P. and K. Johnsgard.* Dragons and Unicorns. *(St Martin's, 1982); Odell Shepard.* The Lore of the Unicorn. *(Harper and Row 1979 reprint); M. Walser.* The Unicorn. *(Marion Boyars/Scribner, 1983).*

Vampire

Together with the golem in his guise as Frankenstein's monster, the vampire has become the world's best-known supernatural monster, the result of decades of horror films capitalizing on the imagination and researches of an Irish author named Bram Stoker. Before Stoker, the vampire legend had attracted attention, and had even become something of a fad in Europe, but it was jumbled, tangled, overgrown. Stoker pruned it, performed some judicious grafting, dressed it up in a richly purple prose, and added Dracula to the list of classic horror stories.

The name of his vampire was borrowed from the name of a fifteenth century Balkan nobleman whose sadistic cruelties justified his name; means 'devil' in Romanian. It was not difficult for Stoker to project the vampire evil onto the ugly actuality of the true story. And he did it so successfully that folklorists are sometimes surprised to find how often he has affected the more modern concepts of vampires.

It is also surprising, considering the wide fame of the vampire motif, to realize that the legend is comparatively young and that it was for a long time highly localized. Corollaries and ancestors of the vampire, several times removed, are fairly plentiful. Evil bloodsucking demons or witches

Rumanian Vampire Beliefs

In the district of Teleorman, on the third day after a death, when people go to the house of mourning in order to burn incense, they carry with them nine spindles, and these they thrust deep into the grave. Should the vampire rise he would be pierced by their sharp points. Another method is to take tow, to scatter it upon the grave, and to set fire to it there, for it is believed that the occupant will scarce venture through the flames. Sometimes the anathema of a priest will confine the vampire in his tomb.

In the Romanati district the vampire is stripped and the naked carrion thrust into a stout bag. The clothes and cerements are sprinkled with holy water, replaced in the coffin which is secured and again buried in the grave. The body is taken away to the forest. The heart is first cut out, and then it is hacked piecemeal limb from limb and each gobbet burned in a great fire. Last of all the heart is flung into the flames and those who have assisted come near so that they shall be fumigated with the smoke. But all must be consumed, every shred of flesh, every bone. The veriest scrap if left would be enough to enable the vampire again to materialize. Occasionally the ashes of the heart are collected, mingled with water and given to sick people as a powerful potion.

At Zarnesti after a female vampire had been exhumed great iron forks were driven through the heart, eyes, and breast after which the body was buried at a considerable depth, face downward.

It is held to be imperative that the vampire should be traced to his lair and destroyed at the very first opportunity. If he is sufficiently cunning to avoid detection so long at the end of seven years he will become a man again, and then he will be able to pass into another country, or at any rate to a new district, where another language is spoken. He will marry and have children, and these after they die will all go to swell the vampire host.

Montague Summers, *The Vampire in Europe*

and blood-hungry ghosts abound in primitive belief. And the ancient world also offers antecedents in the blood-consuming ghosts in the *Odyssey*, in Ovid, and elsewhere.

There is also the demonic Lilith of ancient Hebrew legend, who had many vampire traits, and the Romans conceived of the lamia, a near relation of the vampire, who enticed men sexually and then feasted on their blood. The Arabs believed in blood-eating spirits, and the ancient Irish told of a comparable demon. But none of these creatures was a vampire, as it is now defined, although such legends probably blended and crystallized to give rise to the concept. Almost exclusively a creature of the Slavic regions and Balkan states of eastern Europe, the vampire first made its appearance in its present form in the sixteenth century.

The word 'vampire' comes from various eastern European terms, including the Magyar vampir. By the seventeenth century, the word was on a great many lips; vampire activity seems to have burgeoned rapidly in the Balkans, and to have occurred as far afield as Greece, where fearsome tales of the vrykolakas spread from town to town. Balkan clergy reported the spread of such tales, and their superiors spoke of a new offensive by the Enemy. Then in the seventeenth century a Greek writer named Leone Allacci separated the concept of the vampire from standard Christian demonology.

Travelers began to pick up hints of the new horror, and patched them together in their writings for the rest of Europe. The first stage of the legend's spread was completed in 1746 when a French monk named Dom Augustin Calmet published a learned treatise on vampires.

Late eighteenth century romanticism had fallen in love with the Gothic, and vampires suited the fashion nicely. Goethe wrote some vampire verses and in the following years so did Byron and Southey, Gautier, and Baudelaire.

The vampire soon reached the theater; a successful play in Paris in the 1820s spawned imitators, and as the years passed hardly a stage in Europe lacked its vampire. A singing vampire entertained German opera audiences in 1828; Alexander Dumas wrote a successful stage play on this theme in the 1850s; the London stage also presented vampires, and was in fact still doing so in 1925 with a dramatization of *Dracula*. In 1931 the cinema took over, and assured the immortality of Bela Lugosi who played Count Dracula. But long before that the fashion for vampires had reached a new height in

It is held to be imperative that the vampire should be traced to his lair and destroyed at the very first opportunity.

prose fiction, with the publication in 1847 of a story called *Varney the Vampire*, some 800 pages of horrification, gory action and nauseous over-writing. It was an instant bestseller; but it

Austrian-Hungarian born actor Bela Lugosi (1882–1956) prepares to bite the neck of an unconscious young woman in a still from director Tod Browning's 1931 film, *Dracula*.

was eclipsed at the end of the century when Bram Stoker published his classic blend of folklore and fantasy.

From then on, the vampire's worldwide notoriety was assured. And although other great vampire stories exist, the creature as he is now known is almost indistinguishable from his incarnation as Count Dracula. In studying the folklore vampire it is never possible to get very far away from the evil Transylvanian aristocrat.

It must be remembered that the vampire is a resuscitated corpse, not an immaterial spirit. Primitive people often fail to draw our distinction between the body of someone who has died and the spirit; they may feed the corpse in order to placate the ghost. And it is rarely clear whether tribesmen think of the dead as returning in bodily form or as insubstantial apparitions. This confusion is found to some degree in vampire lore. But basically the vampire is a walking corpse with some of the powers and functions of a noncorporeal spirit.

As a cadaver, the vampire looks cadaverous: lean, pale with the pallor of death, icy cold to the touch. Some tales describe him as skeletal and withered, like an Egyptian mummy, and he may be clothed in a shroud. But more usually he is said to be merely gaunt to an extreme, and to wear normal clothing with perhaps a touch of the theatrical, like Dracula's entirely black costume. His thinness may vanish, in some cases, when he is well fed; when, like a leech, he is horribly swollen with engorged blood. At these times he may be decidedly hot to the touch. But more usually the only sign of life about his face will be the ruddiness of his lips, which are frequently drawn back to display long, pointed canine teeth.

The vampire's eyes gleam, and sometimes flash redly, and his ears may be pointed, as were Dracula's. These

The famed vampire skeleton of Sozopol in Sofia, Bulgaria

features seem to be borrowings from the older tradition of the werewolf; similarly, the vampire will have sharp curved finger nails, eyebrows that meet above the nose, and he will be extremely hairy, with hair on the palms of his hands. His limited diet gives him foul breath but also makes him preternaturally strong despite his thinness.

A few isolated groups of tales add some special features, for extra horror effects. There is the Bulgarian suggestion that a vampire has only one nostril, or the old Polish idea that his tongue has a sharp point or barb. Vampire tales from Greece described the creature as having blue eyes; but this was merely a way of saying that blue-eyed people, rare creatures in Greece, were probably vampires. Anyone who is 'different' in some way has always been a convenient victim when the conforming majority is looking for enemies of the status quo. People with hare-lips, or red hair, or odd birthmarks, and children born with teeth, have all been persecuted for alleged vampirism.

These victims may well have wished that they were vampires, for folklore endows the creature with some impressive supernatural powers. The old eastern European legends underline its character as one of the 'walking dead' by stating that it can get in and out of its grave through 6 feet of soil. According to some Balkan stories, the grave of a vampire is punctuated by numerous small holes, which are channels down to the coffin through which the creature filters up to the surface. This is one of the main examples of the lack of distinction between corpse and ghost: the vampire is a material body with some of the abilities of an immaterial spirit. Hungarian tales overcome the problem by giving vampires the magical ability of changing into clouds of mist, a trick that Bram Stoker borrowed for Dracula; the Count could slip into locked and sealed rooms through the space under a door, or the keyhole, to reach a victim.

The shape-changing powers of the vampire also enable it to turn into various animals, usually noxious or

nocturnal creatures with long-standing supernatural associations. And the vampire will sometimes have such animals at its beck and call, as aides in its evil-doing. Dracula had a pack of wolves under his control to terrify travelers; and the old tales similarly include wolves, or werewolves, among the vampire's animal companions, along with cats, owls, rats, and sometimes even flies. The vampire sometimes changed itself into animals such as these, most often a wolf or a cat. Dracula for instance was able to change into wolf form. And of course he also turned himself into a bat, a metamorphosis that has been emphasized in films. Stoker, however, used the bat sparingly. The old vampire tales of eastern Europe almost never depict the creature assuming this last form.

When the nineteenth century globe-trotting urge sent Europeans as far afield as South America, their travelers' tales sometimes told of the curious fauna of the continent, including a strange bat which fed solely and exclusively on the blood of animals or people. The world reached into folklore to give it its popular name—the vampire bat; and folklore and fiction incorporated it in the supernatural vampire tradition.

One further special power attributed to the vampire, apart from filtering out of a grave or tomb, and shape-changing, is its ability to hypnotize its victims, preventing them from struggling while it feasts, and also from remembering their fearful visitor the next morning. The vampire can therefore return again and again to the same victim, who will complain merely of having had shadowy nightmares and feeling anaemic.

A Stake Through the Heart

According to tradition, if people become aware of the presence of a vampire there is a battery of defenses and reprisals that can be brought into action against it. The creature is bound up in a more extensive array of 'rules', within which it must operate, than any other folklore horror; and these rules contain defences against the vampire. It must of course be active only at night; but because it is a walking corpse, it must not only rest by day but must rest in its own grave or tomb. A few Balkan tales describe vampires moving freely around during the day, but this is generally thought to be cheating. On the other hand, the old tales do not say that sunlight is actively harmful to the vampire; this idea is a contribution of horror fiction, and films.

In fact many things can hurt, or at least ward off, a vampire. It shuns silver, as evil creatures have done since antiquity, and also hates garlic, and the plant's pungent flowers are useful to have at the window, or around the neck, if vampires are about. Since Christian times, the creature has actively feared the crucifix in any form,

an idea that is partly the result of belief that all evil is in some way derived from Satan, the Enemy, and that the symbol of Christ will therefore oppose it. But older tales, from a Devil-oriented age, are sometimes more explicit: theories by European churchmen of the seventeenth century suggested that the corpse which became a vampire was in fact activated, or powered, by a demon from hell, and not by its original soul. Therefore it would especially fear the cross.

Silver, garlic, and the cross are forms of protective magic; but vampire lore also specifies preventive magic which is widely used in lands riddled with the vampire fear. In these regions it seems that every deceased person would be ringed round with charms to bind him into his grave. These often resemble

> *Silver, garlic, and the cross are forms of protective magic; but vampire lore also specifies preventative magic which is widely used . . .*

primitive methods for keeping the dead from rising. The Chiriguono tribe of South America, for instance, fastened a corpse into its grave with pegs, which also kept the ghost down, and some old Slavonic tales suggest thrusting iron skewers through the earth over a grave, so that the corpse would be magically pinned down. The iron works the magic: evil things shun cold iron almost as much as silver. Many European people simply placed a lump of iron in a dead man's coffin, to keep him in his grave. Other methods of ensuring this included putting a branch of hawthorn or some similar sacred tree, or a wreath of garlic flowers, on the coffin.

There are also all the practices by which, in European lore, any ghost is kept down when there is cause to be-

lieve that he may walk—this applies to suicides, executed criminals and so on. They are buried under running water, or at crossroads, or the corpse has a stake driven through its heart. In lands where belief in vampires took precedence even over ghosts, these techniques became charms against vampires.

However, if neither preventive nor protective magic is effective, there are still ways in which the monster can be destroyed. First, though, the vampire must be captured. Few vampires are as gregarious as Dracula, who invited people to stay at his castle, where the truth about him was revealed in several ways: his appearance, his absence by day, or the fact that he had no reflection in a mirror.

If vampire activity broke out in a particular region the locals would repair to the cemetery and examine the graves. Hopefully, they might find one with the small telltale perforations through which the monster filtered up from its coffin. Or they might borrow an old Hungarian test for vampirism. In this a white stallion that has never stumbled and never been to stud is taken to the cemetery; the horse will refuse to walk on a vampire's grave.

If there were no indications above the ground of vampire activity, the hunters would have to open the graves, and look for a corpse that had not decomposed. These trials could take place with perfect safety during the day while the vampire was dormant, but the searchers had to give themselves time to get back indoors before sunset. The uncorrupted corpse would bear additional signs of vampirism: the typical facial appearance, and traces of blood on mouth and face.

Once a vampire has been caught, it can be easily destroyed. For that matter, the monster could be shot with a silver bullet at night, while it was active, provided the hunter could avoid the creature's hypnotic eyes for long enough. Ideally the bullet should be made from a melted-down crucifix, or at least blessed by a priest. A safer method is to find the vampire in its coffin and to employ some homely magic to keep it there. The main technique is to drive a short, sharp stake into its heart.

The tales recommend using sacred wood for the stake, perhaps the thorn, or aspen. According to some traditions only one blow must be used to drive it home, or the 'pinning' magic will not work. Albanian tales suggest using a consecrated dagger, in the shape of the cross, instead of a stake. Other legends recommend that the monster be decapitated as well as staked; and specify that the beheading must be done with the sexton's spade. Sometimes the

beheaded and staked vampire is then conclusively destroyed by the purification of fire.

These powerful defensive and offensive rituals and charms seem to give the living an advantage over the vampire, who at night can be balked by garlic or the cross, and who is wholly at the hunter's mercy during the day. But the vampire has one magical power not mentioned so far. He can recruit his victims into the ranks of vampirism. According to some tales, anyone who dies from loss of blood as the result of a vampire's continued attacks will instantly rise again as a new vampire. Other traditions suggest that even one or two nonfatal attacks by a vampire will cause the victim eventually to rise again after his or her natural death. For every vampire staked and destroyed, several new ones will have been created.

Nor is this recruitment the only way in which vampires can come into

existence. The lands most rife with vampire lore associated many supernatural traditions that are elsewhere ascribed to ghosts with these creatures. In the Balkans, anyone dying in a state of sin, without the Church's blessing, would rise again as a vampire; this category would especially include suicides and ex-communicants. Perjurers and people cursed by their parents, in fact any exceedingly wicked person, might also walk as vampires after their deaths, as would anyone who dabbled in black magic.

According to western European folklore, such evil-doers must come back after death as insubstantial haunts, punished with eternal restlessness for their evil ways, and bound to this earth in a dreadful shadowy immortality. Western European tales also insist that the victims of evil return as haunts; and similarly, in eastern Europe, such victims return, through no

Arsenal for facing vampires

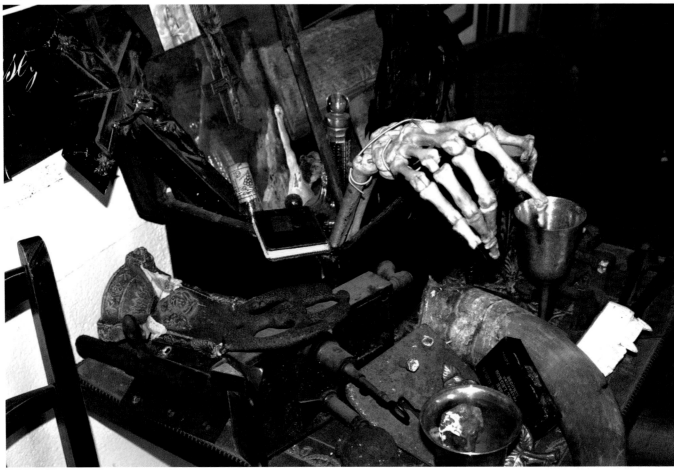

fault of their own, as vampires. A murdered man whose death goes unavenged becomes a vampire (especially in Greek tales); so does a child who dies unbaptized, or a man whose corpse does not receive a Christian burial.

In addition to these borrowings from the older ghost traditions, vampire lore has produced some original ideas about the creation of the monsters. In Romania, for instance, men who are werewolves reappear after death as vampires. Greek legends assert that anyone born on Christmas Day runs the risk of becoming a vampire; and other tales suggest that a seventh son, or a child born with a 'caul', might rise as a vampire after death. According to Romanian tradition, if a vampire stares at a pregnant woman she will give birth to a potential vampire, unless a priest's blessing can cancel out the evil.

Hungry for Blood

The weird assortment of ways in which vampires are bred do not reflect the purpose for which the creature arises. Unlike ghosts, witches, and demons, the vampire is not impelled by any of the familiar evil urges or intentions such as revenge, terrorizing or tempting souls from the righteous path. The vampire is merely obsessively hungry. He seeks blood to give him the pseudo-life he needs to seek more blood.

Folklore contains many instances of the animation of the dead by blood. In the *Odyssey* shadowy phantoms regain substance and the power of speech after drinking blood; witches fed their familiars on their own blood. And there is the story of a seventeenth century French doctor who pumped blood into the severed head of a guillotined prisoner, and was convinced that the head came briefly to life and took on a 'puzzled' expression.

A statue outside the Monkey Forest Temple in Ubud, Bali, Indonesia

The fascination of the vampire legend may be explained, to some extent, by the few nuggets of reality that lurk within the folklore. Some writers, for instance, make much of the parallel between vampires rising from the grave and the prevalence in past centuries of premature burial. Inadequate medical knowledge meant that people were

> . . . *the corpse would have been that of a person buried prematurely who had awoken in the grave and died horribly, trying to claw his way out.*

sometimes buried before they were dead; and folklorists find some possible explanation for the 'uncorrupted corpse' aspect of the legend in this fact.

In the sixteenth and seventeenth centuries it was not uncommon for a number of people in a village to die, apparently inexplicably, from what were then unknown diseases. If a number of graves were later opened, and it was found that one of the recently buried corpses had not yet started to decompose, seemed to have changed

position, and had a frightful expression on its face and blood on its hands, vampirism seemed to be the obvious explanation. In fact, the corpse would have been that of a person buried prematurely who had awoken in the grave and died horribly, trying to claw his way out.

There are also numerous cases of long-dead corpses remaining intact; examples may be found especially in accounts of Christian saints. There is also a supposedly true story from Italy which tells how the body of a woman buried in 1820 was exhumed 30 years later and found to be wholly uncorrupted. One of the exhumers accidentally cut the corpse's leg with a spade, and blood gushed from the wound, as blood is supposed to flow from a vampire when it is staked, after which decomposition set in rapidly. In a superstitious age incidents such as these might well have given rise to a number of 'vampire' tales.

Finally, we must look behind a curtain drawn over the vampire theme by the moralizers of the nineteenth century. In Victorian times explicit accounts of brutality and violence were perfectly proper for widespread dissemination, but anything containing more than a hint of sexuality required censorship. This attitude produced the view that vampire legends are just good gory horror stories, grown out of primitive superstitions about the dead. In fact, vampirism is a blatantly sexual motif, riddled with oral eroticism and sadomasochism.

The old Balkan tales rarely omitted the sexual side of vampirism: married vampires arose from the grave to bestow their terrible attentions on their marriage partners, while those who were unmarried visited attractive young persons of the opposite sex. And it was not solely blood lust that impelled them. But in later tales, and in fiction, the sexual angle was more oblique.

The vampire bites his victims; and anyone with the slightest knowledge of Freud knows that a bite is a sado-erotic kiss; in Dracula the female vampires around Jonathan Harker's bed comment that his health and strength mean 'kisses for us all'. Even the creature's appearance, his thick red lips and unusual hairiness, corresponds to widely-held folk beliefs about excessively sex-oriented people.

Blood is profoundly involved with sexuality in man's psyche, a belief that is reflected in the widespread taboos placed on menstruating women. And modern psychology has shown the predominance of blood and bloodletting in the erotic fantasies of many psychiatric patients.

The British author Maurice Richardson has described the vampire legend as 'a kind of incestuous, necrophilous, oral-anal-sadistic all-in wrestling match'. The vampire embodies repressed sexual wishes and guilts which come 'from the unconscious world of infantile sexuality'. This view may unsettle some people who have enjoyed reading fictions like *Dracula*, or Sheridan Le Fanu's story *Carmilla*

(1872), which has an unmistakable theme of lesbianism. It is these undercurrents which are the main reason for the vampire's staying power, in the forefront of our supernatural horrors.

DOUGLAS HILL

FURTHER READING: David Bischoff. Vampires of the Night World. *(Ballantine, 1981); R. McNally and V. R. Florescu.* In Search of Dracula. *(New York Graphic Society, 1972); Montague Summers.* Vampire in Europe.

Vegetation Spirits

The earliest human beings known to us, those of the Paleolithic or Old Stone Age (c. 30,000 to 10,000 BC), are generally designated 'food gatherers' by anthropologists; for they either found their food in the form of nuts, berries, and roots, or they hunted animals for it. During the succeeding Neolithic or New Stone Age a great transformation of economic activity occurred, which has aptly been called the 'Neolithic Revolution'. Man gradually changed from being a 'food gatherer' to being a 'food producer'. The two basic factors in this change were the invention of agriculture and the domestication of animals. The origins of agriculture have been much debated by scholars; but no generally agreed conclusions have yet been established about how and where this momentous change in human economy was first achieved. We can only speculate about the likely places (for example, the ancient Near East), where wild corn-bearing grasses might first have been purposely planted and tended by man.

This revolution in his economy had a profound effect upon man's life and thought. It led to the establishment of settled communities, from which emerged the first towns and cities; it prompted the formation of the first

Vegetation deities were crucial to Aztec life as well. Close-up of a mural *Quetzalcoatl Gives Indians the Gift of Maize*, located in the Palace of the Governor, Tlaxcala, Mexico

calendars, since seed-time and harvest had to be predicted; and it promoted the invention of writing and a scribal class, as agrarian transactions grew more complicated and required the keeping of accounts and records. The beginnings of all these institutions have been discerned in the ancient Near East.

But the change to an agrarian way of life also deeply affected man's religious ideas. As an agriculturist, he became intimately involved with the annual cycle of Nature's life. He realized that his existence and well-being depended upon the yearly miracle of the germination of the seed-corn, upon its steady growth and the increase of its fruits until harvest. The process of the seasons took on a new significance for him. He saw it as an annual drama of life and death. For in the Near Eastern lands the cycle of Nature's year has the aspect of a dramatic contest between the forces of life and death. Spring comes quickly, clothing the landscape in verdant green, bedecked by flowers. Under the increasing power of the sun

Opposite page:
Monolith of Coatlicue, the Aztec Mother of the Gods (National Museum of Anthropology and History in Mexico City)

the corn quickly ripens to harvest. But as summer advances and no rain falls, vegetation withers and dies, and the ground seems cursed with sterility and death. Yet from this seeming death, vegetation awakens again next spring to a new life, and the miracle of Nature's resurrection provides mankind once more with food.

Son and Lover

But the early peoples of this area saw in the annual rebirth of vegetation a significance deeper than that of the assurance of their food. For them the truth it intimated was twofold, and inevitably they interpreted it in mythic imagery. The idea of a 'Great Goddess', who was the source of all living things, seems already to have found expression in the Paleolithic era in the many carvings of the female form, showing the maternal attributes grossly exaggerated while the facial features were undelineated. This primitive conception of the 'Great Goddess' was naturally associated with the earth, from which all forms of vegetation grew and within which the dead were laid. The vegetation was thus the offspring of the Earth Mother, and it was easily personified as a divine spirit that manifested itself in the trees and grass, and in the corn.

Hence developed the idea of a divine couple who embodied the fecundity of the earth and the crops which it bore, and upon which man's life depended. But the imagery of mother and son did not completely portray the whole complex of Nature's annual cycle. To give birth to vegetation, the Earth Mother had to be impregnated. A variety of imagery suggested itself: the plunging blade of the plough or the fall of rain. Some lines from the Danaids of the Athenian dramatist Aeschylus (c. 499–458 BC) significantly portray the anthropomorphic

images in which the ancient Greeks envisaged the process: 'Love moves the pure Heaven to wed the Earth; and Love (Eros) takes hold on Earth to join in marriage. And the rain, dropping from the husband Heaven, impregnates Earth, and she brings forth for men pasture for flocks and corn, the life of men.'

From such sexual imagery emerged the concept of a virile god who impregnated the Earth Mother with his seed. The form of this deity could vary between the animal and the human. The bull provided an obvious type-figure, and at Catal Hüyük, the oldest known sanctuary (c. 6000 BC) of the Great Goddess, frescoes of bulls and bulls' horns signified the incorporation into her cult of the

> *The dead Osiris was frequently depicted lying supine, with phallus erect and plants sprouting from his body*

principle of male virility. In Greek mythology Zeus, in the form of a bull, carried off Europa, and the Minotaur (half-man and half-bull) was the offspring of the Queen of Crete, Pasiphae, and a divine bull. In these 'faded myths' were probably preserved folk-memories of the associated cults of 'Great Goddesses' and sacred bulls.

Mythic thought is characteristically imprecise, and it easily embraces ambivalent or contradictory ideas. So it is not surprising to find, in many myths of the ancient Near East, a male deity who is both the son and the lover of a fertility goddess. An example of such complex imagery is succinctly expressed in a title of the Egyptian god Amun-Re, descriptive of his relation to the goddess Nut. 'Bull of his Mother, the first on his field',

he impregnated the goddess who gave him birth.

In his role of vegetation god, the offspring of the Earth Mother, this ambivalent male deity was also a 'dying and rising god.' For he personified the annual death of vegetation in the fierce summer heat and drought of the Near Eastern lands, and its resurrection in the spring. As such he became the subject of a complex of myth and ritual. Lamentations commemorated his death as the vegetation withered and died; ceremonies were performed to ensure his return from death; and joyous festivals acclaimed his resurrection as the new green of reviving vegetation appeared in the spring. From this basic drama of death and resurrection, manifest in Nature each year, there stemmed a rich tradition of idea and fantasy which embodied some of the deepest of human emotions—the instinct for life and the fear of death, sexual love and motherhood, the pathos of early death, aversion from the withering touch of time, aspiration for the assurance of immortality.

Life in the Tomb

The ancient Egyptian god Osiris has been regarded by some scholars, most notably by Sir J. G. Frazer, as the classic example of the dying and rising god of vegetation. Subsequent research has not endorsed the view that this was the original character of Osiris; but the deity certainly became closely associated with fertility and the death and resurrection of the corn. This association was graphically portrayed in Egyptian art and ritual. The dead Osiris was frequently depicted lying supine, with phallus erect and plants sprouting from his body. A similar idea inspired other scenes representing the goddess Isis, in the form of a falcon, impregnating herself on the phallus of the dead Osiris. The meaning of such depictions seems clear: Osiris, as the deification of Nature's life-cycle, retained his fertility even in death, from which he triumphantly rose again.

A more spiritually significant idea motivated the making of 'corn-mummies', which were placed in tombs. The specimen found in the tomb of Tutankhamen consisted of an image of Osiris, constructed of wood and linen, which had been filled with mud from the Nile and planted with corn. It was bandaged like a mummy and placed in a wooden box. Enclosed in bandages and coffin, the seeds in this particular example could not have germinated as they did in less elaborate versions, which sprouted with corn in the warm darkness of the tomb, symbolizing the renewal of life after death. But it is probable that they were intended also to assist, by means of imitative magic, in achieving the resurrection of the dead person, buried in the tomb, to a new life.

The significance which the death and rebirth of the seed-corn, per-sonified in a vegetation god, had for man's hope for immortality, invested the annual drama of the alternation of life and death in Nature with a deep emotive significance. The hope which the corn-mummies signified to the ancient Egyptians was presented anew for Christians in the well-known words of St. Paul: 'But someone will ask, "How are the dead raised? With what kind of body do they come?" You foolish man! What you sow does not come to life unless it dies. And what you sow is not the body which is to be, but a bare kernel, perhaps of wheat or of some other grain . . . So it is with the resurrection of the dead. What is sown is perishable, what is raised is imperishable . . . It is sown a physical body, it is raised a spiritual body' (1 Corinthians, chapter 15).

Baal Avenged

The mystique of the annual death and resurrection of vegetation is seen in its clearest and most dramatic form in the cult of Osiris. But the mythologies of other ancient Near Eastern dying and rising gods better illustrate the connection between the god of vegetation and the fertility goddess: those of Adonis, Tammuz, Baal, and Attis.

'Baal' was a title meaning, in Hebrew, 'possessor' or 'lord' of the land. It was used to designate the Amorite god Hadad ('the thunderer'), who personified the winter rains and their accompanying storms. Since the rain was recognized by the Canaanites as an essential factor in the fertility of the fields and the growth of vegetation, Baal was identified with vegetation in its annual cycle of life and death. The mythology of Baal has become known through the discovery of texts, inscribed on clay tablets, at the site of the ancient city of Ugarit, on the Syrian coast north of Beirut. In these texts, which date from the latter half of the 2nd millennium BC, a triad of deities is concerned in the drama of Nature's year. Baal's sister and lover is the fertility goddess Anat, who is generally depicted nude, with the sexual attributes emphasized. The enemy of Baal is Mot, who is the personification of drought and sterility, and hence of death.

Owing to the fragmentary state of the tablets, it is difficult to reconstruct with certainty the myth which described the relations of these deities. It would seem that Baal, for some obscure reason, had to descend into the realm of Mot. Before departing, he had intercourse with a heifer, from which a bull-calf was born: this bestial act may perhaps relate to the association of a bull cult with Baal, which was a feature of the fertility rites of the Great Goddess, already noted.

The disappearance of Baal caused sterility: 'the furrows in the fields are cracked with drought'. Anat took vengeance on Mot for the death of her lover. Seizing Mot, she 'ripped him open with a sword, winnowed him in a sieve, burned him in the fire, ground him with two millstones, sowed him in a field'. This punishment inflicted on Mot has a curious significance; for it parallels the fate of the corn—some being ground into flour for bread; some being sown as seed. What the action signified in the myth is uncertain; but consequent on it, Baal returns to life. It is possible that since Mot had apparently devoured Baal, the sowing of fragments of Mot, intermixed with Baal, caused the resurrection of the dead god of vegetation. The revival of Baal is symbolized in the myth by poetic imagery: 'the heavens rained oil, the ravines ran with honey'. These myths probably served as a kind of libretto to fertility rites, performed each year to assist the germination of the seed-corn and ensure a good harvest. The licentious nature of such Canaanite rites, involving as they did sacred prostitution, was vehemently denounced by the Hebrew prophets.

Tapestry detail; on the left, one-eyed Odin carrying an axe, with a representation of the tree from which he hung; in the centre, Thor, carrying his symbolic hammer in his right hand; on the right, the fertility god Frey holding an ear of corn, Sweden, Viking (twelfth century)

Youthful Lover

Attis was the youthful lover of Cybele, the great mother goddess of ancient Phrygia. The spring festival of the goddess was mainly a ritual commemoration of the death and resurrection of Attis. There are variant versions of the myth accounting for his death, which seems to have resulted from self-castration. It is difficult to make out a coherent myth and ritual complex from these versions and the rites associated with the cult of Cybele and Attis. The fact that the pine was sacred to the young god might indicate that originally he was a tree spirit; it is interesting in this connection to note that an episode in the legend of Osiris concerns a marvellous tree that quickly grew and enshrined his body. Cybele was served by eunuch priests called galli, who were reported to have buried their severed parts in the earth, perhaps to promote the fertility of the Earth Mother. Similarly suggestive are the repulsive rites of the criobolium and the taurobolium, in which a ram and bull, symbols of male virility, were sacrificed, their blood providing a regenerating baptism for initiates into the mysteries of the goddess.

Some scholars have claimed to find in many religions of the ancient Near East a definite 'myth and ritual' pattern connected with the life-and-death cycle of vegetation. According to them, the king represented the vegetation god at the New Year festival, in which the death and resurrection of the deity was ritually enacted in a series of related episodes. These comprised, besides a dramatic representation of the death and resurrection of the god of vegetation, the recitation or symbolic representation of the myth of creation; a ritual combat, in which the triumph of the god over his enemies was portrayed; a sacred marriage; and a triumphant procession, with the king playing the part of the god, followed by a train of lesser gods.

This 'myth-and-ritual' complex, so it is explained, originated from a primitive custom of killing the king when his physical vigour began to diminish; for, since the fertility of the land was magically connected with his virility, it would be disastrous to have an aged impotent monarch. His youthful successor ensured the continuance of the fecundity of the soil by his marriage with the queen or high priestess. These barbaric rites, it is argued, had been gradually transformed into a ritual death and resurrection of the king, which was celebrated each year. In the subsequent sacred marriage, the queen or priestess represented the fertility goddess. The case for the existence of this 'myth and ritual' pattern has not been generally accepted by scholars as proven. But much evidence concerning the reaction of the ancient peoples of the Near East to the death and rebirth of vegetation does suggest that their kings were deeply involved in the annual fertility rites.

Return of the Corn Maiden

In ancient Greece, the famous Mystery cult of Eleusis witnesses to the mystic significance that men there found in the annual drama of the seed-corn.

Stone mask of Xipe Totec, the Flayed Lord, dressed in the skin of a sacrificial victim. In the festival of Tlacaxipeualiztli a sacrificial victim was skinned alive and a warrior danced dressed in the skin. The ceremony symbolized the bursting of the skin of the maize seed. Mexico, Aztec, Late Post Classic (AD 1300–1521)

The two deities connected with this cult differed notably, however, from those of the Near Eastern cults. Instead of a naturally interdependent pair of fertility goddess and vegetation god, the Eleusinian divinities were related as mother and daughter. Demeter, the corn goddess, was the mother of Persephone, the corn maiden. The myth of the abduction of Persephone by Plouton, the lord of the underworld, provided the rationale or explanation of the secret rites performed at Eleusis. Distracted by the loss of her daughter, Demeter forgot her task as the corn goddess. So the ground grew sterile and famine afflicted the race of men, until the supreme god Zeus was obliged to intervene and bid Plouton restore the corn maiden to her mother. But the restoration could not be complete, because Persephone had tasted a morsel of food in the underworld. Zeus ruled, in consequence, that Persephone should spend two parts of the year above ground with Demeter and one part in Hades with Plouton. The return of Persephone brought fruitfulness again to the fields, which soon waved 'with long ears of corn, and its rich furrows were loaded with grain'. There has been much speculation as to the exact significance of this division of the year between Persephone's stay with her mother and with Plouton, but it is generally agreed that the division relates to the life cycle of the seed-corn—perhaps to the time the seed lies buried in the ground until its emergence in the fresh vigorous upsurge of life in the following spring.

In the Eleusinian Mysteries the death and resurrection of the seed-corn was undoubtedly interpreted as presaging a rebirth to a new and immortal life for those who were initiated. Very little is known of the rites which were performed in the great Telesterion or Hall of the Mysteries at Eleusis; but there is evidence that the culminating revelation made to the initiate, who had been subjected to experiences simulating death, was that of 'a reaped cornstalk'. The meaning of the symbol must surely have then been apparent to him, and perhaps that meaning implied an insight similar to that ascribed to Christ in St. John's gospel (12.24): 'unless a grain of wheat falls into the earth and dies, it remains alone; but if it dies, it bears much fruit'. However that may be, the Homeric Hymn to Demeter, which records the Eleusinian myth, ends with the assurance: 'Happy is he among men upon earth who has seen these mysteries; but he who is uninitiate and who has no part in them, never has lot of like good things once he is dead, down in the darkness and gloom.'

> *The sacred union of Virbius and Diana . . . was intended 'to make the earth gay with the blossoms of spring and the fruits of autumn . . .'*

It was Sir James George Frazer who first showed, in *The Golden Bough*, the enormous influence that agriculture has had upon religion. The titles of some of the volumes that make up the work significantly indicate aspects of the theme: The Dying God; Adonis, Attis, Osiris; Spirits of the Corn and of the Wild. In the first volume of the series, *The Magic Art*, Frazer evokes, in a masterly passage, the memory of the mysterious priest-king who served the goddess Diana in her sacred grove at Nemi. This sinister being bore the title Rex Nemorensis, the 'King of the Wood'. Whoever was bold or desperate enough to challenge the 'ghastly priest', proclaimed his challenge by breaking off a bough of the sacred tree—the 'golden bough', according to certain ancient writers.

The Green One

Frazer set himself the task of explaining this strange institution. After a long and involved investigation of ancient literature and folklore, he concluded that 'at Nemi the King of the Wood personated the oak-god Jupiter and mated with the oak-goddess Diana in the sacred grove'. Originally this priest-king was named Virbius, which Frazer translated as 'the Green One'. The sacred union of Virbius and Diana, or the priestess who impersonated the goddess, was intended 'to make the earth gay with the blossoms of spring and the fruits of autumn, and to gladden the hearts of men and women with healthful offspring'. Frazer identified the mystic golden bough with the mistletoe which, growing on the oak, was believed by ancient peoples to be the life or soul of the tree.

In his quest for the origins of the priest-king of Nemi, Frazer was led to investigate a widespread cult of tree spirits which has been practiced in northern lands to make the corn grow. The custom of the Harvest May, observed by various peasant peoples of Europe, is particularly notable. A large branch of may or hawthorn was brought home with the last load of harvest, and decorated with ears of corn. Sometimes it was fastened to the roof of the farmhouse, remaining there for a year, or planted in the cornfield, with the last sheaf tied to it. To those who made it, the Harvest May evidently embodied or represented the spirit of vegetation, upon whose fructifying influence next year's harvest depended.

It was from this primitive belief in vegetation spirits that the custom of the maypole took its origins. The maypole, which the Puritan writer Phillip Stubbes perceptively, if humourlessly, condemned as a 'stinking idol', was the symbol of the vegetation god.

The institution of the May Queen, so essentially associated with the may-pole, preserves an ancient folk-memory of the sacred marriage to promote the fertility of the herds and fields. In the May Day customs the spirit of vegetation was also represented by the Green Man or Jack in the Green. At Knuts-ford in Cheshire, the Green Man still leads the annual procession of the May Queen—a strange and somewhat eerie figure, completely enveloped in greenery.

Frazer collected a mass of evidence from the folklore of many lands expressive of a sense of tragedy at the time of harvest. Sometimes the last sheaf of corn has been ritually threshed and treated as a sacrificial victim, recalling perhaps a human sacrifice that was once made on the harvest field to the god of vegetation. The fate of the corn in its transformation to bread has also been seen as the passion of the Corn Spirit. A Danish folktale describes the sufferings of the rye: 'In the autumn you will be sown, deeply buried in earth; in the spring you will rise; in the summer you will be parched in the sun, drenched in the rain, then cut and dried, carted to the barn and threshed; then, carted to the mill and ground.'

Today in many medieval churches the so-called 'foliate heads' still witness to our ancestors' concern for the spirit of vegetation. These strange emblems, carved in wood or stone, depict a human head with leaves and tendrils sprouting from the mouth and ears.

There are no inscriptions to explain their meaning; doubtless they needed none for people whose lives were so closely bound up with the fields and woods. A faint memory of these old beliefs lingers on in the 'corn dollies' made for harvest festivals. They are the last relics of a tradition that reaches far back to the dying and rising gods of the ancient Near East.

S. G. F. BRANDON

FURTHER READING: J. G. Frazer. The Golden Bough. *(St Martin's Press, 1980 reprint); E. O. James.* The Cult of the Mother Goddess: Seasonal Feasts and Festivals. *(Barnes and Noble, 1959 and 1963 respectively); E. O. James.* The Tree of Life. *(Brill, Leiden, 1966); S. H. Hooke ed.* Myth Ritual and Kingship. *(Oxford Univ. Press, 1958); John C. Gibson.* Canaanite Myths and Legends. *(Attic Press, 1978); G. E. Mylonas.* Eleusis and the Eleusinian Mysteries. *(Princeton Univ. Press, 1961); Findhorn Foundation.* Findhorn Garden. *(Harper & Row, 1975).*

In legend, the werewolf is a living person who has the magical power to change his or her shape.

Wendigo

The Wendigo is a malevolent spirit in the mythology of the Algonquian-speaking peoples of North America, especially dangerous because of its cannibalistic nature, manifesting either as a ogre (qv) or by possession of a human individual. The Wendigo has particularly bleak associations, being identified with the privations of winter and the threat of hunger. The poet, Henry Longfellow, lists the Wendigo as one of the creatures to be destroyed by Hiawatha when the hero is told to—

'Cleanse the earth from all that harms it …. Slay all monsters and magicians, All the Wendigoes, the giants …'

A case came to trial in December 1897 in Ontario where a man was accused of shooting his father thinking that he was destroying the Wendigo who was threatening the group. His defence was that he believed he was firing at a spirit and not a human being. He was found guilty of manslaughter.

Werewolf

In legend, the werewolf is a living person who has the magical power to change his or her shape. In its bestial form it is a terrorizer, a killer, an eater of human flesh. These two elements—metamorphosis and murder—form the basis, and much of the substance, of the legend. But the werewolf's family tree is ancient, vast, and has many spreading branches. Some branches lead to the realm of revenants (those who have returned from the dead), where ghosts and vampires walk; others lead to evil sorcery, witchcraft, and diabolism.

The idea of the werewolf is based on the acknowledgement of 'the beast in man'—our dual nature, which was no doubt as much of a commonplace in the Stone Age as in our Age of Psychoanalysis. Primitive mythology, naturally, makes much of the concept. Sometimes we are said to be descended from original, semidivine animals, and sometimes the primitive feels a mystical and total identity with an animal, in the religious belief called 'totemism.' In folktale, the culture heroes appear in indeterminate, human or animal form, like Coyote and the other tricksters of American Indian myth. And there are numerous tales of intermarriage, when a humanized animal takes a human mate, perhaps producing offspring with the power of shape-shifting. These and other elements of primitive myth established the widespread belief in metamorphosis. When the assumed shape was that of a dangerous animal, a carnivorous enemy of man, the element of murder enters the picture as well, and the werewolf idea begins to emerge.

But not only the werewolf emerges. The world's folklore is full of other were-animals. ('Were' may come from the Old English word for 'man', and the corresponding terms in other languages are mostly similar compounds meaning 'man-wolf'.) Even those lands where the wolf is or was native have tales of other were-creatures: were-bears in Russia and Scandinavia, for instance. Lands without wolves have tales of were-hyenas, were-lions, were-crocodiles, were-jackals. In 1933 a respectable British doctor reported that he had seen two Africans turn themselves into jackals during a ceremony. But the were-leopard dominates the African tradition, assisted by sensationalized tales of the secret cult of the Leopard Men, which gained much attention earlier in this century.

Similarly, were-tigers have been noted in the supernatural lore of India and other Asian lands; were-jaguars and sometimes were-snakes terrorize South American tribesmen. And though occasionally the were-animal is not of the most ferocious species (the Chinese have tales of were-foxes, for instance, rather like the cats or hares that witches are said to become, in European tales), in general the metamorphosis and murder theme predominates.

The Beast in Man

Ancient civilizations provide a number of antecedents for the werewolf. The maenads of ancient Greece flaunted the 'beast in man' in their ecstasies, and apparently sometimes wore wolf masks during their hunts through the forests. Also from Greece comes the legend of Lycaeon, a man who became over-zealous in his worship of Zeus and sacrificed a child to the god, making an offering of the child's flesh. Zeus changed him into a wolf, as punishment. But later there grew up an ecstatic cult of the worship of Zeus Lycaeus, in which the participants wore wolf masks.

Several notable Greek writers, including Herodotus and Plato, gave credence, or at least currency, to the werewolf idea, and so helped its spread into Europe in later centuries. In ancient Rome, Pliny discussed the idea seriously, Petronius mocked it in the *Satyricon*, and Ovid drew the Lycaeon story into the *Metamorphoses*.

Perhaps all the beast-men and wild men, found in folklore all over the world, are also distant kindred of the werewolf: the satyrs and centaurs of Greece, the Abominable Snowman, the human children fostered by animals, as in Kipling's story of Mowgli.

But the metamorphosis and murder is absent, or of minor importance, in such tales. Mowgli is not a werewolf, nor Tarzan a were-ape. More explicitly and directly behind our idea of the werewolf are two strands of folklore from the chillier regions of Europe. Northern peoples generally seem to have viewed the wolf with a fear and hate bordering on hysteria—the kind usually reserved for the worst supernatural monsters. Of course, the wolf was always a dangerous predator that

Drawing of a werewolf in woodland at night. Main illustration for the story *The Werewolf Howls*. Internal illustration from the pulp magazine *Weird Tales* (November 1941, vol. 36, no. 2, page 38)

Werewolf, Lucas Cranach the Elder (1472–1553)

Canada (a man was attacked by wolves in Ontario in 1963), but probably not for long. The hysterical urge to exterminate wolves is well described by the Canadian writer Farley Mowat, in *Cry Wolf,* a book that offers facts about the animal which counter its traditional typecasting as an evil, voracious monster.

No doubt that view will persist, and will pursue the wolf into extinction. Our responses have been conditioned by centuries of horror stories about wolves. Invariably these stories concern the wolf's cruel ferocity and murderousness, and his insatiable hunger. The Bible compares false prophets to 'ravening wolves' in sheep's clothing. A comparable disguise was used by the wolf in the tale of 'Little Red Riding Hood', which is part of the furniture of the mind of nearly every Western European and North American child. There are a number of old wives' tales of hunters caught out in the northern woods as darkness falls, hearing that echoing howl in the distance, approaching; or of that famous Russian sled, from which members of a family are thrown one at a time in vain sacrifices to a pursuing pack. In common catchphrases, villains grin wolfishly, and gluttons wolf down their food. Above all, there is the Fenris wolf, the most terrible monster of Northern mythology, and the eventual killer of Odin himself.

The Fenris wolf points to the second strand of folklore that has contributed directly to the werewolf legend. Scandinavian and Teutonic myth and folklore are and murder. The Norse gods took animal form even more often, it seems, than those of the Greeks. Scandinavian heroes are also often shape-shifters: one Bodvar Bjarhi took the shape of a bear to fight in a great battle in Denmark, recounted in the Norse sagas, and a bear motif appears in the tales of many other heroes. Clearly there is a link here with the

cared little whether its dinner was a prize sheep or the shepherd. But there is more to the fear of the wolf than a mere antipathy to a beast of prey. The wolf seems to be regarded by Europeans as somehow in itself demonic. Wolves are seminocturnal, usually greyish in colour, and move in an almost ghostly silence. They have slanting eyes that glow yellow-green in moonlight, red in reflected firelight. And their chilling, bansheelike howl completes the eerie picture.

So the wolf unsettles us, on some deep atavistic level. Which may explain why even today men seek to exterminate this beast, while intend-ing only to control other predators. The wolf has vanished from America (except Alaska), Britain, Germany, Switzerland, and France. The French suffered terribly from wolves in the past, which explains the abundance of werewolf (*loup-garou*) tales from that country. In 1963 it was thought that a small pack of wolves had been sighted in France; and though some people believed it was just a pack of half-wild dogs, the mere thought of wolves returning to France made international headlines.

Wolves are still said to roam in eastern Europe, in Russia, and in Spain and Portugal. They exist also in 'berserkers' of Scandinavian legend—the warriors who fell into a battle madness that made them preternaturally powerful, causing them to roar like beasts and foam at the mouth. We use 'berserk' to mean that kind of maniacal fury, but it is said to derive from the Old Norse for 'bear-shirt', referring tithe fur garments of these warriors. It was not much of an imaginative step (for their victims especially) to believe that the berserkers not only released the 'beast within' but actually transformed themselves into wild beasts.

The werewolf's impressive European ancestry became focused in the Christian era's dark centuries of superstition and witch hunting. The old horror tales of those centuries showed the witches in possession of the shape-shifting power, conferred on them by Satan. The witches were believed to change into cats, hares, toads, and the like. But the ancient wolf fear rose up too, became projected onto Satan's minions, and led to the idea that werewolves were witches who chose to take wolf form, ravaging the countryside as part of their diabolic duties. So the Renaissance witch trials recorded many gory accounts of werewolfism, especially in France and Germany. Often the 'confessions' of witches asserted that whole sabbaths changed into wolf packs; one old Latvian tale described a 12 day march at Christmastide of thousands of demonic werewolves, led by Satan himself in wolf form.

Sometimes the demonologists argued that werewolves were actual demons or imps, rather than metamorphosed human witches. But a few clearer minds, like that of Reginald Scot, author of *Discovery of Witchcraft* (1584), suggested that shape-shifting was unlikely, that certain kinds of insanity might lead people to imagine that they became wolves. Usually such insanity was ascribed to demonic possession and so although the mental illness known as lycanthropy was recognized quite early, the recognition had little effect on the superstition.

A Belt of Wolfskin

Out of the sixteenth-century obsession with witches and like horrors come some of the world's most famous documented accounts of 'werewolves'. In 1573 a French village was terrorized by a monster that had killed and partially eaten several children. Then a group of villagers rescued another child from an attack by a huge wolf which, they swore, had the face of a local recluse named Gilles Gamier. Gamier was duly induced, by the usual means, to 'confess' to being a werewolf. The

> *In 1573 a French village was terrorized by a monster that had killed and partially eaten several children.*

authorities, who seemed especially incensed that he had engaged in some of his gruesome feasts on meatless Fridays, ordered him to be burned alive.

Even more fearful was the punishment meted out to Peter Stubb, or Stump, in Germany in 1589. Stubb's 'confession' revealed him explicitly as a diabolist werewolf: he shifted his shape by means of a magical 'girdle' or belt of wolfskin, given to him by the Devil. And as a wolf, Stubb went forth on the Devil's work, to wreak 'his malice on men, women and children'. Apparently he had been doing so for some 25 years before he was caught. He sometimes killed livestock, and occasionally men whom he disliked; but he principally preyed on women and girl children, whom (he claimed) he raped, killed, and ate. As a sideline he committed a good deal of ordinary if sinful fornication, as well as incest with his sister and his daughter, and capped his crimes, as the story goes, by killing and eating his own son. Finally he was captured, but the wolfskin belt was not found, which seems to have proved its diabolic origin to the witch-hunters' satisfaction: clearly the Devil had taken it back. Stubb died fearfully, under the most terrible tortures and mutilations.

Somewhat less ugly was the story of Jean Grenier, a clearly mentally defective youth accused of being a werewolf in southwest France in 1603. He brought it on himself, boasting of having killed and eaten many girls; and since several children had been killed in the area, he was believed and brought to trial. He claimed that he shifted his shape by means of a magic ointment and a wolfskin cloak given to him by a 'black man', whom he called 'Maitre de la Foret'. The judges sensibly decided that Grenier was suffering from the mental illness of lycanthropy, though they added that it was caused by demonic possession. Grenier was merely imprisoned for life, in a monastery.

Tell-Tale Signs

Since the days of medieval superstition and demonology, the werewolf legend—like so many others—has become a tangled web of older semi-pagan folklore and Christian strands of belief. But out of the tangle can be extracted a fairly clear picture of the werewolf's nature and habits, as he is known in modern European and American lore, and in those Hollywood films in which Lon Chaney Jr. created the Wolfman.

The creature's appearance is fairly standardized, in the legends. When there are any visual clues that a man is a werewolf, they include extreme hairiness, straight eyebrows meeting over the nose, strong and clawlike fingernails, small, flat ears, or sometimes pointed ears, and the third finger on each hand at least as long as the second.

In wolf form, the werewolf tends generally to be merely an extra-large and ferocious wolf. But in some traditions (including the French) the shape-shifting is not complete, which adds to the werewolf's detectability. Gilles Garnier was said to have retained his human features while in wolf form; other tales speak of werewolves with human hands or feet. In the early twentieth century, according to the French folklorist Claude Seignolle, a French farmer told of seeing two great wolves who conversed in human voices and who took snuff from a box produced from under the tail of one of them.

But it is rare for a werewolf, after the transformation, to be mainly humanoid—as is the Hollywood Wolfman, who after shape-shifting is simply a man with extra hair, teeth and agility. Even in the Middle Ages, when a hairy man began howling and saying he was a wolf, the experts generally agreed that he was mentally ill, suffering from lycanthropy. If he was a werewolf, those experts knew, he would be able to change into a wolf. Still, controversy often arose over occasional lycanthropes who claimed that they did change into wolves, but wore their hair on the inside. In northern Italy in 1541, one such claimant died under the knives of officials probing for proof of his statement.

These were the same kind of officials who generally agreed that werewolves had made a pact with Satan, who then bestowed upon them the power of metamorphosis. But it is clear that the Christian authorities were trying to patch much older werewolf beliefs onto their systematized accounts of devils. They did not succeed entirely: the seams show. For it is obviously

odd and inconsistent that a would-be servant of Satan, who signed that pact, should ask only for the power of shape-shifting. One would have to be a Satanist of very limited ambition to want to be merely a werewolf; after all, any rank-and-file witch could change her shape—as the accounts of sixteenth century witch trials tell us—and a witch could also raise storms, wither crops, fly on a broomstick or other conveyance, and cast a multitude of useful spells.

Of course, much laborious medieval argument arose over whether an actual metamorphosis took place, whether Satan placed the minion's soul in the 'effigy' of a wolf, or whatever. More rewarding, however, are the older, non-Christian ideas about how a werewolf

And Paracelsus wrote that particularly evil, bestial men might return after death as werewolves.

becomes one in the first place. Several of these seem to involve the summoning of a demon to confer the power, but the being who is summoned is quite often obviously an elemental, a pagan spirit (like Jean Grenier's Maitre de la Foret).

How to Become a Werewolf

This conjuring up of an evil spirit is done by a complex ceremony, involving a magic circle, a fire, an incantation or two, application of magical ointment (like the witches' flying ointment) to the nude body, and final donning of a wolfskin cloak or belt. But the shape-shifting power can, in other traditions, come more easily. Sometimes it can come whether you want it or not—if you infringe some taboo. Italian folklore says that if you were conceived at the time of the new

moon or if you sleep outdoors on a Friday under a full moon—you will become a werewolf. An obscure flower will, if eaten, confer the power of metamorphosis, according to Balkan legend; so will drinking from a stream where a wolf pack has drunk. Drinking water from a wolf's paw-print, eating its brains, or eating the flesh of a rabid wolf are do-it-yourself magic for the would-be shape-shifter.

A few ancient writers thought that the power might be hereditary, while others thought that it might grow within a person who lived an especially evil life. An old French tradition tells of priests putting curses on criminals that forced them to be werewolves for seven years. And Paracelsus wrote that particularly evil, bestial men might return after death as werewolves.

The ghost werewolf occurs in a few other places. England's cruel King John was said to have risen after death as a werewolf. And several ghost wolves seen in Britain during the nineteenth century had human features, which identified them as belonging to this species. It seems that this minor aspect of the legend affected Hollywood: the Wolfman was a resurrected corpse, turned into a werewolf by an accidental combining of magical elements like the plant wolf's-bane and a full moon. But the living men with shape-shifting powers vastly outnumber the revenants, in werewolf traditions.

The technique by which the metamorphosis is accomplished is often the same as that by which the power has been acquired: so many legends say that the change requires, each time, the full ritual and summoning of the evil spirit mentioned before. But as always, folklore likes its simple magic too. Often the mere act of putting on the wolfskin belt will cause the change. In a few gruesome variants, the belt is supposed to be of human skin, preferably from a criminal executed on the gibbet. Some French tales say the werewolf must immerse himself in water, besides putting on the belt, in order to change—though elsewhere in Europe, the werewolf is supposed to exhibit a fear of water, a clear transference from the 'hydrophobia' idea of rabies.

Quite often the werewolf changes by stripping himself under a full moon and urinating in a circle on the earth, a technique used by Guy Endore for the hero of his excellent novel *Werewolf of Paris*, as definitive a work for this body of legend as Bram Stoker's *Dracula* is for the vampire. In a few tales, and in Hollywood's films, the full moon alone may affect the change; in a few others, though not as yet in films, stripping nude and rolling about on the ground may do the trick.

Changing back to human form may require the repetition of certain of these actions, like the rolling about or the immersion in water. Some legends say that the werewolf changes back automatically, at daybreak. Most tales agree that the creature instantly changes back to human form if it is injured or killed. From this idea come all those stories in which a hunter

shoots and wounds a marauding wolf, later to learn that some local person has suffered an injury to the same part of the anatomy.

The legends disagree widely on how a werewolf may be injured or killed. In many European tales, it can be caught or destroyed by the same means that would be used against an ordinary wolf. Peter Stubb, for instance, was pursued by men and dogs, and captured when he changed to human form in an attempt to outwit the pursuers. No one seemed surprised that he was as easily killed as any man; many other werewolves in European tales have been simply shot, clubbed or stabbed to death.

In other traditions, however, it seems that the power of the creature must be opposed by some kind of magic. In those traditions where werewolves are believed to be possessed by demons, the holy magic of the Church goes into action, to exorcize them. So a Catholic priest in French Canada is said, in an old tale, to have rescued a man from a *loup-garou* by magically changing it into its human form. And an old legend from colonial New England mentions a simpler exorcism,

when a colonist drove off a pack of werewolves simply by speaking the name of Jesus.

Otherwise, rather more pagan magic is mingled with Christian elements in the werewolf antidotes. In England, Scotland and parts of France the creature is said to be immune to ordinary bullets; although, like vampires and witches, he can be killed by a silver bullet, especially if it is first consecrated in a church. In some instances a cure will be effected if the werewolf is called by his human name, or if he is called three times by his Christian name. French lore says that you may cure the *loup-garou* by taking three drops of blood from him, or merely pricking him to bleeding point, when he is in wolf form; it is not clear how

John Barrymore played the title characters in 1920's *Dr. Jekyll and Mr. Hyde*, with Hyde being an animalistic monster harder to control with each transformation.

The Lupins

In many parts of France, but more especially perhaps in Britanny, Le Meneur des Loups is a well-known figure. He is generally considered to be a wizard, who when the werewolves of the district have met and sit in a hideous circle round a fire kindled in the heart of some forest, leads forth the howling pack and looses them on to their horrid chase. Sometimes he himself assumes the form of a wolf, but speaks with human voice. Gathering his flock around him he gives them directions, telling them what farm-towns are ill-guarded that night, what flocks, what herds, are negligently kept, which path the lonely wayfarer setting out from the inn is taking.

In Normandy tradition tells of certain fantastic beings known as lupins or lubins. They pass the night chattering together and tattling in an unknown tongue. They take their stand by the walls of country cemeteries, and howl dismally at the moon. Timorous and fearful of man they will flee away scared at a footstep or distant voice. In some districts, however, they are fierce and of the werewolf race, since they are said to scratch up the graves with their hands, and gnaw the poor dead bones.

Montague Summers,
The Werewolf

you get close enough to him, in safety. And those who become werewolves involuntarily can cure themselves, it is said, if they have the strength of character to abstain from human flesh for nine years.

Monster from the Mind's Deeps

A fragment of fact is to be found at the roots of the werewolf tradition. It has long been recognized that the mental illness known as lycanthropy is associated with a pathological condition in which the sufferer believes himself to be a wild beast and, as the old case histories show, develops a taste for raw or putrid meat, a desire to howl and run naked through the woods, and sometimes a wish to kill, rape and eat young girls. Although it is a rare malady, it may not have been so rare in past centuries; or perhaps other, more common types of sex murderers and child rapists of the past were assumed to be lycanthropes, the more so because such killings often involve an element of mutilation which might make Europeans think of wolves. Assuredly the werewolf is just as sexual a figure as the vampire. But he lacks the sado-erotic subtlety of the vampire: werewolves are crude rapists and murderers, with a few ghoulish or cannibalistic overtones.

Despite this basis of fact, the werewolf belongs rather in the realm of sado-masochistic fantasies. Robert Eisler has thrown some interesting light on these connections, in a theory based firmly on Jungian ideas. Eisler tries to trace the idea of the werewolf back to prehistory, seeing its origin in a primeval clash of cultures between peaceable, vegetarian early man and the brutal, fur-wearing, carnivorous creature that he was forced (by, say, an Ice Age) to become. The clash left scars on the collective unconscious that have still not healed.

Even in this over-simplified form of Eisler's theory, the argument cannot

be easily dismissed. The werewolf is a monster of the unconscious, one to which folklore and superstition formerly gave fleshly reality and occasionally still do, in modern times: a French farmer in 1930 was accused of changing into a wolf at night; and in 1946 in America a Navaho Indian reservation was terrorized by a murderous beast which was widely reported as a werewolf. (Both Navaho and French traditions are rich in werewolf tales.)

But today the legend has generally retreated to a more subjective reality, without losing any of its horror. Nandor Fodor, the American psychologist and psychical researcher, has collected a number of dreams reported by people under psychoanalysis in which the werewolf theme—metamorphosis and murder—was brutally explicit. 'The old, savage lycanthropic beliefs have been relegated to our dream life where they are still active . . .' Fodor comments, 'the transformation is used symbolically as self-denunciation for secret deeds, fantasies, or desires.'

Coming full circle, these psychological insights merely confirm that age-old and universal truth about the inner duality of man, the ravening beast within each of us. As Lord Byron put it:

Lycanthropy
I comprehend, for without
  transformation
Men become wolves on any slight
  occasion.

History as well as folklore shows that many of us are more than likely to let the beast take over, in an inner 'shape-shifting'.

DOUGLAS HILL

FURTHER READING: B. Copper. The Werewolf: in Legend, Fact and Art. *(Hale, 1977); Robert Eisler.* Man Into Wolf. *(Ross-Erikson, 1978); Montague Summers.* The Werewolf. *(Citadel Press, 1973);* I. Woodward. The Werewolf Delusion. *(Paddington).*

Yeti

Known to the Tibetans as the Yeti or 'mountain spirit', the Abominable Snowman of the Himalayas was first documented by Buddhists. It was depicted as a large man — or apelike creature covered with reddish brown hair and with massive jaw and arms reaching beneath its knees. The beast is named from the Tibetan metohkangmi, the word metoh meaning 'foul' and kangmi 'snowman'. Popular interest in the creature began after a Greek photographer N. A. Tombazi, a member of the British Geological Survey took photographs of a strange manlike creature in the Himalayas in 1925, and burgeoned following pictures taken in 1951 by British climber, Eric Shipton, on Mt. Everest. In January 2013 a Yeti 'sighting' was filmed by an 11-year-old Russian schoolboy when he was with two friends in woods about 18 miles from the Siberian coal mining city of Leninsk-Kuznetskiy, after the boys had spotted massive tracks in the snow; the authenticity of the images has yet to be verified.

For Buddhists the Yeti is sometimes said to be a guardian spirit and is associated with Chen-re-zi, the god of mercy. Another tradition is that it is a creature through which the human soul passes following death, the creature being a link between life and death.

Zombies

One cannot live long in Haiti without hearing talk of zombies, dead bodies brought back to a half-life by magic, and many stories about them have appeared in print. In 1939, for

Opposite page:
Yeti Mask in Kathmandu

Thousands of characterized participants marched on the main avenues of Mexico City as part of the traditional Zombie Walk on 3 November, 2012.

instance, Zora Hurston published a now classic account of a young girl from a well-to-do family who was discovered four years after her death working as a slaver in a shop; she was rescued by French nuns and placed in a nunnery.

The tale was still current in Haiti twenty years later, with several additions: four or five quite different towns were named as the place where she had been found, and some said that her rescuers had been Baptists. They also declared that she had been recognized on account of her bent neck, the result of her having been buried in a coffin too small for her, and by a scar on her foot made by a candle which had overturned and burned her during the wake. But these distinguishing marks are first known in a story told

to the writer Alfred Metraux in about 1950. It concerned a young woman who over-brusquely turned down the amorous advances of a houngan, or Voodoo priest, who bewitched her in revenge, dug her up after her presumed death and used her as a zombie until the Catholic antisuperstition campaign caused him to set her loose.

Whatever the original truth of these stories, their combination has produced something approaching a myth which will probably be gaining credence 100 years from now, because of its apparently factual detail and its compact sense of the superstitions involved. It is certain anyhow that few stories told about zombies are to be taken literally.

Equally important, Haitians delight in telling tall stories about things

supernatural, which serve to amaze their audience and even to convince themselves, if only for a moment. A magistrate, for instance, told a convincing story about a Catholic priest who went blind after seeing a troupe of zombies in the hills, remarking that one shouldn't laugh at such matters. But he immediately followed up his cautionary tale with an eye-witness account of a corpse being dug out of its grave and then re-animated, which was a mere hoax: he examined the grave the following day and found a pipe leading from it to the air so that the supposed corpse—the houngan's accomplice—could breathe before his exhumation.

Few people have actually seen zombies. The following incident was said to have occurred in 1959, and was vouched for by a Catholic priest. (It must be remembered, however, that Voodoo and its superstitions are the great enemy of the Church in Haiti, and that even the most upright of men will slander his enemy in a good cause.) A zombie had come wandering into the village where he lived, entered the courtyard of a house and promptly had his hands tied together by the owner, who took him to the police station. The police wished to have nothing to do with such an ominous creature, and so he was left outside the station for some hours, chewing at his bonds, until he was given saltwater to drink—the instant cure for zombification. He then found his voice again and told his name. His aunt, who was living in the village, was sent for: she not only recognized him but declared she had seen him dead and buried four years previously.

The Catholic priest also arrived on the scene and learnt from the man that he had been one of a large number of zombies set to work by the houngan who had enchanted them. This announcement frightened the police even more, and they sent word to the houngan that he could have his zombie back for a consideration. Two days later, however, the man died, and it was generally presumed that the houngan had murdered him for having spilt the beans. He was arrested, but his wife fled into the hills with the remaining zombies.

The educated classes also tell of zombies, as in Metraux's account of a monsieur whose car broke down outside the house of a houngan. The houngan, assuring him that the matter was no mere accident, invited him inside and showed him a zombie, in whom the monsieur recognized a great friend, dead some six months previously. Full of pity the monsieur offered the zombie a drink, but was stopped

by the houngan who warned him of terrible dangers if he did so.

Return to the Grave

Perhaps the most sensational zombie tale is the one recounted by W. B. Seabrook, about a number of zombies owned by a houngan called Joseph and looked after by his wife. One day, not realizing what she was doing, she gave them salted biscuits to eat. Awoken from their deathly trance and knowing themselves for the walking corpses they were, they made straight for the cemetery, brushing aside all who would stop them. There they hurled themselves upon their graves and tried to dig themselves back into

The most feared consequence of releasing a zombie from his bondage is that he will revenge himself physically and magically upon his owner.

the earth, but turned into carrion as they did so.

The most feared consequence of releasing a zombie from his bondage is that he will revenge himself physically and magically upon his owner. Those who own zombies thus make a point of treating them with great harshness—another point which they have in common with the mentally deranged, for it is normal practice in Haiti to beat lunatics and keep them frightened. The parallel is in fact recognized obliquely by all who claim knowledge of how to make a man into a zombie: there are two major ways, by poison and by enchantment. The plants usually cited as poison are manchineel, whose applelike fruit was often used by resentful slaves in plantation days to kill their owners and their livestock, and datura, the thorn apple, which contains atropine,

and belladonna or deadly nightshade. A further poison can be made from the legendary three drops which escape from the nose of a corpse hung upside down.

Besides these, houngans also prepare a number of leaf powders of different kinds with various magical and, it is said, pharmacological properties. One of these powders, containing pepper wood, is very effective in bringing on possessions by the gods. The powder seems to have no effect other than to stimulate the mucous membranes of the nose, but this is enough to trigger off a dissociation when people are highly suggestible, as they are during a ceremony. It is quite possible, therefore, that such a powder used in the right context can magically zombify a man, by entrapping his soul and leaving him with nothing but his body (called the corpse body in Haitian parlance) and his spirit, also termed the zombie.

Spider into Zombie

Initiates into Voodoo pass through a similar state but with proper safeguards. To become possessed by a god their souls must first be displaced or, as we should say, they must be dissociated. During their initiation, their souls are incubated and finally transferred into a sacred vessel called the *pot de tête*, or head-pot, where they are safe from the attacks of evil-doers and under the protection of the gods. At their death, a rite called *dessounin* is practiced which sends their spirits into the waters of death and again captures their souls in a head-pot to await their spiritual resurrection. An initiate is thus a purified zombie whose activity when possessed is controlled by a god, not a magician.

Significantly enough, the *dessounin* rite is copied by those who want a dying man's zombie. This is done by

136

MAN, MYTH, AND MAGIC

placing a pot, containing twenty-one seeds of pois congo and a length of string knotted twenty-one times, under the pillow of the moribund. After his death the string turns into a spider, and the pot containing it is placed in a dark room. To turn the spider into the dead man's zombie all you need do is to knock three times at the door, taking care to stand with your back to it, and to threaten it with a whip when you give it its orders.

In southern Haiti this kind of zombie is known as a vivi: it is the equivalent of a jinn trapped in a bottle. Another way of making a vivi is to exchange a man's soul while he is still alive for that of a lizard, chicken, butterfly or other small animal. The man is no wiser for the substitution, but the animal which embodies his soul cannot die, and merely vanishes if an attempt is made to kill it. The word 'soul' is probably a misnomer here: a better word is 'talent', for it is men talented in law, accountancy, business, or some such skill who are sought for as zombies, and for whom the dessounin rite is practiced even if they are not initiates into Voodoo proper.

In any case, it is difficult to tell a vivi from a baka, that monster of the supernatural created by black magic to bring luck, power or wealth. Both have to be served in the proper manner or their owner is destroyed by their ungoverned force; both are best invoked in cemeteries. One kind of zombie can be made of a man long dead (by whipping his grave with sticks of pois congo) and is used in several branches of magic: for instance a tired prostitute can have her private parts inhabited by such a 'mort' or dead man, paradoxically to liven them up and make her clients come back for more.

It is to stop this kind of zombification that people enter into Voodoo, have their souls placed in head-pots and undergo the *dessounin* rite. But even this is not enough to stop the corpse answering the magician's voice as it lies in its grave, and being turned into a zombie. In certain parts of Haiti, therefore, the corpse is buried face down with its mouth full of earth, or its lips are sewn together; sometimes a knife is placed in its hand with which it can defend itself. In other places sesame seed is scattered in the grave so that the ghost will be eternally occupied in counting how many there are. As a last resort the corpse is strangled or shot through the head.

Zombies thus come in two major forms: as a body without a soul, and as a soul without a body. These last are not easily distinguishable from magical spells, and both from confidence tricks. The word zombie itself, however, comes from the Arawak Indian term *zemi*, a god or a spirit, which also lies at the origin of the name Baron Samedi, god of the dead: by which we may infer that a zombie is properly to be understood in religious terms, as a body resurrected by spiritual means. It is not impossible for such means to be used for profane ends, nor that a man can truly exist as a body without a soul. So far, however, this is still a moot point.

FRANCIS HUXLEY

FURTHER READING: Zora Hurston. Tell My Horse. (Lippincott, 1938); Francis Huxley. The Invisibles. (Humanities, 1966); Alfred Métraux. Voodoo in Haiti. (Schocken, 1972); W. B. Seabrook. The Magic Island. (Folcroft, 1977).

Banquet with Corpses

In the centre of the room was an elegantly set table with damask cloth, flowers, glittering silver. Four men, also in evening clothes, but badly fitting, were already seated at this table. There were two vacant chairs at its head and foot. The seated men did not arise when the girl in her bride-clothes entered on her husband's arm. They sat slumped down in their chairs and did not even turn their heads to greet her . . .

As she sat down mechanically in the chair to which Toussel led her, seating himself facing her, with the four guests ranged between them, two on either side, he said, in an unnatural strained way, the stress increasing as he spoke:

'I beg of you . . . to forgive my guests there . . . seeming rudeness. It has been a long time . . . since . . . they have . . . tasted wine . . . sat like this at table . . . with so fair a hostess . . . But, ah, presently . . . they will drink with you, yes . . . lift . . . their arms, as I lift mine . . . clink glasses with you . . . more . . . they will arise and . . . dance with you . . . more . . . they will.'

Near her, the black fingers of one silent guest were clutched rigidly around the fragile stem of a wine-glass, tilted, spilling. The horror pent up in her overflowed. She seized a candle, thrust it close to the slumped, bowed face, and saw the man was dead. She was sitting at a banquet table with four propped-up corpses.

W. B. Seabrook, *The Magic Island*

Opposite page:
A former member of Tonton Macoute displays a cross and skull pendant in Haiti

Glossary

Abstruse   Hard to understand, puzzling.

Alacrity   Eagerness and the ability to conceptualize quickly.

Amalgam   A combination made up of different elements or traits.

Amatory   Actions and feelings of love and desire.

Apparition   An image or figure of a spirit or ghost.

Baleful   Containing hostility, harm, or wickedness.

Barrows   A large mound of earth and stones covering an ancient grave.

Burlesque   Played out with exaggeration for comic effect.

Dogmatism   Believing that a set of rules or doctrine is true without questioning it.

Eminent   High ranking, greatly respected, especially in a particular field.

Exuberance   A feeling of great excitement and positive energy.

Formidable   Powerful and difficult to the point of causing fear or respect.

Funerary   Pertaining to ceremonies for burying the dead.

Grotesque   Hideous and shockingly ugly.

Harbinger   A creature, person, or occurrence that signals an upcoming event.

Hominid   An upright, two-footed primate; usually a person, but also a creature bearing a resemblance to a human.

Impudence   Being rude, cocky, or bold to the point of being offensive.

Lamentably   With the quality of being sad, unfortunate, or regrettable.

Malevolence   Action that is wicked, in the spirit of wrong-doing.

Pernicious   Harmful, even deadly.

Personifications   Seeing and assigning human characteristics to something that is not human, such as animals, spirits, inanimate objects, or ideas.

Pilfering   Stealing by small degrees.

Placate   To calm or soothe someone who is angry, or who is prone to anger.

Polytheistic   Having a belief system that includes multiple gods and goddesses.

Presage   A sign or foreshadowing that indicates something (often bad) is about to occur.

Progenitor   The original ancestor of a given family or people.

Propitiated   Having gained the good opinion of a person, deity, or spirit by doing something to please them.

Reminiscent   Something that calls to mind or suggests the memory of an earlier occurrence, experience, or state.

Reprehensible   Bad, shameful, or wrong in nature.

Sylvans   Dwellers of the woods and forest.

Tutelary   Acting as a guardian or protector.

Unequivocal   Without a doubt, absolutely certain.

Usurp   To take leadership or power by force.

Virulent   Particularly aggressive and harmful.

Visitant   An alien, extraordinary, or supernatural being appearing before humans.

Vituperative   The quality of being verbally abusive and offensive.

Wizened   Wrinkled and gnarled by aging.

Index

122, 127
Green Man 126
gremlins 66
Grendel 85
Griffins 66–68, 67, 68
grimoires 33, 72
Gryphons *see* Griffins
Gwion Bach 94

H
Hades 14–15
hags 37
Haiti 132, 134–135, 137
hamadryads 26, 84
Hand of Glory 100
harbingers of death 12, 36, 52, 73, 79
Harpies 6, 68–70
Harvest May 125
haunts 49, 53
    see also ghosts
Havemand 80
Hawaii 25
Hedley Kow 37
heliodromos 87
Hell 35
    harrowing of Hell 66
heraldry 24, 25, 86, 109
Hercules 14, 15, 24, 58, 66, 72
hero-giants 61
Herodotus 86, 88, 94, 127
Hesiod 15, 16, 58, 65, 91, 97–98
Hill, Betty and Barney 10
Himalayas 8, 9, 113
Hinduism 23, 85, 100, 106
Hittites 16, 107
hobbits 23
hobgoblins *see* goblins
hobs 36, 44, 46
Holland 80
Homer
    Iliad 16, 23, 69
    Odyssey 16, 58, 65, 69, 84, 94,
        96–97, 98, 119
Homeric Hymns 125

homunculus 64, 70–71, 70
horror films 71, 114, 115, 115, 131
horses 50, 69, 85
    water horses 80
    winged horses 16, 66, 85–86
    see also unicorns
human sacrifice 23, 25, 124, 126
Hungary 117
hybrid creatures
    Abominable Snowman 9, 127, 132
    basilisk 12, 12
    centaurs 13–14, 98, 127
    Chimaera 16
    dragons 18–25, 18, 19
    Echinda 14
    Garuda 106
    Harpies 68–70
    Lei Kung 106
    Manticore 79
    mermaids and mermen 44, 79–80,
        79, 81, 83, 99
    Typhon 14, 18, 58, 72
    unicorns 109–114
Hydra 16, 71–72, 71

I
Iamia 115
Iceland 25
imps 34, 38, 72
incantations 41, 72, 72
incubi 30–31, 108
India 79, 106, 109
Indonesia 100
Inuit 59
invisibility, power of 28, 65
Iran 22–23, 68
Ireland 12, 15, 36, 42, 43, 46, 74, 80,
        95, 100, 115
Isle of Man 41, 50, 102
Isis 122–123
Ixion 14

J
Jack and the Beanstalk 85

Jack in the Green 126
Japan 24, 25, 77, 85, 106
Jason and the Argonauts 14, 69, 98
Java 100
Jenny Green Teeth 80
Jewish tradition 22, 29–30, 57, 62–64,
        74, 109, 111, 115
    see also biblical references

K
kallikantzaroi 14
kelpies 37, 42, 73, 80
Kenya 106
ki-lin 113
King of the Auxcrinier 80
knockers 27
kraken 73–74, 73
Kumbhakarna 57

L
La Belle Rosalie 50
Lady of the Lake 43
lake dwellers
    Lady of the Lake 43
    Loch Ness Monster 74–77, 75
    Mhorag of Loch Morar 77
    Muc-sheilche of Loch Maree 77
    Ogopogo 77
Le Meneur des Loups 131
Lei Kung 106
Leopard Men 94, 127
leprechauns 36, 74
Leviathan 13, 33, 74
lights, ghostly 50–51
Lilith 115
little people *see* fairies
Little Red Riding Hood 128
lizard cult 23, 24
Loch Ness Monster 74–77, 75
Loew, Rabbi Judah 64, 65
Loki 25, 27, 59
Lucifer 33
Lycaeon 127
lycanthropy 77, 129, 130, 132

sexual motifs 10, 30–32, 108, 111–
    112, 120, 122
shape-shifting 77, 92–95, 116, 128,
    129, 130
    see also werewolves
Shellycoat 37
Sherpas 9
ships, phantom 48, 50
Siberia 77
Sibyl 14
Siegfried 22, 24, 101, 103
Silenus 90
Simon Magus 70
Simurgh 106
Sindri 27
Sirens 79, 96–99, 96–97, 98, 99
skunk ape 8, 13
sleepers 100–103, 100, 101
Sleeping Beauty 42, 100, 101
Sleipner 85
Smaug 23
Sorcerer's Apprentice 64
spells 33, 48, 74, 95
Sphinx 16
spriggans 42
statues, giving life to 62
subterranean races 103–105
succubi 30, 31–32
Sumerian mythology 19, 23, 24
superman 61
Sweden 77, 107, 108
Switzerland 27

T
Talmud 62, 111
Telchines 92
telepathy 54, 56
Teutonic mythology 24, 26, 27, 51,
    59, 80, 101, 103
Thetis 83–84
Thor 27, 59
thunderbirds 105–107, 105
Tibet 113
time slips 43

Titans 14, 58
Tityroi 92
trains, ghost 50
treasure guardians 23–24, 24, 25, 26,
    61, 68, 74, 102
tree spirits 125
trolls 107–109, 107, 108
trow 107
Tsonoqa 84
Typhon 14, 18, 58, 72

U
Uchaishravas 85
the unconscious 46, 53, 54, 132
underworld *see* ghosts; Hades; Hell
undines 44
unicorns 8, 109–114, 110–111, 112,
    113
Unidentified Flying Objects (UFOs)
    9, 10
United States 9, 13, 15, 50, 51, 52

V
vampires 51, 114–120, 115, 119
    destruction of 117–118
    Dracula 18, 115, 116, 117, 120
    glaistigs 37
    protection against 117
vegetation spirits 120–126
Vietnam 25
Visvarupa 23
vivi 137
Voodoo 134, 135, 137
vrykolakas 115

W
Wales 12, 41, 80, 94, 102
water creatures
    Hydra 16, 71–72, 71
    kelpies 37, 42, 73, 80
    kraken 73–74, 73
    Leviathan 13, 33, 74
    mermaids and mermen 44, 79–83,
        79, 81

Naiads 83, 84
Nereids 83, 84
Oceanides 83
undines 44
see also lake dwellers
Wendigo 126
were-bears 94, 127
were-hyenas 84, 127
were-tigers 94, 127
werewolves 93, 94–95, 116, 119,
    126–132, 127, 128
    appearance 129–130
    destruction of 131–132
    metamorphosis 130–131
wife-stealing 108
wild men *see* Abominable Snowman;
    Bigfoot
Will o' the Wisps 37
wisdom and knowledge 13, 26
    dwarfs 26
witches 33, 34, 35, 51, 129
    Devil's marks 34
    familiars 34
    pacts with Satan 34
    shape-shifting 129, 130
wolves 116, 128
    see also werewolves

X
Xipe Totec 124

Y
Yang and Yin doctrine 25
Yarthkins 42
Yeti 8, 9, 132, 133
Ymir 27, 59

Z
Zeus 14, 58, 68, 84, 91, 92, 94, 107,
    122, 125, 127
Zimbabwe 106
zombies 132, 134–137
Zu 19, 25

Author List

Contributors to *Man, Myth, and Magic: Legendary Creatures and Monsters*

Rev. E. A. Armstrong is an authority on the folklore of birds and animals. Formerly Vicar of St Mark's Cambridge; Armstrong is the author of *The Folklore of Birds; The Wren; Bird Display and Behaviour*, and others.

Richard Barber is the author of *Arthur of Albion; Henry Plantagenet; The Knight and Chivalry*; and co-author of a dictionary of fabulous beasts.

S. G. F. Brandon was Professor of Comparative Religion, Manchester; and the author of numerous books including Man and his *Destiny in the Great Religions; Creation Legends of the Ancient Near East; History, Time and Deity; The Judgment of the Dead; The Trial of Jesus of Nazareth*; Brandon also edited the *Dictionary of Comparative Religion*.

K. M. Briggs was the former President of the Folklore Society; author of *The Anatomy of Puck; Pale Hecate's Team; The Fairies in Tradition and Literature; Dictionary of British Folk-Tales*, and others.

Alexander Eliot is the author of *Socrates; Creatures of Arcadia*, and others.

June Grimble is a journalist and broadcaster.

Ellic Howe is a specialist in the prehistory of German National Socialism; and the author of *Urania's Children; the Strange World of the Astrologers,* and others.

Francis Huxley, British anthropologist, was well known for his books *The Invisibles* (a study of voodoo); *The Way of the Sacred;* and *The Raven and the Writing Desk.*

Douglas Hill is the author of *Magic and Superstition; Return From the Dead; The Supernatural* (with Pat Williams); *The Opening of the Canadian West; Regency London*, and others.

Christina Hole was an hon. editor of Folklore; books include *English Folklore; English Custom and Usage; English Folk Heroes; A Mirror of Witchcraft; Witchcraft in England*; edited the *Encyclopedia of Superstitions.*

Eric Maple is the author of *The Dark World of Witches; The Realm of Ghosts; The Domain of Devils; Magic, Medicine and Quackery; Superstition and the Superstitious.*

Venetia Newall is a folklorist, traveler and lecturer; hon. secretary of the Folk-Lore Society; author of *An Egg at Easter.*

David Phillips is freelance journalist and broadcaster, as well as former head of the BBC Greek service.

E. D. Phillips was a Reader in Greek, the Queen's University of Belfast.

Sandy Shulman is a novelist, and the author of *Dreams.*

C. Nelson Stewart is author of *Bulwer Lytton as Occultist; Gem-Stones of the Seven Rays,* etc.

R.J.Zwi Werblowsky was Professor of Comparative Religion and the History of Jewish Thought at the Hebrew University of Jerusalem. He studied in Switzerland and taught in England before joining the Hebrew University in 1956, and wrote numerous books and articles on comparative religion, the Cabala, and Jewish mysticism.

R. F. Willetts was a Professor of Greek, Birmingham; and the author of *Aristocratic Society in Ancient Crete; Cretan Cults and Festivals*, and more. In addition, Willetts edited the *Law Code of Gortyn.*